The Zondervan Family Cookbook

The Zondervan Family Cookbook

by Patricia Gundry

ZONDERVAN PUBLISHING HOUSE
Grand Rapids, Michigan

The Zondervan Family Cookbook
Copyright © 1988 by Patricia Gundry

Zondervan Books
are published by Zondervan Publishing House
1415 Lake Drive, S.E.
Grand Rapids, MI 49506

Library of Congress Cataloging in Publication Data

Gundry, Patricia.
  The Zondervan family cookbook.

  Includes index.
  1. Cookery. I. Zondervan Corporation. II. Title.
TX714.G86 1988   641.5   88-20751
ISBN 0-310-25380-2

Many of the pictures used in this volume were
copied or adapted from *Ready-to-Use Food and Drink
Spot Illustrations*, edited by Susan Gaber (Clip Art
Series), copyright © 1981 by Dover Publications,
New York, N.Y. Used by permission.

Printed in the United States of America

    89 90 91 92 93 94 / DH / 10 9 8 7 6 5 4 3 2

CONTENTS

♥ **How to Use This Book & Welcome** 6

♥ **Acknowledgments** 9

♥ **First of All**
APPETIZERS 11
BEVERAGES 23
SALADS 31
SOUPS 55
FRAGRANT LOAVES AND OTHER BREADS 71

♥ **More Substantial Fare**
STRATAS, OVEN OMELETS, SOUFFLES, AND
FRENCH TOAST 115
LUNCH AND LIGHT SUPPER DISHES 125
Pizza 136
Chili 145
Sandwiches 149

♥ **Main Dishes**
CHICKEN 153
PORK 177
BEEF AND LAMB 189
SEAFOOD 223

♥ **Vegetables and Side Dishes** 231

♥ **Sweet Things**
COOKIES 255
DESSERTS 297
CAKES 339
PIES 373
CANDY AND SWEET SNACKS 393

♥ **Miscellaneous** 401
DIGESTIBLES 402
INDIGESTIBLES 409
Index of Recipes 411

WELCOME

Welcome to *The Zondervan Family Cookbook.* This is a cookbook unlike any other you have seen. It *is* a *cook*book all right, but it is much more. I like to think of it as a book of resources, from many families to yours.

A few years ago when the idea for *The Zondervan Family Cookbook* was born, I was thinking about the difficulties families have now. It is not easy, as I am sure you know, to have a successful and satisfying family life. Many distractions disrupt family life, many forces seem to be pulling the family in different directions, threatening to pull it apart.

As I was thinking about the problems families face, I began wondering about possible solutions, helps, resources for families. And I thought, *Families need to be able to share resources with each other, so that what one has discovered others can use and enjoy also.* Applying the principle of starting where you are to make changes, I looked around to see what I might do to help make that possible. As a cookbook collector for many years, an experienced mother-of-four, and a writer, I realized that a cookbook-resource book about food, eating, and family food times could be a very good means to share some of those resources—because food and eating are at the heart of family life.

So I set out to collect from the families that I have access to resources to share with your family and all families everywhere. It so happens that through my publisher, Zondervan Publishing House, I have access to some

How to Use This Book

Recipes appear on the left side of each page; stories and informational notes on the right. It's really two books in one, you can read and use them separately or together. The following graphic symbols indicate special categories, making it possible to scan for and quickly find certain types of recipes and notes.

You may want to create your own symbols to identify recipes you want to try, have tested and liked, or that you find particularly suitable for some purpose, such as: Prepare Ahead, Take With, or Entertaining.

 Taster's Choice, *especially good, according to our testers and tasters.*

of the most innovative and interesting families anywhere.

The people from whom I requested recipes and information shared enthusiastically, because they thought it was a wonderful idea, and because they are gracious and generous people. One author, Kalman Toth, copied and sent me forty-eight recipes for delicious authentic Hungarian cuisine from his wife's files. She was ill and unable to select only a few for him to send, so he copied a wealth of them for me to choose from—and said he would send more if I wished him to.

Zondervan Publishing House grew from the idea and effort of two brothers, Pat and Bernie Zondervan, into the large corporation it is today. Because of the Dutch heritage of the Zondervan brothers and of many Zondervan employees who live in the Grand Rapids area, quite a few Dutch recipes appear in this book. Because missionaries often become authors, there are interesting and unusual international recipes here. Because families love and cherish food from their ethnic heritage, many delicious ethnic dishes have found their way into the following pages. And because families love what is easy, simple, and good, there are many, many of those recipes here too.

This book is not a "balanced" cookbook with a certain number of recipes in each category. I could have done that, but it would have necessitated discarding many good recipes. Families may eat a balanced diet, but their special favorites cluster in larger amounts in certain categories. There is a higher proportion of recipes for cookies and pizza, for example, than you would find in most other cookbooks. Because families love

 Child Helping, *recipes developed for or lending themselves to being prepared by children and adults together.*

 Quick and Easy

 Natural Foods

 Convenience, *utilizing packaged and prepared foods.*

 Christmas

 Birthdays

 Candlelight

 Microwave

The following symbols indicate

�». **recipe is continued on next page**

◄◄ **note refers to accompanying recipe**

♥

pizza, and nothing is so good as hot cookies, fresh from the oven, with a glass of cold milk.

So, from my family, the Zondervan family of authors and employees, and the Zondervan founders' families—from our hearts and our treasured collections of favorites, from our experiences—we send our best, this book, from our family to yours. ♥

ACKNOWLEDGMENTS

Producing a cookbook is a longer and wider job than one would think. Along the way, many people have made meaningful contributions.

My very largest thanks must go to all the kind, clever, and generous people who submitted recipes and notes years ago. Special thanks to Paul Hillman, my original publisher, who loved the idea and encouraged me with his enthusiasm throughout the testing of recipes, and waited and waited patiently for the finished book. Thanks too to Carol Holquist for her imaginative and capable assistance, to Judy Markham and Julie Link, who were both editors on the project, and to Bob Hudson, who inherited the whole thing. Louise Bauer and Rachel Hostetter deserve bouquets for internal design, art, and paste-up, and Terry Dugan for the cover design.

Zondervan editors and staff have dutifully and diligently eaten their way through test recipes and are heavier for it. Thank you all for you competence, courtesy, and friendship.

And to my own staff a very special thank you. Without my son and chief editorial assistant, David Gundry, who tested and advised expertly and word-processed endlessly, this book could have been produced—but it's an awful thought.

Sincere appreciation also to my daughter, Ann Gundry Teliczan, whose family ate their way through seafood and various other items. Hugs to my longsuffering in-house assistants, son Jon Gundry and friend Betsy Kamel.

My husband Stan also deserves a pat on the back and a squeeze for just the right advice at just the right time, and for carrying all those food containers and stacks of paper to and from work.

Thanks everyone, and get ready, as soon as I've recovered, I'm starting the next one. ♥

Pat Gundry, Grand Rapids, Michigan, 1988

APPETIZERS

Guacamole 12
Fresh Salsa 12
Thick Mexican Salsa 13
7-Layer Sabrosa Spread 13
Wild Bean Spread 14
Janeen's Cheese Spread 14
Beth's Cheese Ball 15
Joanne's Vegetable Dip 15
Crabby or Shrimpy Dip 16
Shrimp Dip 16
Spinach Dip 17
Cheese Pops 17
Hot Sausage Balls 18
Cheese Straws 18
Vegetarian Pizza 19
Japanese "French Fries" 20
  Ginger-Soy Sauce, Lemon-Soy Sauce 20
Chinese Fried Walnuts 21

Guacamole

**2 or 3 ripe avocados (don't use the very large
    ones with the light green shiny skins;
    they don't make the best guacamole)**
1 or 2 teaspoons grated onion
juice of ½ fresh lime
1 or 2 tablespoons Heinz chili sauce
generous pinch of salt
¼ teaspoon crushed red pepper

Peel and seed avocados and place in a mixing
bowl. Add remaining ingredients and mash with a
fork or potato masher until thoroughly mixed and
of desired consistency. Refrigerate to blend flavors
and chill. Serve with tortilla chips.

Patricia Gundry

Fresh Salsa

**2 or 3 large, ripe tomatoes, cored, peeled, and
    chopped**
1 small onion, grated
¼ teaspoon crushed red pepper
salt, to taste

Mix together. Serve with tortilla chips.

Patricia Gundry

Fresh Salsa

◄ *Salsa is highly individual and
varied, so make it a few times
and adjust the amounts to find
the combination you like best.
But mix it up an hour or two
before you eat it, if you can, so
the flavors can marry, as they
say.* ♥

Patricia Gundry

Thick Mexican Salsa

2 (8 ounce) cans tomato sauce
1½ teaspoons sugar
½ teaspoon salt
¼ teaspoon black pepper
¼ teaspoon oregano
dash celery flakes or 1 stalk celery, diced
2–3 cloves garlic, minced fine
1 large onion, diced
2 jalapeno peppers, sliced
1 fresh tomato, peeled and diced

Combine ingredients, put in saucepan, and simmer until onion is translucent.

JOYCE LEENSVAART

7-Layer Sabrosa Spread

1 large can refried beans
2 or 3 avocados, peeled and seeded
1 tablespoon lemon or lime juice
½ cup mayonnaise
½ cup sour cream
¼–½ package taco seasoning mix
2 fresh tomatoes, chopped
1 bunch green onions with tops, chopped
1 can black olives, chopped
6–8 ounces shredded Cheddar cheese

Mash avocados with lemon or lime juice. Blend mayonnaise, sour cream, and taco mix. Spread ingredients on serving dish in layers in order given. Serve with tortilla chips or corn chips.

Variation: For a lighter version, mix several drops of Louisiana Hot Sauce or Tabasco sauce with refried beans and omit mayonnaise, sour cream, and taco seasoning.

JOANNE BOER

Wild Bean Spread

1 large can red kidney beans
1 small jar sweet pepper relish
1 clove garlic, grated
1 tablespoon white horseradish
1 teaspoon dry mustard
2 or 3 tablespoons mayonnaise
sour cream (optional)
Tabasco sauce (optional)

Rinse and drain beans thoroughly. Partially or thoroughly mash beans, as desired. Drain off and discard some of liquid from sweet pepper relish. Mix all ingredients, including sour cream and Tabasco sauce, to taste, if desired.

ANNETTE & ROGER NICOLE

Janeen's Cheese Spread

12 ounces cream cheese
2 jars Old English cheese
1 jar Roka cheese
½ teaspoon Worcestershire sauce
¼ teaspoon Tabasco sauce
¼ teaspoon garlic salt
¼ teaspoon onion salt

Soften cream cheese with electric mixer. Add Old English and Roka cheese a jar at a time and mix. Add remaining ingredients and mix until of spreading consistency. Serve as a dip or spread, with favorite crackers.

JANEEN SHUPE

Entertaining

When you entertain, do not leave out the children. Include them in your entertainment, at least most of the time. It will be an enriching, growing, and maturing experience for them. Be sure to include at least some foods you know they will enjoy eating. ♥

JANE & PAUL MICKEY

Beth's Cheese Ball

1 (8 ounce) package cream cheese, softened
½ cup mayonnaise
5 slices bacon, fried crisp and crumbled
1 tablespoon chopped green onion
½ teaspoon dill weed or dill seed
⅛ teaspoon pepper

Combine cream cheese and mayonnaise, mix well. Add remaining ingredients (or bacon can be reserved and used to coat outside of ball), mix well. Form into ball and chill overnight.

ELIZABETH BROWN

Joanne's Vegetable Dip

1 cup sour cream
½ cup mayonnaise
1 tablespoon wine vinegar
1 tablespoon A-1 steak sauce
¼ teaspoon Tabasco sauce (optional)
½ teaspoon garlic powder
1 teaspoon salt
¼ teaspoon pepper

Combine all ingredients and refrigerate until served. Can be made ahead of time.

JOANNE BOER

Crabby or Shrimpy Dip

1 (8 ounce) package cream cheese, softened
¼ cup mayonnaise
2 tablespoons catsup
2 tablespoons minced onions
1 tablespoon lemon juice
½ teaspoon Worcestershire sauce
1 (7½ ounce) can broken shrimp, drained, or
    crab meat, bones removed

Blend all ingredients except shrimp with electric mixer at medium speed until fluffy. Drain shrimp and add to mixture, mixing at low speed. Chill thoroughly. Remove from refrigerator 15 minutes before serving. Serve with chips, crackers, or assorted raw vegetables.

WILMA ZONDERVAN TEGGELAAR

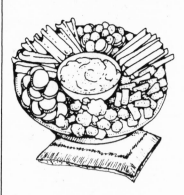

Shrimp Dip

2 (3 ounce) packages cream cheese, softened
1 (10¾ ounce) can tomato soup
1 cup salad dressing or mayonnaise
½ cup diced celery
½ cup diced green pepper
½ cup diced onion
1 (4¼ ounce) can broken shrimp, drained and
    cut up

Combine cream cheese and tomato soup by slowly adding soup to cream cheese, mixing well, or mix in blender or food processor. Add salad dressing. Mix well. Stir in celery, green pepper, onion, and shrimp. Refrigerate. Serve with crackers.

DOUG & SHARON KUIPERS

Spinach Dip

1 package frozen chopped spinach (thawed
   and drained)
1 cup sour cream
1 cup mayonnaise
2 green onions, chopped
1 package dry vegetable soup mix
½ cup sliced water chestnuts

Combine and refrigerate overnight. Serve in hollowed out round sourdough or pumpernickel loaf, surround with large bread cubes.

GRACE & DEAN MERRILL

Cheese Pops

MAKES 5 dozen.

1 jar stuffed green olives
½ cup butter, softened
2 cups shredded Cheddar cheese
1 cup flour
⅛ teaspoon salt
¼ teaspoon paprika
½ teaspoon Worcestershire sauce

Mix all ingredients except olives and knead into a soft dough. Mold a small amount of dough around each olive. Freeze on a cookie sheet. (Once frozen, they may be stored in a plastic container.) *Do not bake until thoroughly frozen.* Bake at 350F for 15 to 20 minutes. Serve hot accompanied by vegetable juice cocktail or hot consommé.

JOY MACKENZIE

Fireplace Picnics

We have picnics on a blanket on the floor in front of the fire in the fireplace, with potted plants and rubber bugs for atmosphere. ♥

RACHEL & LARRY CRABB

Hot Sausage Balls

1 pound raw (hot-flavored) bulk sausage
3 cups biscuit mix
10 ounces extra sharp cheese, grated
4 or 5 drops Tabasco sauce

Combine all ingredients. Form into bite size balls (they expand during baking so be sure to form them smaller than you want them to be when done), place on cookie sheet. Bake 15 minutes at 375F. Balls can also be formed and frozen ahead of time. Bake frozen sausage balls 20 to 25 minutes at 400F.

LATAYNE SCOTT

Cheese Straws

1 cup grated sharp Cheddar cheese
1 cup flour
⅛ teaspoon pepper
1 cube butter
4 teaspoons heavy cream, or milk

Mix together with a fork, as for pie crust. Roll out thin, cut in narrow strips 2 inches long and ⅓ inch wide—a pastry wheel is a great help here. Bake at 400F until a very delicate brown, about 10 minutes.

DONNA FLETCHER CROW

Vegetarian Pizza

2–3 packages crescent roll dough
½ to ⅔ cup mayonnaise
2 (8 ounce) packages cream cheese
1 tablespoon dill weed or dill seed
1 tablespoon dried onion, presoaked
¼ cup grated Parmesan cheese (optional)
assorted vegetables cut in bite size pieces,
    such as:
cherry tomatoes (halved)
broccoli
cauliflower
green pepper
mushrooms
olives
cucumbers

Line jelly roll pan with crescent roll dough, making sure edges of pieces are firmly pressed together. Bake 8–10 minutes at 400F, allow to cool. Combine mayonnaise, cream cheese, dill, onion and Parmesan cheese if desired, spread on baked, cooled crust. Add vegetables and cut into small squares. For smaller batch, use one package crescent roll dough and one half of remaining ingredients in a 7"x11" baking pan.

SHARON & JAMES ENGEL

Entertaining

Having guests is usually an event that involves the whole family, even if the children will not be included in the meal itself. We do not feel that guests should have to take us just as we are, but that they deserve special effort on the part of everyone. If company is coming, we have the children give their rooms a special cleaning, even if it is unlikely that the company will go there. We use special dishes, sometimes rearrange furniture to make seating more comfortable, etc. Our children are in most cases expected to greet the guests and spend a few minutes in conversation, then they may go on to their studies or other activities if these are pressing, or if their presence is not called for. When the guests leave, the children are expected to come and say good-bye. There are a few occasions when the word to the kids is, "Stay out of sight. We don't want to hear from you unless there is a fire." But we usually prefer to include them, and hope they will continue to feel that company deserves the best they can provide. ♥

BARBARA BUSH

Japanese "French Fries"

SERVES 4 or more

juice of 1 lemon
2 quarts water
1 large eggplant
1 cup flour, or as needed
oil for frying

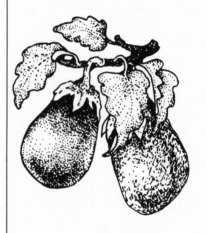

Mix lemon juice and water and set aside. Peel eggplant (use a stainless steel knife) and cut it into ½ inch thick batons resembling thick French fries. Drop the pieces into the lemon water to prevent discoloration.

Heat oil to 375F. Drain eggplant pieces and pat dry. Put flour into a large, clean paper bag, add eggplant pieces, close the top of the bag and shake vigorously. Empty bag onto a wire rack and shake off loose flour.

Drop the pieces into hot oil in batches (do not add more than will cover ⅓ of the surface of the oil at a time) and fry until golden brown. Remove, drain and serve with Ginger-Soy Sauce or Lemon-Soy sauce.

Ginger-Soy Sauce

1″ piece fresh ginger, grated
½ cup soy sauce

Mix well and use for dipping.

Lemon-Soy Sauce

2 tablespoons lemon juice
½ cup soy sauce

Mix well and use for dipping.

ROBERT FARRAR CAPON

Chinese Fried Walnuts

MAKES 4 cups

6 cups water
4 cups walnuts
½ cup sugar
salad oil
salt

In a 4 quart saucepan heat water to boiling. Add walnuts and boil 1 minute. Rinse walnuts under running hot water, drain. Wash saucepan and dry well.

In a large bowl, with a rubber spatula stir warm walnuts with sugar until sugar is dissolved. If necessary, let mixture stand five minutes to dissolve sugar.

Meanwhile, in same saucepan over medium heat, heat about 1 inch salad oil to 350F on deep fat thermometer (or heat oil according to manufacturer's directions in a deep fat fryer set at 350F). With slotted spoon, add about half of walnuts to oil. Fry 3 to 5 minutes or until golden, stirring often.

With a slotted spoon, place walnuts in a coarse sieve over a bowl to drain; sprinkle very lightly with salt. Toss lightly to keep walnuts from sticking together. Transfer to a cookie sheet to cool. Fry remaining walnuts. Can be stored for up to two weeks in a tightly covered container.

JANET KOBOBEL

My husband and I both work. So do our two teenage daughters. Many times our family has a difficult time eating meals together on any consistent basis. Both of our daughters work at fast food restaurants. When they work the dinner shift we will visit them at work. We sometimes treat ourselves to dinner out where they work. Often we will give one or both of them a ride to work early and eat dinner out together. ♥

KATHY LYNN (in cooperation with David, Jeanine, and Michelle)

BEVERAGES

Elegant Frosty Punch 24
Request Punch 25
Oriental Punch 25
Punch du Jour de Blender 26
Wassail 27
Russian Tea 28
Ed's Mongolian Tea 28
Spice Tea 29
Hot Cocoa Mix 29

Elegant Frosty Punch

Large Recipe:

SERVES 150–175

6 quarts orange juice
6 cups lemon juice
2 (46 ounce) cans pineapple juice
12 cups simple syrup (add 5 lbs. sugar to 6
    cups water, boil)
7 quarts ginger ale
1 gallon pineapple sherbet

Small Recipe:

SERVES 75

3 quarts orange juice
3 cups lemon juice
1 (46 ounce) can pineapple juice
6 cups simple syrup (add 2½ lbs. sugar to 3
    cups water, boil)
3½ quarts ginger ale
½ gallon pineapple sherbet

Mix juices and cooled sugar syrup (large recipe makes about 14 quarts without the ginger ale). Pour into clean, empty half gallon milk cartons and freeze. Large margarine containers also make good freezer containers. Remove from freezer and let stand at room temperature 2–3 hours before serving. To serve, place in large punch bowl and add ginger ale, using one quart ginger ale to every 2 quarts (half gallon) punch. Add pineapple sherbet (approximately ⅓ at a time) for an elegant, frothy, tasty punch.

DAVID M. MARTIN

Request Punch

Large Recipe:

SERVES about 50 people.

3 (46 ounce) cans Hawaiian Punch
3 quarts ginger ale
1 (46 ounce) can apple juice
1 gallon raspberry sherbet (or another kind)

Family Batch:

1 (46 ounce) can Hawaiian Punch
1 quart ginger ale
2 (6 ounce) cans apple juice
1 quart raspberry sherbet

MRS. LOUIS GOLDBERG

Oriental Punch

1 cup water
2 cups sugar
2 (46 ounce) cans pineapple juice
2 cups orange juice
1 cup lemon juice
4 quarts chilled ginger ale
1 orange, thinly sliced, for garnish

Boil water and sugar together for 5 minutes. Set aside to cool. Reserve 2 cups of the pineapple juice. Pour the rest into ice cube trays and freeze. Combine reserved pineapple juice, orange juice, lemon juice, and sugar water and chill. To serve, put frozen pineapple juice cubes in punch bowl, add fruit juices and ginger ale. Decorate with orange slices.

NAOMI & JIM RUARK

Request Punch

◄≪*In one of the pastorates where my husband served, I received a recipe for a very tasty punch from a person who catered at many weddings. When I serve this punch people often ask for the recipe because of its distinctive flavor.* ♥

MRS. LOIS GOLDBERG

Punch du Jour de Blender

You can vary this punch according to what you have on hand.

1 (46 ounce) can pineapple juice
juice of 1–3 lemons
1–3 bananas, fresh or frozen strawberries,
 peaches, raspberries or other fruit, alone
 or in any combination. (It helps to allow
 the frozen fruit to thaw slightly first.)

Pour enough pineapple juice into a blender or food processor to puree fruit in. Add fruit and blend. Add sugar and water to taste. Pour the blended mixture into one or two pitchers and mix together by pouring punch back and forth between the two. Taste and add more of any of the ingredients if you like, returning enough punch to the blender or food processor to blend in more fruit.

You can substitute a citrus-flavored soft drink for the lemon juice, but I think real lemon juice tastes best.

Patricia Gundry

Wassail (WAH-sul)

1 gallon apple cider
1 cup brown sugar
1 (6 ounce) can frozen lemonade concentrate*
1 (6 ounce) can frozen orange juice
   concentrate*
1 tablespoon whole cloves
1 tablespoon whole allspice
1 teaspoon nutmeg
cinnamon sticks
lemon slices

In a large kettle, combine cider, sugar, lemonade and orange juice concentrates. In a piece of cheesecloth, tie together cloves and allspice and add to cider mixture. Add nutmeg and simmer, uncovered, 20 minutes. Remove cheesecloth bag. Serve hot. Decorate with cinnamon sticks and lemon slices. Makes about 16 servings.

Editor's note: The recipe can be made either by using the concentrates undiluted (as in the original recipe) or diluted according to the instructions on the cans. We tested it both ways and both were delicious. The undiluted version is just more powerful!

DEB WRIGHT

Wassail

◄ *This is my favorite recipe. I clipped it out of the* Detroit Free Press *when I was still in college. Every Christmas morning, we open our gifts and drink wassail. (One year it was quite memorable; the cider was a little harder than we were planning on!) Anyway, it really is delicious!* ♥

DEB WRIGHT

Russian Tea

2 cups instant orange drink mix
1 scant cup powdered instant tea
2 cups sugar
1 teaspoon ground cloves
1 teaspoon cinnamon

   Mix well and store in an airtight container. Use one tablespoon per cup of hot water.

JOYCE LEENSVAART

Ed's Mongolian Tea

1½ cups instant orange drink mix
1¼ cups instant tea
1⅓ cups sugar
½ cup powdered lemonade mix
¾ teaspoon ground cloves
¾ teaspoon cinnamon
¼ teaspoon nutmeg

   Combine all ingredients. Store in an airtight container. Use 1 tablespoon of mixture per cup of hot water.

ED AND RUTH VAN DER MAAS

There is something almost sacramental about sharing good food together around the table. The emotional warmth, the obvious love of a well-prepared meal, the sharing together—you say something about the value of people in the way you serve food and the expectation that everyone in the family be present to enjoy it together. ♥

GLADYS HUNT

Spice Tea

A spicy citrus tea

1 cup instant orange drink mix
¾ cups sugar
1 cup dry lemonade mix
1 cup powdered instant tea
½ teaspoon ground cloves
½ teaspoon cinnamon
½ teaspoon nutmeg

Mix all ingredients. Store in an airtight container. Use 2 rounded teaspoons per cup of hot water.

Joyce Leensvaart

Hot Cocoa Mix

1 cup unsweetened cocoa
2 cups powdered sugar
3 cups instant nonfat dry milk
1 cup dry nondairy creamer

Combine cocoa, sugar, dry milk and creamer in a large bowl. Stir until well blended. Store in jars, covered. Use 4 tablespoons to a cup of boiling water.

Variations: For a richer drink, use 2 cups nondairy creamer. For an interesting mocha flavor, add ½ cup powdered instant coffee. 4 cups instant dry 2% or whole milk may replace the nonfat dry milk and nondairy creamer.

Joyce Leensvaart

SALADS

Tabouli 32
Three or Four Bean Salad 33
Meri's Many Bean Salad 34
Mexican Chef's Salad 35
Layered Vegetable Salad 36
Betty's Salad and Dressing 37
Scandinavian Summer Salad 38
    Sour Cream Dressing 38
Cole Slaw De Luxe with Dill Dressing 39
Uldine's Light Avocado-Carrot Salad 40
Crunchy Salad 40
Olivia's Broccoli-Mushroom Salad 41
German Broccoli Salad 41
Potato Salad 42
Grandma Lou's Hot Potato Salad 43
Rotini Salad 44
Tuna Cooler 44
Sour Noodles 45
Cooperation Salad 46
Sunny Carrot Salad 47
Mandarin Orange Salad 48
Quick Picnic Salad 48
Hot Fruit Salad 49
Holiday Cranberry Salad 49
Cucumber Salad 50
Orange-Pineapple Salad 51
Apricot Nectar Gelatin Salad 51
Cranberry Jell 52
Jiffy Cranberry Salad 52
Van Raalte Dressing 53
Red Dressing for Tossed Salad 53
Poppy Seed Dressing 54

Tabouli

"An especially good summer salad and a complete meal if served with chickpeas, feta cheese, and bread or crackers. Begin preparation at least 3 hours ahead of serving time. It is preferable to begin in the morning, and fine to start the night before."

SERVES 6–8

1 cup bulgur wheat
1¼ cups boiling water
1 teaspoon salt (or less, to taste)
¼ cup fresh lemon and/or lime juice
1 teaspoon crushed fresh garlic
½ cup chopped green onions
½ teaspoon dried mint, crumbled finely, or ⅓
    cup finely chopped fresh mint
2 medium tomatoes, diced
1 cup *fresh* parsley, finely chopped, packed in
    the cup
freshly ground black pepper, to taste
¼ cup good olive oil

Optional ingredients:

Add one or more as desired

½ cup coarsely grated carrot
½ cup cooked chickpeas
1 cucumber or summer squash, chopped
1 green pepper, chopped
radishes, thinly sliced

In a bowl combine bulgur, boiling water and salt. Cover and let stand 15–20 minutes. Meanwhile, squeeze lemon and/or lime juice, crush garlic, chop green onions, and crumble or chop mint. Add to wheat mixture and mix thoroughly. Refrigerate 3 hours or more. Just before serving, add tomatoes, parsley, pepper, olive oil, and any optional ingredients desired.

Serving suggestions:

Line a shallow bowl with cabbage leaves or firm lettuce leaves and spoon tabouli into the center.

Garnish with crumbled feta cheese and ripe olives

Good with charcoal-grilled meats or roast lamb.

WENDY & ROBERT MANLEY

Three or Four Bean Salad

"Make it a day in advance."

1 (16 ounce) can cut green beans
1 (16 ounce) can wax beans
1 (16 ounce) can dark red kidney beans
1 (16 ounce) can chickpeas
½ cup thinly sliced green pepper
¾ cup sliced green onions, with some tops
   included
½ cup wine vinegar
⅔ cup sugar
½ teaspoon salt
½ teaspoon freshly ground pepper
¼ teaspoon dill weed
½ teaspoon tarragon
¼ teaspoon celery seed
½ cup oil

Drain green beans and wax beans, drain and rinse kidney beans and chickpeas. In a large bowl or jar place beans, chickpeas, green pepper and green onions. Mix remaining ingredients together and add to the above. Store in refrigerator, stirring occasionally (important) to make sure all beans are marinated. To serve, use a slotted spoon to place bean mixture in serving dish.

WILMA ZONDERVAN TEGGELAAR

We have had many family dinners together at my daughter's house. We consider it the ultimate experience in taste, vitamins, minerals, enzymes, and artistry. She serves broiled chicken or fish but does not settle for one vegetable or salad as accompaniments, but for seven or eight beautifully arrayed vegetables on a huge platter. She puts it together in a flash because the vegetables are already washed, in crispers in the refrigerator all set to go. With a flair of her own, she tosses spoonfuls of oil and lemon juice with a generous pinch of herbs through a variety of salad greens and tops it all with pecan halves. While she is doing this, she has white and red cabbage wedges, whole medium sized carrots and thick slices of zucchini cooking in her steamer for 5 minutes. She garnishes the platter with large clumps of sprouts, watercress, parsley, and sliced green pepper. Her dessert consists of a colorful bowl of cut up fresh fruit embellished with kiwi slices and served with wedges of Brie or Camembert. ♥

ETHEL RENWICK

Meri's Many Bean Salad

Great for a picnic, as it can be served right from the jars it is prepared in.

"In Ethiopia we had to start by cooking the beans, and there were no blenders. This is U.S.A. adapted."

Use any combination of canned beans (approximately 1 pound size cans).

Suggestions:

Cut green beans
Cut golden wax beans
chickpeas
dark red kidney beans
light red kidney beans
white kidney beans (canellini)
pinto beans (may be tough)

For each 3 cans of beans you will need:

1 green pepper, cut in chunks (or 3–4
    tablespoons frozen)
1 small onion, cut in chunks (or 3
    tablespoons frozen)
¼–½ cup sugar (I use part sugar substitute)
½ teaspoon ground pepper
½ cup vinegar
½ cup oil

Drain beans and place in large jars, preferably large mouth, for ease of handling, layering the different types to make interesting color combinations. (A quart jar holds about 3 cans.) In an electric blender, liquefy remaining ingredients, blending until mixture is creamy in appearance. Pour over beans in jars, cover, and tip jars or shake to distribute liquid mixture over all beans. Refrigerate for several hours or days before serving, inverting jars (if tightly covered) or stirring to make sure all beans are marinated in liquid.

MERILYN & MILTON FISHER

To our three children Ethiopia was home for a number of years. For several of those years our home was in a large, square, one story stacked stone house with very high ceilings, and a "ker-koro" (corrugated iron) roof. We moved to this house in the town of Gorei (population 5,005 while we 5 were there) in the month of November, during the rainy season. This meant that we had to carry with us by airplane as many fresh vegetables as we could fit into a large Ethiopian basket, since we had to plant and raise a garden for any vegetables we would need in the future. We also had to airfreight any canned goods, sugar, and flour, as trucks for freight could not pass through to Gorei until late January when the mud roads were sufficiently dry.

There was a period of three weeks between the time our supply of fresh vegetables ran out and the garden began to produce. For those three weeks the only vegetable available locally was a pumpkinlike type of squash. As you may guess, it was a couple of years before we could face this kind of squash again! ♥

MERILYN & MILTON FISHER

Mexican Chef's Salad

Also known as Taco Salad, this mixture has several variations, but basically consists of cooked ground beef, mixed with a seasoning, and then with fresh cold salad ingredients and tortilla chips.

1 pound ground beef
1 can enchilada sauce, or ½ package taco
    seasoning mix combined with 1 (8 ounce)
    bottle Thousand Island dressing, or 1 (8
    ounce) bottle French dressing (Use only
    one of these seasoning choices, not all
    three.)
1 head lettuce, cut up
1 onion, chopped
1–4 tomatoes, chopped, or ¾ box cherry
    tomatoes
4–8 ounces shredded Cheddar cheese
1 green pepper, chopped (optional)
1 avocado, sliced (optional)
1 can kidney beans, drained (optional)
tortilla chips

Brown ground beef, drain grease. If using enchilada sauce, add and simmer 10 minutes (kidney beans may be added and simmered with ground beef also). If using other seasoning choice, mix with ground beef. Mix seasoned ground beef with remaining ingredients, except tortilla chips. Five minutes before serving add tortilla chips and toss.

LAURIE GOTT
MRS. DAVID KOK
SANDY & STEVE GRUNLAN

Layered Vegetable Salad

A very popular salad, layered salad is particularly useful for prepare-ahead meals. The recipe below contains the basic elements, plus variations from four different contributors.

SERVES 8–10

1 head lettuce, torn up, chopped, or shredded
⅓–1 cup sliced celery
1 medium onion or 1 bunch green onions, chopped, or thinly sliced
1 green pepper, chopped or thinly sliced
1 can water chestnuts, drained and sliced
1 (10 ounce) package frozen peas, uncooked (or 1 medium sized can English peas, well drained)

Dressing choices:

1. 2 cups salad dressing or mayonnaise.
2. 1 cup mayonnaise, ¼ cup sour cream, pinch of sugar.
3. 2 cups mayonnaise, 1 teaspoon lemon juice.

Topping choices:

1. Mix together ⅓ cup Parmesan cheese, 1 teaspoon seasoned salt, ¼ teaspoon garlic powder, 2 teaspoons sugar. Top with ½ pound bacon (fried and crumbled), tomato slices, wedges, or halved cherry tomatoes, and bean sprouts.
2. Bacon bits, grated yellow cheese.
3. ½ pound bacon (fried and crumbled), 4 hard-boiled eggs (sliced or chopped), 1½ cups grated Cheddar cheese.
4. 2 hard-boiled eggs (chopped), bacon bits, 2 tablespoons grated Parmesan cheese. ➨

It was early 1979 when I first realized that people love to eat. I don't particularly, nor does my wife, Yolanda, so neither of us had ever given it much thought. To us, eating is something you do to keep your stomach from growling and to keep from dying. We especially don't like to cook. Both of us would be quite content to absorb nutrients from the air so we could go about our lives and work without the interruption of fixing and eating meals. That doesn't mean we're bad cooks. Mediocre, but not bad.

When I was a bachelor (until 1976) I had two specialties. The Absolutely Incredible Exploits of the Adventuresome Uncle Goopy was a picnic ham a la Roast 'n Boast with diverse fixin's on the

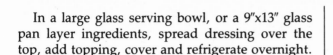

In a large glass serving bowl, or a 9"x13" glass pan layer ingredients, spread dressing over the top, add topping, cover and refrigerate overnight.

JOHN BOYKIN
MARY & PAT ZONDERVAN
LAURIE GOTT
M. G. BOEHMS

Betty's Salad and Dressing

Salad:

lettuce, as desired
spinach, as desired
1 can bean sprouts, drained
3 hard boiled eggs, chopped
5 slices crisp bacon, crumbled

Dressing:

¼ cup vinegar
⅓ cup catsup
1 tablespoon Worcestershire sauce
1 tablespoon grated onion
½ teaspoon salt
⅔ cup sugar
¼ cup brown sugar
1 cup oil

Wash, dry and tear in pieces lettuce and spinach. Add bean sprouts, chopped eggs, and bacon. Prepare dressing by mixing ingredients in an electric blender. Or mix ingredients in a bowl or shake in a tightly closed jar, adding oil after other ingredients are well mixed and mixing again by shaking jar or using egg beater in a bowl. Pour dressing over salad, toss, and serve.

RONNIE CARDER

side. Toenail Pudding consisted of macaroni, cheese, hamburger, corn, tomato sauce, and any leftovers in the fridge. Yolanda doesn't let me make the latter anymore, lest doing so give me an occasion for saying the dish's name out loud. She couldn't bear that.

Because of our divergent schedules (I'm an editor, she's a college instructor), Yolanda and I rarely eat breakfast or lunch together. As long as I have to eat, I like to make lunch a private time to hide in a corner and read. A sandwich, taco or slice of pizza will do, and I couldn't tell you ten minutes later what I'd had. A book of E. B. White essays or a newspaper is fine company for lunch.

So dinner tends to be our only meal together. Yolanda is usually cooking it when I come home, so we use that cooking time to start telling each other about our respective days. (When I was single I used to put on the TV news or an

Scandinavian Summer Salad

1 head Boston lettuce, torn in pieces
2 tomatoes, skinned, seeded, and cut into large cubes
8 radishes, sliced
1 tablespoon fresh chopped chervil
1 tablespoon fresh chopped parsley
1 teaspoon chopped chives
1 tablespoon chopped dill
8 mushrooms, sliced
4 slices smoked salmon (optional)
2 tablespoons butter

Mix lettuce, tomatoes, radishes, and herbs, refrigerate. Just before serving, saute mushrooms, and salmon, if desired, in butter. Toss salad with Sour Cream Dressing, add hot ingredients and serve immediately.

Sour Cream Dressing:

Make ahead and chill.

1 cup sour cream
2 teaspoons tarragon vinegar
1 tablespoon white vinegar
1 teaspoon grated horseradish
½ teaspoon salt
generous sprinkle of ground pepper

Mix ingredients, chill, and add to salad.

JOIE & MIKE VANDER WALL

album while fixing dinner. Now that time is for us.)

Dinner is our best time to just talk. It's a continuation of the cooking talk. Yolanda has a great interest in health (she never says her shoulder hurts; it's her scapula) so her conversation often drifts to subjects like cleft palate, facial lacerations, and autopsies. I don't share her interest in such things, particularly during the spaghetti, so I generally interrupt with a spirited analysis of the defensive strategies of a crack third baseman.

Whatever the topic, we have developed one habit that means a lot to both of us: we don't let the end of dinner mean the end of the conversation. Let the dishes sit; we'd rather keep talking. We can always soak the dishes later; we won't necessarily be able to pick up the threads of the conversation later. So we often just stay put for another fifteen or twenty minutes, enjoying each other's company. Those are among our best times together. ♥

JOHN BOYKIN

Cole Slaw De Luxe with Dill Dressing

SERVES 6

1 cup unpeeled, cored, and diced tart apples
2 teaspoons lemon juice
3 cups finely shredded red and green
    cabbages
¾ cup raisins
½ cup thinly sliced celery
⅓ cup sliced red onions
1 medium carrot, peeled and shredded
2 green onions with tops, sliced
¼ cup coarsely chopped walnuts

In a large bowl, toss apples with lemon juice. Add remaining ingredients, add Dill Dressing, toss to blend thoroughly, cover and chill.

Dill Dressing:

½ cup sour cream
½ cup mayonnaise
2½ tablespoons red wine vinegar
1½ tablespoons sugar
2 teaspoons dillweed
½ teaspoon salt
¼ teaspoon black pepper

In small bowl whisk together sour cream, mayonnaise, red wine vinegar, sugar, dillweed, salt, and pepper. Makes 1 cup.

LENA & DAVID EWERT

Uldine's Light Avocado-Carrot Salad

SERVES 6

3 avocados, diced
2 grated carrots
1 small green pepper, diced
½ cup sunflower seeds
Salad greens of your choice, as desired
Fresh parsley or lemon peel for garnish

Dressing:

1 tablespoon minced onion (optional)
2 tablespoons apple cider vinegar
¼ cup salad oil
juice of ½ lemon
¼ teaspoon Vege-sal (from health food store)

Toast the sunflower seeds. Then mix with avocado, carrot, and green pepper. Mix dressing ingredients. Put avocado mixture on a bed of greens, add dressing and garnish with fresh parsley or lemon peel.

ULDINE BISAGNO

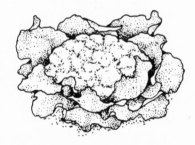

Crunchy Salad

1 pound fresh cauliflower
1 pound fresh broccoli
¼ cup bacon bits
1–2 cups Ranch style salad dressing
croutons, mildly seasoned

Clean vegetables and cut or break into bite-sized pieces. Add bacon bits and dressing and marinate for an hour or two in the refrigerator. Toss lightly and serve with croutons.

MARTIN & SHERRY SINGER

Crunchy Salad

◀ We noticed that typical potluck fare at church meant an abundance of casseroles and Jello salads—nothing that went "crunch." So we were pleased to find this salad for those who enjoy broccoli and cauliflower. ♥

MARTIN & SHERRY SINGER

Olivia's Broccoli-Mushroom Salad

3 medium bunches fresh broccoli
1½ pounds fresh mushrooms
2 large green onions with tops

Dressing:

1 cup oil
¼ cup vinegar
1 teaspoon salt
1 teaspoon celery seed
½ cup sugar
1 teaspoon onion powder
1 teaspoon paprika

Combine dressing ingredients and set aside at room temperature for 1 hour, then refrigerate. Slice mushrooms and green onions, break broccoli into flowerets, mix together. Cover and store in refrigerator. Pour dressing on salad and let stand in refrigerator 1 hour. Toss about 30 minutes before serving.

Olivia & Paul Hillman

German Broccoli Salad

8 slices bacon, fried crisp and crumbled
½ cup onion, chopped medium fine
½ cup raisins
½ cup nuts (optional)
1 large bunch fresh broccoli, tops only

Dressing:

1 cup mayonnaise
½ cup sugar
2 teaspoons vinegar

Combine salad ingredients. Mix dressing, add amount desired to salad, toss and serve.

Linda Fallin

Potato Salad

SERVES 8–10

8 medium to large white potatoes
5 eggs
¼ cup finely chopped green pepper
⅔ cup finely chopped green onions
1¼ cups sliced celery
1 cup sliced radishes, plus radish roses for
   garnish
¾ cup chopped cucumber (optional)
paprika

Dressing:

1¼ cups mayonnaise
¼ cup salad dressing
½ teaspoon dry mustard
1 tablespoon prepared mustard
3 tablespoons lemon juice
½ teaspoon sugar
1 tablespoon pickle relish
1¼ teaspoon celery seed
salt and pepper, to taste

Peel and boil potatoes until just tender, drain and stove dry, cool in refrigerator. Hard boil eggs, peel and refrigerate to cool. Prepare dressing, mixing all ingredients together. Prepare green pepper, onions, celery, radishes and cucumbers. When cool, chop hard cooked eggs (slicing 1 or 2 and reserving for garnish). Mix vegetables, eggs and dressing. Garnish with sliced hard cooked eggs and radish roses and sprinkle with paprika. Cover and refrigerate all day or overnight so flavors can blend.

WILMA ZONDERVAN TEGGELAAR

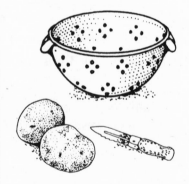

Grandma Lou's Hot Potato Salad

SERVES 6

7 or 8 potatoes suitable for boiling, unpeeled
1 teaspoon salt
6 slices bacon, diced
1 medium onion, diced
1½ tablespoons flour
¼ cup sugar
¼ cup vinegar, more if desired
1 cup water
1 teaspoon salt
pepper, to taste
⅓ cup undiluted evaporated milk
½ cup sour cream (optional)
hard-boiled egg, and/or parsley or minced
    chives for garnish

Scrub potatoes, place potatoes, salt, and water to cover in a saucepan, and boil about 20–25 minutes. Do not overcook or potatoes will fall apart. Drain, peel while still warm and cut into cubes or slices.

Fry bacon in skillet until just golden, remove bacon and set aside. Drain excess grease and saute onions in remaining bacon grease in skillet. In a bowl, combine flour and sugar, stir in vinegar and water slowly, add salt and pepper. Stir into onions and boil gently for a few minutes until thickened, stirring frequently. Add bacon.

Add evaporated milk and stir until well mixed—do not allow to boil. Pour over warm potatoes and mix gently with a wooden spoon. Add sour cream, if desired, and taste for seasoning. Garnish with sliced hard-boiled egg, and/or parsley and minced chives.

LYDIA HEERMANN

Grandma Lou's
Hot Potato Salad

This recipe is one my dear mother-in-law bequeathed to me. It was served at every picnic. I believe the ingredient which makes it different is the addition of sugar, which I haven't found in other potato salads. The ingredients can be changed to suit individual tastes.

We have discovered the flavor is better when the salad is served warm, and often warm it slightly in the oven if it has been necessary to refrigerate it. ♥

LYDIA HEERMANN

Rotini Salad

This salad should be made a day ahead.

1 box rotini pasta, cooked and cooled
1 medium onion, chopped
1 cup diced celery
¼ teaspoon celery salt
¼ teaspoon celery seed
½ teaspoon turmeric
salt and pepper, to taste

Dressing:

1 pint mayonnaise
1 cup water
½ cup vinegar
1 cup sugar

Combine salad ingredients. Mix dressing ingredients and add to salad. Cover and store in refrigerator until serving time.

BETTY DRESCHER

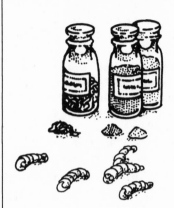

Tuna Cooler

2 cups uncooked macaroni
¾ cup chopped celery
¼ cup finely chopped onion
¼ cup chopped green pepper
1 (6 ounce) can tuna, drained and flaked
1 (17 ounce) can peas, drained
1 (2½ ounce or 4 ounce) jar mushrooms,
   drained

➤→

Tuna Cooler

←This is a great recipe for picnics or summer potlucks. I discovered it when Darrell and I were poverty-stricken newlyweds, and I was a real novice in the kitchen. It was inexpensive and easy then, and I still like it for the same reasons. ♥

DEBBIE BARR

Dressing:

1¼ cups mayonnaise
¼ cup catsup
¼ cup milk
1 teaspoon salt
¼ teaspoon pepper
¼ teaspoon chili powder (optional)
⅛ teaspoon celery salt

For garnish: add paprika and fresh parsley

Cook macaroni, rinse, and drain. Turn into large bowl. Combine with celery, onion, pepper, tuna, peas and mushrooms. Add dressing, toss gently to combine. Chill 2 to 4 hours. Garnish with paprika and fresh parsley. Keep chilled.

DEBBIE BARR

Sour Noodles

16 ounces pasta (noodles, mostaccioli, macaroni, shells, etc.)
1 cup vinegar
1 teaspoon salt
1 teaspoon pepper
1½ cups sugar
2 teaspoons prepared (or dry) mustard
1 medium onion, cut into chunks
½ teaspoon garlic powder
1 medium cucumber, peeled and cut into chunks
1 tablespoon parsley flakes
½ cup vegetable oil

Cook pasta, drain and cool. In a blender, mix remaining ingredients (except oil) thoroughly, until all have been incorporated into the liquid. With blender on add oil, slowly. Place pasta in a large bowl and mix in liquid. Cover and refrigerate overnight. Stir again before serving.

SUELLEN STOOKEY

Cooperation Salad

4 or 5 yellow apples, cored and cut into
    small pieces
2 carrots, coarsely grated
¼ cup raisins
2 tablespoons shredded coconut (optional)
chopped nuts (optional)
¼ cup plain yogurt
1–2 tablespoons honey

Several family members can cooperate on this
(hence the name). Divide activities up, such as:
(1) coring and slicing apples (one of those neat
little gadgets for this task is helpful and fun);
(2) cleaning and grating carrots (be careful with
little fingers on this one); (3) measuring and
mixing yogurt and honey together (this dressing
can be served separately if the salad is eaten right
away); (4) measuring and stirring in raisins, coconut and nuts.

Mix all ingredients together. Store in refrigerator in an airtight container.

Everyone helps with cleanup while having a
whistling contest.

Whistling contest:

(Better for older children, to avoid frustration.)
Pick a short tune such as "Mary Had a Little
Lamb" or "This is the Way We Wash Our
Clothes." See who can whistle the whole tune the
fastest. Two or three people start on "Go!" (You
can have the youngest family member say "Go.")
The tune must be recognizable.

Who can whistle the tune twice without laugh-
ing? Who can whistle it highest—and lowest?

Anyone who knows "Whistle While You
Work" teach it to everyone.

AUDREY HINTEN

Cooperation Salad

◄ *Cooking is an excellent
medium for fostering closeness
and cooperation in a family.
Our son Rocky (now six) has
been helping me cook since he
was three. It takes patience, but
is very rewarding for us both.
He and I developed this recipe
together. Vary the amounts of
any ingredients to your own
taste.* ♥

AUDREY HINTEN

Sunny Carrot Salad

 Quick & Easy

SERVES 4

2½ cups grated raw carrots
½ cup raisins (optional)
¼ – ½ teaspoon salt, if desired
Orange Squash, or thawed undiluted orange
juice concentrate (if orange juice
concentrate is used, you may need to add
a bit of sugar or honey)

Mix carrots, raisins, and salt, if desired. Add enough Orange Squash or orange juice concentrate to moisten. Toss to blend.

MERILYN & MILTON FISHER

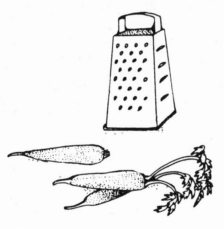

"Interesting Things"

The first person (designated by dad) reports on his most interesting experience during the last twenty-four hours. This may include something unusual which happened to him or his friends . . . a surprisingly good grade . . . the homerun that won the ball game . . . a compliment . . . the unexpected letter . . . some wonder of nature . . . the place where he felt God closest . . . big breaks . . . bad breaks . . . little breaks in the routine . . . somebody's trauma . . . an aching heart . . . something read . . . what a friend said—humorous, sad, sharp . . . maybe a complaint . . . or a deal for the family's voting . . . the good, the bad, the ugly; any of these will do.

Each person takes his turn around the table. Although no one is permitted to repeat what has been said before, new slants and different versions are acceptable. When each has had

Mandarin Orange Salad

1 bunch romaine lettuce, torn in bite-sized
   pieces
1 red onion, thinly sliced
1 can mandarin orange slices, chilled and
   drained (fresh orange sections may be
   substituted)
jicama, chopped (optional)
Italian or poppyseed dressing

Combine lettuce, onion, orange slices and
jicama, if desired. Toss with Italian or poppyseed
dressing.

MARY ANN HOWARD

Quick Picnic Salad

SERVES 8–10

1 can apricot or peach pie filling
1 (8 ounce) can mandarin orange slices,
   drained
1 (20 ounce) can pineapple chunks, drained
2 cups miniature marshmallows
2 bananas
seedless grapes (optional)
other fruit, fresh or canned (optional)

For a picnic, you can chill the cans of fruit and
pie filling and take along in a food cooler, mixing
salad just before serving. Mix all ingredients
together, slicing and adding bananas last.

To make at home, mix all ingredients except
bananas, cover and chill in refrigerator. Just before
serving slice and add bananas.

LA VERNE MADVIG

his turn, seconds and thirds are
admissible. All this leads to
many questions, plus
considerable traffic in ideas.
   Several good things come
from this practice.
   Each person opens up his
soul a bit for all to see what's
going on inside. During the
"cave" years this is particularly
important. (In the early teens
our children seemed to withdraw
for a time. We call these the
"cave" years.) Since there is a
twenty-five cent fine for the
nonparticipant, everyone makes a
noble effort. Those who wonder
where the fine money goes will
be interested in this: it has been
so long since anyone had to
pay, no one can remember.
Families who feel a dearth of
intercommunication will find
"interesting things" a powerful
stimulant. ♥
   (Excerpted from You Can Be
a Great Parent, Charlie Shedd,
p. 74; copyright 1970, Waco,
Texas: Word. Originally
published as Promises to
Peter.)

Hot Fruit Salad

"Especially good for brunch on cool fall mornings."

1 can applesauce
1 can mandarin orange slices, drained
1 can apricots, drained
1 can pineapple chunks, drained
1 can cherry pie filling

Topping:

½ cup brown sugar
1 teaspoon cinnamon

Layer fruit and pie filling in a casserole in the above order. Mix brown sugar and cinnamon together and sprinkle over the top. Bake at 325F for 60 minutes. Serve hot.

Lois & Caryn Dykstra

Holiday Cranberry Salad

"This is best if made a day ahead."

Equal portions of the following:

cranberries, ground (frozen or fresh)
celery, chopped
pecans, chopped
apples, chopped (a tart variety)
crushed pineapple, well-drained
sugar

Combine, cover and refrigerate until served.

Frances & Curtis Vaughan

Cucumber Salad

1 package lime flavored gelatin
½ cup boiling water
1 medium cucumber, unpeeled, shredded
1 small onion, grated
½ cup mayonnaise or salad dressing
1 teaspoon vinegar
½ teaspoon horseradish (important)
salt, to taste
1 pound cottage cheese

Garnish:

mayonnaise
paprika
cucumber slices
radish halves

Dissolve gelatin in boiling water. Add shredded cucumber, onion, mayonnaise, vinegar, horseradish, salt, and cottage cheese. Mix. Refrigerate in a pan or individual molds until firm. (Keep refrigerated.) Garnish just before serving with a cucumber slice and radish half on a dollop of mayonnaise sprinkled with paprika.

WILMA ZONDERVAN TEGGELAAR

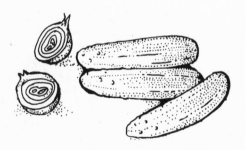

Play "Thirteen"!

When our boys were growing up in pre-dishwasher days, we played "Thirteen" on special occasions when we had extra people and extra dishes. Everyone had the privilege (?), guests included, of wiping 13 dishes. Five pieces of silverware counted as 1. This can be played with dishwashers, too. Each player clears 13 things from the table and stacks. Another puts 13 items in the dishwasher or washes 13 items that won't fit in. Lots of fun and the kitchen is cleaned up in a hurry! ♥

MATILDA NORDTVEDT

Orange-Pineapple Salad

1 tablespoon (1 envelope) gelatin
¼ cup cold water
1 (8 ounce) can crushed pineapple, undrained
1 tablespoon honey
1 cup orange juice
2 carrots, grated
1 stalk celery, finely chopped

Garnish:

orange slices

   Soften gelatin in cold water. Bring pineapple and liquid from can to a boil. Add softened gelatin and stir until dissolved. Add honey, orange juice, carrots and celery. Chill until set. Decorate with orange slices if desired.

MATILDA NORDTVELDT

Apricot Nectar Gelatin Salad

1 (12 ounce) can apricot nectar
1 (3 ounce) package lemon flavored gelatin
⅓ cup water
1 tablespoon lemon juice
1 (11 ounce) can mandarin orange slices,
   drained
½ cup, or more, seedless green grapes, halved
¼ cup, or more, unpeeled apple, chopped

   Bring apricot nectar to a boil; add gelatin, stirring until dissolved. Stir in water and lemon juice. Chill until the consistency of unbeaten egg whites. Stir in orange slices, grapes and apple. Pour into an oiled 4-cup mold. Chill until firm.

JANE & PAUL MICKEY

Cranberry Jell

1 (3 ounce) package raspberry flavored gelatin
1 (3 ounce) package lemon flavored gelatin
1¼ cups boiling water
1 (10 ounce) package frozen red raspberries,
   partially thawed
1 cup lemon-lime soda
1 (14 ounce) jar cranberry-orange relish

Dissolve gelatin in boiling water. Add partially thawed raspberries and stir gently until mixed. Slowly stir in soda. Add cranberry-orange relish. Pour into a 6½ cup mold. Chill until firm.

DORIS RIKKERS

Jiffy Cranberry Salad

"This takes only a few minutes to mix up, and is a tasty dish for the holiday season."

1 (3 ounce) package cherry flavored gelatin
½ cup boiling water
1 can jellied cranberry sauce
1 cup plain yogurt
½ cup chopped walnuts
1 cup miniature marshmallows
1 banana, diced

Dissolve gelatin in boiling water. Add remaining ingredients, pour into an 8"x8" pan and chill until set.

CARLA MOCKABEE

Meal time at our house is important. The stage is often set by lighted candles and an attractive table setting—why wait for a party? Every day should be a celebration. Often humor pervades and we tell funny stories or jokes. Proverbs 17:22 should be present at every meal. "A merry heart doeth good like a medicine." ♥

MARY ANN HOWARD

Van Raalte Dressing

¾ cup vinegar
½ cup catsup
¾–1½ cups sugar
1 teaspoon salt
½ teaspoon ginger
½ teaspoon paprika
1 small onion, diced
2 cups oil

Mix all ingredients together in an electric blender until smooth and well blended. Refrigerate. Shake or stir well before serving.

Mrs. David Kok

Red Dressing for Tossed Salad

¼ cup vinegar
¾ cup sugar
½ teaspoon dry mustard
1 cup oil
1 cup catsup
½ teaspoon celery seed

In an electric blender or with an electric mixer mix together vinegar, sugar, and mustard. With mixer or blender running, slowly add oil. Stir in catsup and celery seed. Chill before serving.

Evelyn Bence

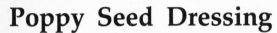

Poppy Seed Dressing

⅓ cup vinegar
1½ teaspoons onion juice
¾ cup sugar
1 teaspoon dry mustard
1 teaspoon salt
1 cup oil
1½ tablespoons poppy seeds

In an electric blender or with an electric mixer mix together vinegar, onion juice, sugar, mustard, and salt. With blender or mixer running, gradually add oil. Stir in poppy seeds.

Mrs. T. T. (Bennie) Crabtree

SOUPS

Judith's Cream of Mushroom Soup 56
Carrot Mushroom Soup 57
Uldine's Mushroom Soup 57
Winter Bean Soup 58
Twyla's Quickie Stew 59
Vegetable Beef Soup 60
Mab's Meaty Soup 61
Cabbage Borscht 62
Cheese and Broccoli Soup 63
French Onion Soup 64
Tuna Soup 64
Clam Chowder 65
Matzo Ball Soup 66
Farina Dumplings 67
Judith's Cream of Chicken Soup 68
Chicken-Rice Soup 69
Chicken Soup Hunt 70

Judith's Cream of Mushroom Soup

SERVES 4 to 6

½ lb. mushrooms
4 tablespoons butter (½ stick)
½ cup celery, diced
¼ cup onion, diced
2 tablespoons chopped fresh parsley
2 cups chicken stock
2 tablespoons flour
1 cup milk
pepper to taste
¾ teaspoon salt
⅛ teaspoon paprika
3 tablespoons dry white wine

In a small saucepan saute mushrooms in 2 tablespoons of the butter. Remove and place in an electric blender, add celery, onion, and parsley and blend until finely chopped. Return mixture to saucepan, add chicken stock and simmer, covered, for 20 minutes. While mixture is simmering make a white sauce in a medium sized saucepan: melt remaining butter, add flour, stir and cook for ½ minute. Gradually add milk, stirring constantly. Bring to a boil, stirring frequently. Cook 1 minute. Pour the mushroom stock slowly into the white sauce, stirring until smooth. Add remaining ingredients and cook at medium heat, stirring constantly, heating to just below a boil.

H. JUDITH & Dr. ROLAND HARRISON

Carrot Mushroom Soup

SERVES 4 or 5

2 tablespoons butter or margarine
1 onion, chopped
1 cup fresh mushrooms, sliced
3 carrots, sliced
5 cups chicken broth
1 tablespoon curry powder
1 tablespoon lemon juice
salt, to taste
chopped parsley, to taste

Saute onion in butter. Add remaining ingredients; simmer until carrots are tender.

EVELYN BENCE

Uldine's Mushroom Soup

SERVES 4 to 6

4 tablespoons butter
2 tablespoons onion, grated
½ lb. fresh mushrooms, thinly sliced
1 quart chicken stock
1 teaspoon salt
1 pint half and half
2 tablespoons cooking sherry

Saute onions in butter, until soft. Add mushrooms and cook, covered, 5 minutes over low heat. Add chicken stock, cover, and let simmer for 15 minutes. Add sherry and half and half and reheat—do not simmer. Good with a topping of unsweetened whipped cream.

ULDINE BISAGNO

Cooking and Listening

Although we all share dinner duties (setting the table, getting out the milk, etc.) I find the time I am in the kitchen preparing dinner is a good time to listen to one read or another chatter on about the day. In other words, the preparation and clean-up time can be valuable family together times, too. ♥

CAROL KUYKENDALL

Winter Bean Soup

SERVES 6

2 cups bean mixture*
2½ to 3 quarts cold water
ham hock, soup bone, or beef chunks
1 clove garlic, pressed
2 sliced onions
4 cups tomatoes
1 bay leaf
salt, pepper, oregano, and thyme to taste

Bean mixture:

Combine equal parts of the following:

great northern beans
small red beans
green split peas
yellow split peas
speckled limas
black-eyed peas
kidney beans
baby limas
garbanzos
black beans
barley
soy beans
pea beans
lentils
mung beans
pinto beans

Soak 2 cups of bean mixture in cold water overnight. Combine all ingredients in a large pot or Dutch oven, add additional water to cover. Simmer until beans are tender. Remove bay leaf before serving.

SANDRA DRESCHER LEHMAN

Winter Bean Soup

◄ The bean mixture makes a colorful assortment. It's fun to make a double batch and give away jars of it as Christmas gifts. It's a good stew to simmer all day in the crock pot. ♥

SANDRA DRESCHER LEHMAN

Twyla's Quickie Stew

Quick & Easy

"SERVES 10 hearty eaters *twice*."

**3 pounds lean ground beef
1 (gallon) can Veg All mixed vegetables
1 (3 pound) can chili (beans and meat) or 1
    (3 pound) can pork and beans
any leftover vegetables, gravy or meat in the
    refrigerator
2 packages beef stew seasoning mix
additional seasoning to taste, if desired
flour and water to thicken, if desired**

Brown ground beef in a large pan or Dutch oven. Add Veg All, chili or pork and beans, leftovers, and seasonings. Simmer together 30 minutes or longer, stirring frequently. Thicken with flour and water, if desired.

TWYLA LUBBEN

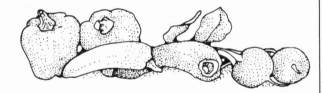

Quick & Easy

Quickie Stew

As a mother of eleven adopted children plus another 59 who have slept beneath our roof, I have learned much about food and families. It isn't so much what *you* serve as how *it's* served.

Mealtime should be without stress. If there is a relaxed atmosphere it matters little how simple the meal. At age 57 years I had 5 little ones, 6 years and under. I was too busy folding diapers to worry about exotic dishes, yet the family grew to be healthy individuals. Now at age 71 and 77 my husband and I are adopting our eleventh baby and I still cook very plainly. No junk food. Soft drinks are only for the flu. Instead we thrive on good thick stew, meat loaf, and Swedish meat balls (because we can't often afford steak). We eat turkey and crisp browned chicken along with green fresh vegetables and fresh fruit. ♥

TWYLA LUBBEN

Vegetable Beef Soup

1 large beef shank
1 tablespoon salt
1 onion, cut in chunks
8 cups water
1 medium potato, cut in small pieces
2 stalks celery, cut up
2 small onions, cut in chunks
1 small can stewed tomatoes
¼ cup Minute Rice
½ teaspoon pepper
2 bay leaves
½ teaspoon basil
½ teaspoon thyme
1 tablespoon parsley flakes

Combine first 4 ingredients in a large pot or Dutch oven, bring to a boil and simmer for 2 hours. Remove meat from bones and return to broth. Add remaining ingredients and simmer 2 to 4 hours. Taste and add more salt if desired. Remove bay leaves before serving.

KATHY THOMPSON

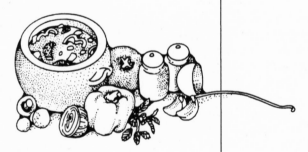

Mab's Meaty Soup

"Although I love to eat, I'm not a good cook. However, there is one thing I make that seems to be a hit with all my family—soup. Here's how I do it:"

SERVES 4 or 5, or two people 2 days. (The second day it's better.)

½ to 1 lb. cubed stewing beef or 2 meaty
      beef ribs
1 tablespoon oil
5-6 cups water
2 carrots, diced
1 large potato, diced
1 onion, diced
2 stalks celery, diced
1 fresh tomato, peeled and diced (or 1 small
      can tomato sauce)
2 tablespoons frozen beans
2 tablespoons frozen peas
2 tablespoons frozen corn
1 beef bouillon cube
garlic, salt, and pepper, to taste

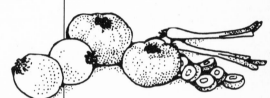

In a pressure cooker, brown the meat in oil, uncovered. Browning time on low is about half an hour, stirring and turning the pieces often. Add water and pressure cook according to manufacturer's instructions fifteen minutes. (If you don't have a pressure cooker, use a large saucepan or Dutch oven and simmer meat until tender.) Following cooker directions, let off steam. Add remaining ingredients. Cover and simmer an hour—at least—the longer the better. Before eating, if possible, refrigerate so you can take off all fat. Remember, fat makes fat.

MAB GRAFF HOOVER

My family is grown and gone—but we had one rule for all meals—no quarreling at the table. My husband and I tried never to discuss bills or anything else unpleasant at mealtime, and we tried not to put the children on the spot about their shortcomings while we were eating. ♥

MAB GRAFF HOOVER

Cabbage Borscht

"Good as a main dish served with fresh baked bread or rolls, with apple pie for dessert. The soup is even better warmed up."

2–3 pounds soup bone with some meat (beef or chicken)
2 quarts water
2 carrots, finely cut (optional)
1 medium head cabbage, finely chopped
4 medium potatoes, cubed
1 medium onion, cut up
1 teaspoon salt
10 peppercorns
1 small bay leaf
dill and parsley, to taste
dash of cayenne pepper
dash of paprika
1 to 1½ cups tomatoes (or substitute 1 can tomato soup or tomato sauce)
½ cup heavy cream or sour cream

Simmer soup bones in water in a large saucepan or Dutch oven for 1½ to 3 hours, until meat is tender. When meat is cooked, remove bones. Add enough water to make about 2 quarts of broth. Add carrots, cabbage, potatoes, and onion. When vegetables are tender, add tomatoes and seasonings, bring just to a boil, remove from heat, and add the cream just before serving. Can be frozen and reheated. (You may want to remove bay leaf before serving.)

LENA & DAVID EWERT

Cheese and Broccoli Soup

2 green onions, with tops
2 small carrots, cut up
2 stalks celery, cut up (or celery seed, to
    taste)
1 cup water
1 chicken bouillon cube
¼ cup margarine
3 cups milk
¼ cup flour
⅛ teaspoon pepper
8 ounces Velveeta or American cheese, grated
1 bunch cooked, chopped broccoli (you may
    wish to omit stalks)

Place green onions, carrots, celery and water in blender and chop until fine. Place in pot and add bouillon cube and margarine. Simmer 10 minutes. Mix flour, pepper and one cup of milk in blender, add to cooked mixture. Add remaining milk and cook on medium heat, stirring until thickened. Lower heat and add cheese, stirring until melted. Do not boil. Add broccoli and serve.

SHIRLEY BLEDSOE

Economy

It's a game with me to find a sale item for which I also have a cents-off coupon. Coupons are stored in a shoe box and organized in recycled envelopes. I write my grocery lists on recycled envelopes, and place coupons in the envelopes while shopping. ♥

DOROTHY & DAVIS A. YOUNG

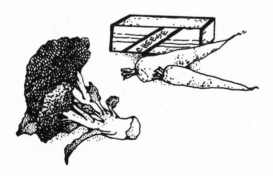

French Onion Soup

3 lbs. onions, sliced
1 stick (½ cup) butter
1 teaspoon pepper
2 tablespoons paprika
1 bay leaf
2 teaspoons salt
¾ cup flour
1 cup white wine
3 quarts beef bouillon
French bread
Swiss cheese, sliced

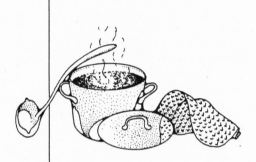

In a large pot simmer onions in butter over low heat for 1½ hours, stirring frequently. Add pepper, paprika, bay leaf, and salt. Mix flour with wine and stir in. Cook on low heat 10 minutes. Add bouillon and simmer 2 hours. Remove bay leaf. Cool, and refrigerate overnight. Heat soup to serve. Place a slice of Swiss cheese in the bottom of individual serving bowls. Top soup with 1" thick slices of French bread topped with additional slices of Swiss cheese. Place under broiler to melt cheese.

BARBARA & STEPHEN G. COBB

Tuna Soup

"Don't let the tuna fish turn you off—it is really delicious!"

1 cup onions, diced
3 tablespoons margarine
3 cups water
½ teaspoon basil
1 teaspoon salt
¼ teaspoon pepper
2 cups uncooked egg noodles
½ pound cheese, cut in chunks
1 (7-ounce) can tuna, drained
2½ cups milk

➤→

In a large pot or Dutch oven, saute onions in margarine. Add water, basil, salt and pepper and bring to a boil. Add noodles, simmer, covered, about ten minutes. Remove from heat and add cheese, stirring until melted. Add tuna and milk, heat to serving temperature. Do not boil.

OLIVIA & PAUL HILLMAN

Clam Chowder

1 (10 ounce) can whole clams
1 (6½ ounce) can minced clams
8 ounces (2 cubes) butter or margarine
1 cup chopped celery
1 cup chopped onion
4 cubes chicken bouillon
3 cups diced potatoes
2 cups water
1 cup flour
4 cups milk
1 cup half and half
salt
pepper

Drain clams and reserve juice, set aside. In a large pot or Dutch oven, saute celery and onion in 4 ounces of the butter (1 cube). Add clam juice, bouillon cubes, potatoes, and water. Simmer until potatoes are cooked. Melt remaining butter (1½ cubes), and mix with flour. Add to soup. Add milk, clams, half and half, salt and pepper, to taste. Heat to serving temperature. Do not boil.

Variation:

Omit clams for potato soup.

RONNIE CARDER

Listed below are a few of the things we have done as a family to make mealtime warm and special.

1. "The Neater Eater Award." When our children were small we would choose one of them who we felt was working at being a neat eater. Awards ranged from candy and gum, to special privileges.

2. "You Are Special." Some evening my husband will choose one of our family members to be special for the night. Each of the other family members must say at least one specific thing they like about our special person.

3. "Changing Places." Everyone sits in a different person's seat for the mealtime and acts like that person would act. A real eye opener.

4. "Choosing Right." My husband has on some occasions told a story to the children that has a moral ethical choice involved. The children discuss the options and decide on what God would have them do if they had the choice. We then talk about Bible verses that relate to the situation. ♥

RONNIE & DAVE CARDER

Matzo Ball Soup

"Living in Chicago 12 years, I learned to make Matzo Ball Soup from scratch . . . and still serve it with much pleasure to all my friends. They love it! It is unbelievably delicious!"

SERVES about 4 people

1 chicken
2 carrots, sliced
2 stalks celery, sliced
1 small onion, cut up
2 eggs
½ cup matzo meal
1 teaspoon salt
fresh parsley or cilantro

To prepare broth:

Cut up chicken, put in boiling water, add carrots, celery, and onion, and simmer until chicken is tender. Pour off broth and allow to cool. Remove fat from broth and save for preparing matzo balls and other cooking. (I keep some in my freezer all ready to use.) Use cooked chicked for another recipe.

Matzo Meal:

Buy a box for less than one dollar at your grocery store. The recipe is on the box: Manischewitz Matzo Meal (salted or unsalted).

To prepare matzo balls:

Beat eggs with fork, add 2 tablespoons melted chicken fat (from the chicken you boiled). Mix matzo meal with salt and add to egg mixture. When well blended, add 2 tablespoons chicken broth and mix. Cover and place in refrigerator for at least 20 minutes.   ➤➤

While conducting a prayer workshop in Tucson, Arizona, I was the guest in a home where there were two teenage boys. Their parents practiced conversational prayer, having been in my classes in Taiwan on my visit there in 1969. But I was surprised to find them doing all four steps while their hot meal was waiting on the table. I stole a glance at the boys and noticed they took part without enthusiasm and as briefly as possible.

Later, as their mother cleared the dining room and took care of the kitchen, I slipped into the living room where the boys were. I asked if they liked those long prayers before they ate.

Now, using a 2 or 3 quart pot, bring salted water to a brisk boil. Reduce heat, and into the slightly bubbling water drop balls formed from the above mixture. Wet or oil your hands, and make the balls about the size of a walnut.

Cover and cook 30–40 minutes. You can make these the day before, or hours before. When ready to serve, heat broth and add matzo balls. Allow to simmer for a few minutes until heated.

ROSALIND RINKER

Farina Dumplings

½ cup water
6 tablespoons margarine
¼ teaspoon salt
¼ teaspoon nutmeg
¾ cup Cream of Wheat cereal
2 eggs
soup
chopped parsley, for garnish

In a saucepan bring water and margarine to a boil. Add salt and nutmeg. Slowly stir in Cream of Wheat. Cook slightly, then cool while preparing soup. Add eggs to Cream of Wheat mixture and beat well. Drop by tablespoonsful into boiling soup. Cover and simmer 10 minutes, or until dumplings are set. Spoon into bowls and sprinkle with chopped parsley.

JEAN SHAW

Wouldn't they like it better after they ate. They both lifted their heads and flashed eager smiles at me. "Do you think you could manage it?" Of course I could and did. The parents had never once thought of the effect upon the boys.

In finding the right time for your family, be sure you think about the children and what effect it will have on them. There is a right time and a wrong time for each family. ♥

ROSALIND RINKER (from Making Family Devotions a Priority)

Judith's Cream of Chicken Soup

"My own creation."

SERVES 4 to 6

¼ cup chopped onion
¼ cup chopped celery
1–2 tablespoons butter
½ cup cooked chicken, chopped
2 cups chicken stock
2 tablespoons flour
2 tablespoons butter
1 cup milk
⅛ teaspoon paprika
¾ teaspoon salt
¼ teaspoon chopped parsley
2–3 tablespoons dry white wine

In a small saucepan saute onion and celery in butter. Remove and place in electric blender, add chicken and blend until finely chopped. Return mixture to saucepan, add chicken stock and simmer 20 minutes. While mixture is simmering make a white sauce in a medium sized saucepan: melt butter, add flour, stir and cook for ½ minute. Gradually add milk, stirring constantly. Bring to a boil, stirring frequently. Cook 1 minute. Slowly add broth mixture to white sauce, stirring until smooth and creamy. Add paprika, salt, parsley, and wine. Heat to just below boiling.

H. JUDITH & DR. ROLAND HARRISON

Chicken-Rice Soup

"This delicious soup came into being when my children asked for tasty soup without anything 'gross' in it. We enjoy blueberry muffins with this soup for an easy supper."

4 quarts water
1 teaspoon salt
3–4 chicken breasts
1 can condensed chicken-rice soup
2 tablespoons chicken bouillon granules
1 tablespoon minced onion
2 teaspoons dried parsley flakes
1 bunch celery, sliced or chopped (use most of the leaves too)
4 or 5 carrots, sliced or chopped
¾ cup uncooked rice

In a large pot or Dutch oven simmer chicken in water and salt until tender. Remove chicken, discard skin, remove meat from bones and cut into bite-size pieces. Return cut-up meat to broth and add remaining ingredients. Simmer, covered, 3–4 hours. Taste, and correct seasonings.

DIANE BRUMMEL BLOEM

We try to avoid disturbing or problem-centered conversation at dinner time. It is our time to check in with each other and share what is happening in our lives. I don't think we have ever spelled out the ground rules, but over the years we have come to understand that everyone participates in the conversation. We don't just eat, and no one person monopolizes the time. My husband may ask a quiet family member, "Well, Gary, how has your day been?" If someone has been someplace out of the ordinary routine, he will generally ask, "What was your favorite thing?" He sometimes puts a little list at his place at the table to remind him to inform family members of up-coming events or to remind himself to get necessary information from them. I have been told by various people over the years that our family talks to each other more than others. I don't know about that, but I do know that we have a whole arsenal of comments that mean

Chicken Soup Hunt

Quantities in this recipe are determined by how much broth you begin with. The soup should be nicely filled with vegetables and meat.

chicken broth
chopped onion
chopped celery, including the leaves
chopped carrots
green pepper (optional)
zucchini (optional)
rice (about ¼ cup)
salt, to taste
8–10 whole peppercorns
2 tablespoons white cooking wine
cooked chicken, chopped, chunked, or
    shredded

The secret to good soup is to let it simmer a long time so that all the flavors blend. Add the chicken meat just before serving. Serve with corn bread and you have a nutritious meal.

GLADYS HUNT

nothing to others but that can cause a family member to double up in laughter. This common ground comes from sharing every part of our lives with each other, and a significant amount of that sharing takes place around the dinner table. ♥

BARBARA BUSH

FRAGRANT LOAVES
AND OTHER
BREADS

Yeast Bread

Elaine Watson's Sunday Morning
Bread 73
90-Minute No-Knead Bread 74
White Bread 75
Parmesan Cheese Loaf 76
Salesman's Garlic Bread 76
Pan Rolls 77
Dinner Rolls 78
Walnut Honey Buns 79
Quick Cinnamon Rolls 80
Mrs. Howard's Rolls 81
Frosted Cinnamon Rolls 82
Ice Box Buns 83
Weihnacht Stollen 84
Honey Oatmeal Bread 85
Honey Wheat Bread 86
Swedish Limpa Rye Bread 87
Bagels 88
Olie Bollen I 89

Quick Bread

Olie Bollen II 90
Peanut Butter Lovers' Wheat Germ
Muffins 90
6 Week Bran Muffins 91
Shirley's Whole Wheat Muffins 91
Golden Raisin Buns 92
Sharon Engel's Blueberry Muffins 93
Butter Pecan Waffles 94

Annie's Yogurt Waffles 95
Buttermilk Pancakes 95
English Pancakes 96
Swedish Pancakes 96
Powerful Whole Wheat Pancakes 97
Best Biscuits 98
Olivia's Corn Bread 98
Jane's Corn Bread 99
California Zucchini Bread 100
World's Best Walnut-Zucchini Bread 101
Swedish Almond Bread 102
Blueberry Buckle 103
Blueberry Oatmeal Bread 104
Carrot Bread 105
Date Bread 106
Boston Brown Bread 107
Hibernia Bread 108
Irish Soda Bread 109
1, 2, 3 Counting Banana Bread 110
Best Banana Bread Ever 111
*Ursula's Cinnamon Topped Banana
    Bread* 112
Easy Cinnamon Rolls 113

Elaine Watson's Sunday Morning Bread

"For breakfast before church I sometimes served a bread I had made on Saturday. It is good fresh, but it is also very good sliced, spread with butter, and browned slightly under the broiler. Serve with apple sauce or apple butter."

MAKES 1 round loaf

1 package dry yeast
⅓ cup lukewarm water
2½ cups white flour
2 cups whole wheat flour
1¼ teaspoons salt
1 tablespoon sugar
1½ cups milk, scalded and cooled to
   lukewarm
¾ cup chopped walnuts
½ cup butter or margarine

Mix yeast into water until dissolved. Add butter to scalded milk to melt as milk cools. Mix dry ingredients together, reserving ½ cup white flour. Gradually add milk and yeast to dry ingredients. Mix well. Add nuts. Knead in the remaining ½ cup flour (using whole wheat instead of white flour if a heavier bread is desired).

Cover, let rise until double. Punch down. Knead five minutes. Form dough into a ball and place on baking sheet sprinkled with cornmeal.

Let rise 20 minutes. Slash top once with sharp knife. Place in center of preheated 425F oven with a pan of hot water at the bottom of the oven. After a half hour, remove the water and reduce heat to 300F. Bake 30 minutes more.

ELAINE WATSON

Sunday Meals

While the children were growing up, Sunday dinner after church was a family dinner, eaten formally at the dining room table. I prepared the meal, but one son mashed potatoes, one son set the table (correctly), our daughter made salads or prepared a relish tray, and my husband helped wherever he was needed. As they grew older the children helped with soup, the main course, and dessert, too.

Everyone worked together to clean up.

Then everyone was "free" for the rest of the day. Especially Mother.

In the evening each child always prepared his or her own favorite meal, which usually ranged from pancakes to pizza, all put together in the kitchen (never reheated or frozen foods), and usually eaten between bouts with homework or TV.

Sometimes they would share the

90-Minute No-Knead Bread

No-knead loaf bread needs vigorous stirring or some other pounding or stretching action to develop the gluten in the flour. If it is not developed sufficiently the bread will not rise well or hold its shape during baking. This bread has a coarser texture than kneaded varieties. But served hot from the oven, it is quite good.

MAKES one loaf

1 cup warm water
1 package yeast
1 teaspoon salt
2 tablespoons sugar
1 tablespoon oil or melted shortening
about 2½ cups flour

Dissolve yeast in warm water. Add salt, sugar, oil, and about half the flour. Stir vigorously for 1 minute, stir in the rest of the flour, adding enough to make a soft dough. Let stand for 15 minutes. Turn out on a floured surface and beat with a wooden spoon or rolling pin for one minute, folding dough over when it becomes flattened. Form into a loaf and place in a greased 9"x5" loaf pan. Cover and let rise in a warm place for about 30 minutes, until doubled. Bake at 400F for 30 minutes.

LATAYNE SCOTT

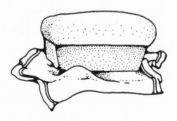

results, and our daughter's chocolate chip cookies would follow pizza or hamburgers and an exotic salad. Cooking one's favorite food never ceased to be a treat, it seemed, and the obligatory cleaning up of the kitchen followed pretty easily. Hearing one child harass another into getting the stovetop clean again, rather than having to have parental oversight out there, was music to my ears. Sometimes I got a cookie or a slice of pizza, too.

Adults, of course, seldom need a lot of calories at the end of the day—especially after a big Sunday dinner—so a quick sandwich with fruit and tea usually appealed to my husband and me, and to any guest who might have dropped by that evening. Or a bowl of popcorn—often shared with the children, who were hungry again before going to bed. ♥

ELAINE WATSON

White Bread

"Although this recipe makes two loaves, plan on having one eaten right away when it's hot!"

1¾ cups milk
1 tablespoon butter
1 tablespoon or 1 package dry yeast
½ cup warm water
2 tablespoons sugar
2 teaspoons salt
5½ cups flour

Scald milk, add butter to hot milk to melt, then cool to lukewarm. Dissolve yeast in water. In a large mixing bowl combine sugar, salt, milk, butter, and yeast mixture. Stir in flour one cup at a time until the dough is stiff enough to knead. Knead 8–10 minutes, adding a little flour when it becomes sticky. Form dough into a ball, place in greased bowl, cover, and let rise until double. Punch down and let dough rest 10 minutes. Divide in two, form into loaves, and put in 2 greased and floured 9"x5" loaf pans. Cover and let rise to the top of the pans. Bake 25–30 minutes at 350F. When nicely browned, remove from oven and brush tops with butter. Remove from pans and try at least one piece while hot!

JANICE KEMPE

There is an indescribable feeling of warmth and coziness when I enter a home which is full of the smell of homebaked bread!

I remember certain smells and sounds in my home when I was a child which made me feel safe and happy. I remember opening the door and smelling either something good that was baking or the smell of a hot iron as my Mom pressed the shirts, sheets and handkerchiefs. The sounds of dishes clinking in the kitchen or of the vacuum cleaner in another room made me feel good—I don't know why. Maybe it was proof that someone was busy making things right, making my home good, taking care of my needs and filling my world with love and caring. If I close my eyes and bring those little loving touches to mind, all of the feelings of home come flooding back and fill my eyes with tears of joy.

Making my children feel that same, wonderful warmth that I knew as a child is a priority in my life, and one of the things I've found that never fails to bring everyone together in the kitchen in a hurry is when I announce, "The bread's done." ♥

JANICE KEMPE

Parmesan Cheese Loaf

For one loaf of French or Italian bread

¾ **cup butter, softened**
¼ **cup Parmesan cheese**
1 small clove garlic, crushed (or ¼ teaspoon
instant minced garlic)
¼ **teaspoon dried basil**
1 tablespoon chopped fresh parsley (or 1½
teaspoons parsley flakes)
1 loaf French or Italian bread, unsliced

Blend together first five ingredients. Slice bread diagonally, and spread blended ingredients on bread slices. Reassemble in loaf form and wrap securely in aluminum foil. Heat in oven until butter is melted, or grill on rack over medium hot coals, turning frequently, about 20 minutes, or until butter melts.

JOANNE BOER

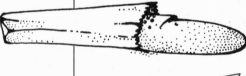

Salesman's Garlic Bread

Gordon Penner, a Zondervan salesman, says he can always get garlic bread when he's traveling. If they say they don't have any, he tells them to do the following:

Butter bread, sprinkle with garlic salt, place bread under the broiler, on the grill, or in the microwave.

Pan Rolls

Makes about 30 medium-sized rolls

2 cups warm water (120F–130F)
2 tablespoons or 2 packages dry yeast
½ cup sugar
½ cup butter, melted
2 teaspoons salt
4½ to 5 cups flour

Dissolve yeast in water. Stir sugar into yeast mixture. Add butter, salt, and half of flour, stir well. Add as much of the remaining flour as needed to make a soft dough. Knead on a well-floured surface about 5 minutes. Cover dough and allow to rise in a warm place until double in bulk. Divide into walnut sized pieces and place in a greased, 9-inch square baking pan. Cover and let rise until double. Bake 15–20 minutes at 425F.

This dough can be refrigerated up to a week if punched down regularly.

Latayne Scott

In retrospect, as we were training the children and trying to help them appreciate the Lord's Day as special we developed a custom of having candlelight at supper time. This was fun and the children as well as their parents enjoyed this custom. ♥

Pearl and John Sanderson, Jr.

Dinner Rolls

1 package yeast
1 tablespoon sugar
¼ cup warm water
¾ cup scalded milk, cooled to lukewarm
2 tablespoons oil or melted shortening
1 egg, separated
1 teaspoon water
3 cups flour
½ teaspoon salt

Dissolve yeast and sugar in warm water. Add warm milk, half the flour, salt, and beat until smooth. Blend egg yolk with 1 teaspoon of water and stir into mixture. Beat egg whites until stiff and add to batter. Add remaining flour and oil, mix well. Cover and let rise in a warm place until doubled in bulk. Punch down, form into rolls in desired shape, and place on greased baking pan. cover and let rise until doubled. Bake at 400F for 15 to 20 minutes.

Marilyn & Marvin K. Mayers

I shop weekly with a neighbor. We carefully check the newspaper for the weekly specials and usually shop at 5-6 stores. We also have a chance for a good visit, having been neighbors for some 35 plus years. ♥

Bertha G. Taylor

Walnut Honey Buns

A nice combination of light whole wheat roll and honey-walnut upside-down topping. You may need to place another pan or a sheet of foil under the baking pan near the end of the baking time to catch drips from the topping.

MAKES one dozen muffin shaped rolls.

1 package yeast
¼ cup warm water
1¼ cups flour
1 cup whole wheat flour
½ teaspoon salt
⅓ cup margarine
½ cup milk, scalded and cooled to warm
¼ cup honey
1 egg, beaten

Topping:

⅓ cup honey
¼ cup light brown sugar
¼ cup margarine
½ cup chopped walnuts

Dissolve yeast in warm water. Mix flour, whole wheat flour, and salt. Cut in margarine with pastry blender or two knives. Add dissolved yeast, honey, and beaten egg. Stir to mix. Cover and let rise in a warm place until doubled. While dough is rising prepare topping by boiling first three ingredients together in a small saucepan for one minute. Sprinkle chopped walnuts in muffin tins. Pour hot topping syrup over nuts. When dough is ready to place in pans, divide into twelve pieces and place on topping. Allow to rise until almost doubled. Bake at 375F for 20 minutes. Cool in pan 10 minutes. Invert, and serve warm.

ELIZABETH & SCOTT PHILLIPS

Quick Cinnamon Rolls

In this recipe the yeast is not dissolved before adding it to the other ingredients, and the buttermilk is added at a higher temperature (120F–130F) than usual for yeast bread recipes.

MAKES 12 rolls

1 cup buttermilk (or milk mixed with 1 teaspoon vinegar or lemon juice)
3 tablespoons oil
3 cups flour
1 package yeast (regular or fast rising)
¼ cup sugar
½ teaspoon salt
¼ teaspoon soda
2 tablespoons water
¼ cup melted butter
½ cup brown sugar
1 teaspoon cinnamon
½ cup chopped nuts (optional)

Scald buttermilk, add oil, and set aside while you mix together 1 cup of the flour, yeast, sugar, salt, and soda in a mixing bowl. Add buttermilk and oil and beat well by hand or with an electric mixer. Stir in enough additional flour to make a stiff dough, turn out on a floured surface and knead until smooth and elastic, adding more flour as needed. Let dough rest while you prepare baking pan. Butter 12 muffin cups or one 8" round cake pan. Mix water with half (2 tablespoons) of the melted butter and half (¼ cup) of the brown sugar. Divide mixture among muffin cups or spread in the bottom of a cake pan. Roll out dough into a 12"x15" rectangle and spread with remaining melted butter. Sprinkle remaining brown sugar, cinnamon, and nuts, if desired, over dough. Roll up as for jelly roll and cut in 12 equal pieces. Arrange in muffin cups or cake pan, cover, and let rise in warm place until doubled. Bake at 350F about 25 minutes. Turn upside down and remove from pan immediately.

DONALD HENRY

Mrs. Howard's Rolls

These rolls are quite sweet, so you may want to reduce the sugar slightly if you prefer a less sweet roll.

MAKES about 36 muffin-shaped rolls

2 cups warm water
1½ packages yeast
2 eggs
½ cup sugar
3 tablespoons shortening, softened or melted
2 teaspoons salt
5 cups flour
butter or margarine for tops

Mix warm water with yeast. Stir until dissolved. Add eggs, sugar, shortening, salt and half of flour. Beat vigorously for about one minute. Add remaining flour and mix until smooth. Cover and let rise in a warm place until doubled. Stir dough down and fill greased muffin tins about ½ full. Let rise until about double. Put a dot of butter or margarine on each roll. Bake at 400F for 15 to 20 minutes. Dough can be stored in refrigerator for a couple of days.

ISABELLE & KENNETH BARKER

NEVER, but NEVER go shopping for groceries when you're hungry. Every shelf in the store will reach out to you with appetizing items and resistance will be nil. ♥

LYDIA HEERMANN

Frosted Cinnamon Rolls

MAKES 27 rolls

½ cup milk
½ cup sugar
1 teaspoon salt
¼ cup butter or margarine
½ cup warm water
2 packages yeast
2 eggs, beaten
4½–5 cups flour

Sugar mixture:

¾ cup brown sugar
¾ cup sugar
3 teaspoons cinnamon
1 cup chopped walnuts

Frosting:

1 pound confectioner's sugar
2 tablespoons melted butter
1 teaspoon almond extract
1 teaspoon vanilla
5–6 tablespoons milk

Scald milk; stir in sugar, salt and butter; cool to lukewarm. Measure warm water into large warm bowl. Sprinkle yeast into water; stir until dissolved. Stir in lukewarm milk mixture, beaten eggs, and half the flour; beat until smooth. Stir in enough remaining flour to make a slightly stiff dough. On lightly floured surface knead dough until smooth and elastic, about 8 minutes. Place dough in a greased bowl, cover and let rise in a warm place until doubled, about 1 hour. Punch down and divide dough into thirds. Roll each third into a 9" x 14" rectangle. Spread each third with ⅓ of the combined sugar mixture. Roll up

➤➤

Christmas

◄◄ *Christmas Eve always means hot apple cider and snacks, the singing of carols around the tree, and the reading of the Christmas story. Christmas morning and Easter morning breakfasts consist of homemade cinnamon rolls and scrambled eggs with ham, sausage, or bacon.*

D. G. KEHL

each rectangle like a jelly roll. Seal edges. Cut each roll into nine 1″ pieces. Place rolls in 3 greased 9″ cake pans. Cover and let rise until double, about 30 minutes. Bake at 350F for about 25 minutes. Mix together frosting ingredients and spread on warm rolls after removing from oven.

D. G. KEHL

Ice Box Buns

MAKES 24 rolls

1 package yeast
2 tablespoons warm water
½ cup sugar
2 cups milk, scalded and cooled to lukewarm
2 beaten eggs
1 teaspoon salt
5½ cups flour
½ cup melted butter or shortening

Combine yeast, water, and sugar. When yeast is dissolved, add warm milk, eggs, and salt. Then add about half of the flour, mix well. Add melted butter or shortening, mix. Then add remaining flour. Mix until smooth. Cover and place in refrigerator overnight.

Take out and divide dough into three pieces. Roll each piece out on a floured surface into a circle about 11″ in diameter. Cut into 8 pie shaped wedges. Roll up each wedge beginning at widest point. Place on greased baking sheet. Cover, let rise in a warm place until doubled. Bake 15 to 20 minutes at 350F.

PATRICIA GUNDRY

Weihnacht* Stollen

(*Christmas, in German)

"Our favorite sweet bread on Christmas morning—with cups of hot coffee."

MAKES one large stollen or two smaller ones

1 cup milk
½ cup sugar
1 teaspoon salt
½ cup warm water
2 packages yeast
5 cups flour
¼ teaspoon nutmeg
1 cup (½ pound) butter, softened
2 eggs, beaten
½ cup citron, finely chopped
½ cup glacé cherries, sliced
1 cup sliced blanched almonds (optional)
1 cup raisins
grated peel of 1 lemon
½ teaspoon cinnamon
2 tablespoons sugar
melted butter
confectioner's sugar

Scald milk, add sugar and salt, and let cool to warm. Dissolve yeast in warm water. To cooled milk add dissolved yeast, nutmeg, and 1 cup of flour. Beat until smooth. Cover and let rise in a warm place until doubled. Add ¾ cup of the butter (reserving ¼ cup), beaten eggs, citron, cherries, almonds, raisins, and grated lemon peel. Stir in three more cups of flour and turn out on a floured surface. Knead until dough is smooth and elastic (about 5 minutes) using as much of the remaining cup of flour as needed. Let dough rest for 5 minutes, then roll out into one 18"x12" oval or two 15"x9" ovals. Spread remaining ¼ cup of butter on oval(s) and sprinkle with a mixture of 2 tablespoons sugar and ½ teaspoon cinnamon.

➤→

Fold dough over like an omelet and place on a greased cookie sheet. Curve ends slightly to form a crescent. Brush tops with melted butter, cover and let rise until doubled. Bake at 350F for 25 to 35 minutes for smaller stollen, 35 to 40 minutes for large, or until golden brown. Remove from oven and dust with confectioner's sugar.

LENA & DAVID EWERT

Honey Oatmeal Bread

MAKES 2 loaves

2 cups boiling water
½ cup mild flavored honey
2 tablespoons butter
2 teaspoons salt
1 cup old-fashioned rolled oats
1 package yeast
½ cup lukewarm water
2 cups whole wheat flour
2 cups unbleached white flour

In a large mixing bowl, stir together boiling water, honey, butter, salt and oats. Set aside for one hour before adding other ingredients. Dissolve yeast in warm water. Add dissolved yeast to oatmeal mixture. Add flour gradually, beating well. Cover and let rise in a warm place until doubled. Turn dough out on a floured surface and knead until smooth and elastic, adding more flour as needed. Shape into two loaves. Place in buttered 9"x5" loaf pans, cover, and let rise until doubled. Bake at 350F about 40–45 minutes. Tops should be well browned and loaves sound hollow when tapped. Remove from pans and, if desired, glaze with the following: brush tops of loaves lightly with honey and sprinkle with uncooked oats.

ULDINE BISAGNO

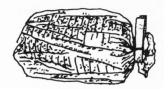

Bag Closures
To tightly close bread wrappers or any plastic type bag containing food use a clip type clothes pin. This saves time. ♥

MARY ANN HOWARD

Honey Wheat Bread

MAKES 2 loaves

1½ cups water
2 packages yeast
2 tablespoons sugar
¼ cup butter
½ cup honey
2 teaspoons salt
1 cup (8 ounces) soft curd or cream style
    cottage cheese
5½ to 6 cups flour
1 egg
1 cup whole wheat flour

Heat water in medium saucepan until luke-warm. Remove ½ cup of water to a small bowl, add yeast and sugar, stir, and set aside. To water remaining in saucepan add butter and heat until butter melts. Remove saucepan from heat and add honey, salt, and cottage cheese. Make sure mixture in pan is warm, but not hot. Transfer mixture to a large mixing bowl and add 1 cup flour, egg, and dissolved yeast. Beat with an electric mixer for 2 minutes at medium speed. By hand, stir in whole wheat flour and enough all-purpose flour to make a stiff dough. Turn out on a floured surface and knead until smooth and elastic (about 2 minutes). Place in a greased bowl, cover, and let rise in a warm place until doubled. Punch down dough, divide, and form into two loaves. Place in two greased 9"x5" loaf pans, cover and let rise until doubled. Bake at 350F for about 40–50 minutes, until golden brown, or until loaves sound hollow when tapped.

SHIRLEY SCHOLTEN

We have rotating table grace. A different member of the family prays at each meal. A short time is given for silent prayer as we reflect on any sin in our life and confess before we pray and eat. One time our son was silent longer than usual before he prayed. Then we all wanted to know what he had been doing that day. ♥

MARY ANN HOWARD

Swedish Limpa Rye Bread

MAKES 2 round loaves

1½ cups warm water
2 packages yeast
¼ cup molasses
⅓ cup sugar
2–3 teaspoons salt
2 tablespoons oil or soft shortening
grated peel of one orange
2 tablespoons anise seed
2½ cups rye flour
2¼–2¾ cups flour

Dissolve yeast in warm water. Stir in remaining ingredients. Turn out on floured surface and knead until dough is soft and springy and not sticky, adding more flour as needed. Put dough in a greased bowl, cover, and let rise in a warm place until almost doubled. Punch down, and let rise again until doubled. Form into two flattened balls, and place on a greased baking sheet. Cover and let rise until doubled and bake at 350F for 20–35 minutes.

JANET KOBOBEL

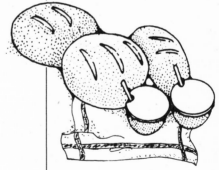

Bagels

MAKES 15 bagels.

2 packages yeast
4¼ to 4½ cups flour
1½ cups warm water
3 tablespoons sugar
1 tablespoon salt

Dissolve yeast in water. Add 1¾ cups flour, sugar, and salt to yeast mixture. Beat with an electric mixer at low speed for ½ minute, then at high speed for 3 minutes. By hand, stir in enough remaining flour to make a moderately stiff dough. Turn out on a floured surface and knead until smooth. Cover and let rest for 15 minutes. Cut into 15 portions and shape into balls. Punch a hole in the center of each ball and stretch to enlarge the hole. Cover and let rise 20 minutes. In a large kettle, combine 1 gallon of water and 1 tablespoon sugar. Bring to a boil and reduce to simmer. Cook bagels, 4 or 5 at a time for 7 minutes, turning once. Drain and place on a greased cookie sheet. Bake at 375F for 30 to 35 minutes.

For variety—

Whole Wheat Bagels: Replace half of flour with whole wheat flour.
Onion Bagels: Add ½ cup finely chopped onion to dough.
Raisin Bagels: Add ½ to 1 teaspoon cinnamon and ½ cup finely chopped raisins to dough.

SANDRA DRESCHER LEHMAN

Bagels

◄▥ *Fun to make with children or other friends. You can slice and freeze bagels for a quick snack to pop in the toaster. Top with butter or cream cheese. Good for coffee breaks or when unexpected guests come by.* ♥

SANDRA DRESCHER LEHMAN

Olie Bollen I (Fat Balls)

"This is a very traditional Dutch recipe. On 31 December, almost every family in the Netherlands makes these, and when you walk through the streets on that day, you can smell the aroma everywhere."

3 cups flour
2 cups warm milk (scalded, then cooled)
2 packages or 2 tablespoons yeast
2 tablespoons lukewarm water
2 eggs, beaten
2 teaspoons sugar
1 teaspoon salt
1 teaspoon cinnamon
2 cups raisins
2 cups chopped apples
oil for frying
confectioner's sugar

Put flour, salt and cinnamon in a large mixing bowl. Stir in milk, beating well with a wooden spoon. Dissolve yeast and sugar in lukewarm water. Stir eggs and dissolved yeast into flour mixture. Add raisins and chopped apples. Cover and let rise in a warm place for about an hour, until double. Heat oil to 375F. Drop batter by tablespoon into hot oil. When brown on one side, turn over. Drain on paper towels. Serve sprinkled with confectioner's sugar.

DINY & CASE DAMSTEEGT

Some Unorthodox Ideas About Using Mealtimes Profitably

A Different Approach to "Family Breakfasts"

Much has been written about mealtime as a "family event," a time for growing together and sharing in the family. We have found in our family, however, that mealtimes can also be used to provide the individual attention that children need in a busy family.

For years I had thought that a "family breakfast" should be our ultimate goal in the morning. I pictured it as a delicious, nutritious meal, with everyone gathered and chatting happily about plans for the day, followed by something devotional or inspiring. This, I felt, would

Olie Bollen II (Fat Balls)

1 cup sugar
2 eggs
4 cups flour
4 teaspoons baking powder
2 teaspoons oil or melted shortening
1½ cups milk
1 to 2 cups raisins
oil for frying

Plump raisins in boiling water, then drain and allow to cool. Combine all ingredients, mix well. Drop by heaping tablespoon into deep fat heated to 375F. The olie bollen should turn over by themselves when one side is done.

JOYCE LEENSVAART

Peanut Butter Lovers' Wheat Germ Muffins

⅔ cup packaged biscuit mix
⅓ cup wheat germ
¼ cup sugar
1 egg, slightly beaten
⅓ cup water
2 tablespoons peanut butter
½ teaspoon vanilla

In mixing bowl combine biscuit mix, wheat germ, and sugar. In another bowl combine beaten egg, water, peanut butter, and vanilla, mixing with egg beater. Add to dry ingredients, stirring only until dry ingredients are moistened. Fill greased muffin tins ⅔ full, and bake at 375F for 20–25 minutes or until golden brown.

Microwave: 2–2½ minutes on High, turning half way through cooking time.

DONALD HENRY

be a good way to start everybody's day. This ideal, however, never seemed to materialize. Either my husband had breakfast meetings, or I wasn't organized enough, or someone wasn't in a happy mood. For years the ideal of the family breakfast eluded me.

A couple of years ago I discovered an approach which seems to suit our family better. Realizing that everyone seems to be ready to eat at a different time anyway, I began to feed each child as he came out to the kitchen. Andrew, our early riser, always appears first, dressed and ready. We have pleasant chats while I work on breakfast or make lunches. After he has eaten, his brother Jamie, a later riser, appears. We then have a nice visit while he eats. My husband gets ready for class before breakfast and usually arrives last. Timothy, our toddler, often sleeps until everyone else is gone! This approach may seem somewhat unorthodox, but it has helped to

6 Week Bran Muffins

"For any meal or snack time, this recipe has been the answer. Beautiful, homemade muffins in 20 minutes."

MAKES 50 muffins

5 cups flour
5 teaspoons soda
3 cups sugar
1 (15 ounce) package Raisin Bran
1 cup melted shortening or oil
1 quart buttermilk
4 eggs, beaten

Mix all ingredients together in *large* container. Refrigerate, covered, for from 4 hours to 6 weeks. To bake, fill greased muffin tins and bake at 400F for 15–20 minutes.

ANN & VERNON GROUNDS

Shirley's Whole Wheat Muffins

MAKES 12 muffins

1½ cups whole wheat flour
½ teaspoon salt
2 teaspoons baking powder
½ teaspoon soda
½ teaspoon cinnamon
½ cup brown sugar
½ cup raisins
1 cup sour milk
1 egg, beaten
2 tablespoons melted butter

In mixing bowl mix dry ingredients together and add raisins. Make a well in center of ingredients. Pour in milk, eggs, and melted butter. Mix well. Fill greased muffin tins ½ to ⅔ full. Bake at 375F for 25 minutes.

SHIRLEY SCHOLTEN

create a much more peaceful atmosphere in the morning. Each child has had at least some one-on-one contact with a parent, and has been allowed to follow his own time-table in getting ready.

In doing individual breakfasts like this I have also discovered that it is easy to give everyone what he wishes for breakfast. Thanks to an electric frying pan, it is equally easy to offer eggs or French toast in addition to the old favorite cereal, and if there is pancake batter made up in the refrigerator that is also an option. For this one meal, at least, I can easily "cater" to everyone's desires!

Getting up in the morning and going out to face the world is, I feel, a difficult part of the child's day. Ideally they should be sent out of the nest with tummies that are full and spirits that are quiet and nourished, as well. Our "individual breakfasts" have helped us to achieve this goal.

Also, if my husband is not

Golden Raisin Buns

These hollow rolls are similar to cream puff shells and particularly good frosted.

1 cup water
½ cup butter or margarine
1 teaspoon sugar
¼ teaspoon salt
1 cup flour
4 eggs
½ cup golden raisins, plumped in hot water, and drained

Lemon Frosting (optional):

1 tablespoon butter
1½ tablespoons cream, or undiluted evaporated milk
1 cup confectioner's sugar
½ teaspoon lemon juice
½ teaspoon vanilla

Combine water, butter, sugar, and salt in a saucepan; bring to a boil. Add flour all at once, then over low heat beat with a wooden spoon about 1 minute, or until mixture leaves the sides of the pan and forms a smooth, thick dough. Remove from heat. Continue stirring (about 2 minutes) until mixture cools slightly. Add eggs one at a time, beating after each until mixture has a satiny sheen. Stir in plumped raisins. Drop by heaping tablespoonfuls, about 2 inches apart, on a greased baking sheet. Bake at 375F about 30–35 minutes, until golden brown and firm. (Be sure to bake until crisply done on the outside, or they will fall as they cool and be gummy and inedible inside.) Cool slightly and, if desired, frost while still warm.

going to be home for dinner, I do "individual dinners." While one finishes a favorite television show or does homework, I'll eat with the other. Especially if our preschooler is also watching TV or is busy, the older child and I have a delightful "dinner for two" and a time for real sharing. Then we switch and I drink tea while the other child eats, and we also have a nice time of being together. As I write this I realize that this is not a plan that has been discussed with the children, or of which they are aware! As far as they are concerned it just "happens." I think that in a large, busy family, sometimes there is so much togetherness that it is important to be alert to opportunities to do things with each child alone. Surprisingly, mealtimes have provided us with those opportunities. ♥

Phyllis & James Hurley

Lemon Frosting:

In a small saucepan melt butter, stir in cream. Remove from heat, add confectioner's sugar and stir until smooth. Stir in lemon juice and vanilla.

"I add the frosting for a treat. Mostly I just serve them plain with butter. The kids love these for their dinner bread."

SHEILA HUIZMAN

Sharon Engel's Blueberry Muffins

MAKES 24 muffins

1 pint blueberries (1¾ cups) fresh or frozen
3 cups flour
1¾ cups sugar
1 tablespoon baking powder
½ teaspoon salt
(½ cup) butter or margarine
2 eggs
1 cup milk
1 teaspoon vanilla
2 tablespoons (scant) melted butter

Cut butter into flour, sugar, salt, and baking powder. Set aside 1 cup of mixture. To all but 1 cup of flour mixture, add milk, eggs, and vanilla. Beat until smooth. Fold in blueberries. Fill muffin cups with batter. Drizzle melted butter over reserved cup of flour mixture and toss with a fork. Sprinkle on top of muffin batter and bake at 375F about 25–30 minutes, or until golden brown.

SHARON & JAMES ENGEL

Butter Pecan Waffles

Rich and filling.

MAKES six large or twelve medium waffles

1 **package yeast**
5 **cups flour**
⅓ **cup sugar**
¾ **teaspoon salt**
2 **teaspoons soda**
1 **quart buttermilk**
¾ **cup melted butter**
4 **eggs**
¾ **cup pecans (or blanched almonds), finely chopped**

In a large bowl, mix dry ingredients, add liquid ingredients, beat in eggs, mix until batter is well blended but still lumpy. Stir in chopped nuts. Cover bowl and let rise in a warm place until bubbly (about 30 minutes), or refrigerate overnight. Bake batter in a preheated waffle iron. After they are baked place in a single layer directly on racks in 300F oven for at least 5 minutes, or until time to serve. Or cool waffles completely on racks, wrap, and freeze for up to one month. Reheat, without thawing, in toaster.

DIANE HEAD

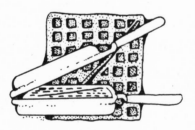

Butter Pecan Waffles

◄≪ *There is nothing our family loves more than a Saturday morning* big *breakfast. Sundays through Fridays are often so hectic we grab breakfast on the run. But Saturdays are our days to indulge in a relaxing time around the table together while enjoying such "big breakfast" delights as Strawberry Crepes (see page 322), "Dutch Babies" (see page 116), or Butter Pecan Waffles.* ♥

DIANE HEAD

Annie's Yogurt Waffles

MAKES 2½ large waffles

2 eggs
1 cup plain yogurt
2 tablespoons oil
1 cup whole wheat flour
1 teaspoon soda
½ teaspoon salt
¼ cup water (approximately)

Mix together eggs, yogurt and oil. Add flour, soda and salt. Mix together until smooth. Add water, adding additional water if necessary to make the right consistency for your waffle iron.

PHYLLIS & JAMES HURLEY

Buttermilk Pancakes

This recipe makes a very thin batter and very thin pancakes. For thicker pancakes reduce buttermilk to ¾ cup.

1 cup flour
1 teaspoon baking powder
¼ teaspoon soda
¼ teaspoon salt
1 tablespoon sugar
1 egg
1 cup buttermilk, or milk soured with 1
    tablespoon vinegar per cup
¼ cup oil or melted shortening

In a mixing bowl sift or stir together dry ingredients. Combine egg and buttermilk and add to dry ingredients, mixing well. Stir in oil or melted shortening. Pour on hot griddle or skillet. Cook until lightly browned on underside, turn over and cook other side. Serve hot with butter and syrup or other topping.

JOANNE BOER

English Pancakes

MAKES about 16 large thin pancakes

2 cups flour
1 teaspoon salt
4 eggs
4 cups milk
1 or 2 lemons
sugar

Sift flour and salt into a large mixing bowl and make a well in the center. Add eggs, and with a wire whisk, mix them in gradually to avoid lumps. Keeping the mixture as smooth as possible, add about half the milk. Beat thoroughly, then gradually stir in the rest of the milk.

Melt just enough lard in a thick frying pan to coat the bottom and sides; pour off any surplus. When the fat is hot, pour in a little batter, just covering the bottom of the pan. Cook the pancake until it is golden brown on the underside, then toss it or turn it over. Cook the second side, remove to plate, and sprinkle with sugar and a squeeze of lemon, and roll up. Serve at once.

JILL BRISCOE

Swedish Pancakes

"This recipe was given to us by a dear friend who acquired it from his Swedish grandmother. Our family enjoys them not only for breakfast occasionally, but for a light Sunday night supper. My husband loves them best with fresh blueberry sauce but they are delicious with any syrup— even plain!"

½ cup butter, melted
2 cups sifted flour
¼ cup sugar
1 teaspoon salt
4 eggs
3 cups milk

➤➤

Pancake Tuesday

◄≪*When we lived in England and our children were growing up, a special day in February was set aside for "Pancake Tuesday." Everyone made bowls of pancake mix as per recipe. In the small villages in England, pancake races were held. All the mothers, wearing their best aprons, ran the race, pan in hand. They had to flip the pancake 3 times before they hit the finishing line (or before the pancake hit the finishing line!). The whole village turned out for the event and a great time was had by all.*

Since we have lived in America, we have forgone the race but enjoy the pancakes. I usually keep the meal for holiday times when we are all together and can enjoy a nostalgia trip! ♥

JILL BRISCOE

Melt butter and set aside to cool. In a large mixing bowl sift or stir together flour, sugar and salt. Make a well in the center. Add eggs, and with a wire whisk gradually mix them in. Add milk slowly, beating well, until smooth. Just before cooking, stir in the melted butter. Pour from a pitcher onto a hot rounded skillet or griddle (no need to grease skillet). Tilt the pan to spread batter. Batter will be very thin and pancakes are flat.

OLIVIA & PAUL HILLMAN

Powerful Whole Wheat Pancakes

MAKES 15 pancakes

1 cup whole wheat flour
¼ cup soya flour (or add another ¼ cup
  whole wheat flour)
½ cup instant nonfat dry milk
1 teaspoon salt
2 teaspoons baking powder
¼ teaspoon soda
2 cups buttermilk or yogurt
3 eggs, beaten
4 tablespoons oil or melted margarine
¼ cup wheat germ

Into mixing bowl sift together flour, soya flour, dry milk, salt, baking powder, and soda. Add liquid, beaten eggs, and oil and mix thoroughly. Stir in wheat germ. Bake on lightly greased hot griddle. Use ¼ cup batter for average size pancakes.

PHYLLIS & JAMES HURLEY

Best Biscuits

MAKES about 18 biscuits

2 cups flour
4 teaspoons baking powder
½ teaspoon cream of tartar
½ teaspoon salt
2 tablespoons sugar
½ cup shortening
1 egg
⅔ cup milk

Sift flour, baking powder, cream of tartar, salt, and sugar into bowl. With pastry blender or 2 knives, cut in shortening until of cornmeal-like consistency. Pour milk into flour mixture slowly. Add egg and briefly stir to mix. Turn out on a floured surface and knead five times. Roll to ½" thickness and cut with round biscuit cutter. Bake on ungreased baking sheet at 425F for 10–15 minutes.

KAY & DON GLENN
LATAYNE SCOTT

Olivia's Corn Bread

1½ cups cornmeal
1 cup flour
2 teaspoons baking powder
1 teaspoon soda
1 teaspoon salt
2 eggs
5 tablespoons oil
2 cups buttermilk

Heat 2 tablespoons of the oil in a 10" cast iron skillet. (If you don't have one you can also bake it in a 9" square baking pan.) Mix remaining ingredients until almost smooth. Pour into hot skillet. Bake at 375F about 30 minutes.

OLIVIA & PAUL HILLMAN

Jane's Corn Bread

"This is my own version because I like a coarser texture and nutty flavor the whole wheat flour seems to give. This delicious bread is quite sweet, so you may want to reduce the honey to 1 or 2 tablespoons if you prefer a less sweet cornbread."

1 cup yellow cornmeal
½ cup unbleached white flour
½ cup whole wheat flour
1 tablespoon baking powder
½ teaspoon salt
1 egg
¼ cup honey
¾ cup milk

Combine all ingredients; batter will be lumpy. Pour into well-greased 10″ cast iron skillet, a special cast iron pan divided into pie-shaped wedges, or 9″ square baking pan. Bake at 375F for about 25 minutes, or until golden brown. Cut into wedges or squares, serve hot.

JANE PEART

"Hoecake"

When the snow outside is two feet deep and we can't fly South, about six couples in our church who are from the South get together for an old fashioned Southern feed.

Everyone brings something Southern—greasy beans with ham hock, mustard greens with sliced boiled eggs, blackeyed peas with chopped onions, potato salad with plenty of pickles, corn chowder, hams cooked in paper sacks, homemade biscuits, and sweet potato pie.

My contribution to the meal is always hoecake. (One of the guys calls my thing Dog Mush—they feed the dogs under the table.) My father taught me how to make hoecake—and he

California Zucchini Bread

"We enjoy the moistness and tang pineapple lends to 'plain old zucchini bread.'"

Try making this bread with carrots or half zucchini and half carrots, 1 cup of each. We tested it that way and found it an interesting and delicious mixture.

MAKES 2 loaves

3 eggs
1 cup oil
2 cups sugar
2 teaspoons vanilla
2–3 cups (lightly filled, not packed) shredded
    zucchini, and/or carrots
1 (8¼ ounce) can crushed pineapple, well
    drained
3 cups flour
2 teaspoons soda
½ teaspoon baking powder
1 teaspoon salt
1½ teaspoons cinnamon
¾ teaspoon nutmeg
½–1 cup chopped raisins (optional)
½–1 cup chopped nuts (optional)

With an electric mixer, beat eggs until frothy. Add oil, sugar, and vanilla, continue beating until foamy. With a spoon, stir in zucchini (and/or carrots) and pineapple. In a separate bowl combine flour, soda, salt, baking powder, cinnamon, and nutmeg. Stir gently into zucchini mixture. Add raisins and nuts, if desired. Bake in 2 greased and floured 9"x5" loaf pans at 350F for 60 minutes or until a toothpick inserted in the center comes out clean. Cool in pans for 10 minutes. Turn out on wire racks and cool thoroughly before slicing. This bread freezes well.

got the recipe from a black woman who helped rear him on a farm in Kentucky.

Hoecake is nothing but white cornmeal and butter—just what you don't want if you want to lose weight.

To prepare, boil water, stir the boiling water into the cornmeal until a paste is formed. Then, pour the paste into boiling butter in an iron skillet and spread evenly. Keep shaking the skillet to keep from sticking. When one side is nice and crisp, flip over (add more butter) and do the other side. Oh, I forgot, you've got to add salt—when you made the paste—plenty of salt.

Hoecake may not be the most nutritious, but the excuse it affords me to tell about my upbringing is well worth it.

Daddy made hoecakes every Sunday, and sometimes during the week—to spread the food around. I especially remember hoecakes when we lived on the farm, Cedar Hill, Texas, during the early part of the war

For high altitudes: reduce oil to ¾ cup, reduce sugar to 1½ cups plus 2 tablespoons, increase size of canned pineapple to 13½ ounces.

SHERRY & MARTIN SINGER

World's Best Walnut-Zucchini Bread

"This is a moist, hearty bread—our favorite. My husband, Robert, likes it for breakfast."

MAKES 3 small or 2 large loaves

3 **eggs**
2 **cups sugar**
1 **cup oil**
3 **cups peeled, shredded zucchini squash (fill cups lightly, do not pack)**
2 **teaspoons vanilla**
1 **teaspoon salt**
1 **teaspoon soda**
1 **teaspoon baking powder**
1 **teaspoon cinnamon**
3 **cups flour**
1 **cup coconut, shredded or grated**
1 **cup walnuts, coarsely chopped**

Stir ingredients together in the order given. Bake at 350F in 3 small 8"x4" or 2 large 9"x5" well greased loaf pans for about 45 minutes for small pans and 60 minutes for large pans, or until a toothpick inserted in the middle comes out clean. Cool 10 minutes before removing from pans.

DIANE BRUMMEL BLOEM & ROBERT BLOEM

(Second World War). We raised chickens and sold eggs, milk, and "fryers" to the little corner grocery stores in Dallas.

Mama made my shirts out of Purina feed sacks and I made new soles for my shoes every morning out of cardboard before walking to school.

As I look back, these were the greatest days of my life. We were rich in everything that matters. We had a God-fearing family that read through the Bible every year together, an old fashioned Methodist church, lots of love, and each other. What more could a kid ask for? ♥

LYMAN COLEMAN

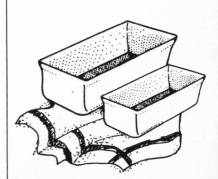

Swedish Almond Bread

MAKES 2 large or 3 small loaves

1 cup margarine
2 cups sugar
2 eggs
1 teaspoon almond extract
4 cups flour
½ teaspoon baking powder
½ teaspoon soda
½ teaspoon salt
1 cup sour cream

Cream together sugar and margarine; add eggs and almond extract. Sift or stir together dry ingredients, and add alternately with sour cream. Bake in 3 small 8"x4" greased loaf pans or 2 large 9"x5" greased loaf pans, at 325F for about 50 minutes for small pans, 60–70 minutes for large pans. Remove from pans while still warm and wrap in foil or plastic bags. Be sure and wrap the loaves before they are completely cool, and keep wrapped, because this bread dries out easily if left unwrapped.

CAROLYN NYSTROM

Blueberry Buckle

¾ cup sugar
¼ cup butter, softened
2 eggs
½ cup milk
1½ cups flour
2 teaspoons baking powder
½ teaspoon salt
¼ teaspoon cloves
½ teaspoon nutmeg
2 cups (1 pint) blueberries

Topping:

½ cup sugar
⅓ cup flour
½ teaspoon cinnamon
¼ cup butter, softened

Either with an electric mixer or by hand, thoroughly mix first 4 ingredients. Stir in next 5 ingredients. Fold in blueberries. Spread batter in a greased 9″ square baking pan. Mix topping ingredients together until crumbly and sprinkle over batter. Bake at 375F about 45–50 minutes.

SUE HALL

Lazy Susan

Getting tired of passing salt, sugar, ketchup, etc.? Put a lazy susan in the middle of the table with all the frequently asked for items on it. ♥

RONNIE & DAVE CARDER

Blueberry Oatmeal Bread

MAKES 1 loaf

2 cups flour
1 teaspoon baking powder
1 teaspoon soda
1 teaspoon salt
½ teaspoon nutmeg
1 cup quick oats, uncooked
⅓ cup shortening
2 eggs
¾ cup light brown sugar
1 cup buttermilk or milk soured with 1
    tablespoon vinegar per cup
½ cup walnuts or pecans, chopped
1 cup blueberries (if frozen, thaw and drain)

Into a large bowl sift flour with baking powder, soda, salt, and nutmeg. Stir in oats. In a small bowl, with an electric mixer beat together shortening, brown sugar, and eggs at high speed until smooth and fluffy. Blend in buttermilk at low speed. Add to dry ingredients, stirring until just blended. Gently fold in nuts and blueberries. Bake in a greased 9"x5" loaf pan at 350F for about 60 minutes. Cool in pan for 10 minutes, then turn out on a wire rack to cool completely. Wrap well with aluminum foil or a plastic bag to keep bread moist.

ELIZABETH BROWN

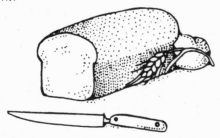

Carrot Bread

MAKES 1 large or 2 small loaves

½ **cup oil**
1 **cup sugar**
2 **eggs**
1 **cup raw carrot, finely shredded**
1½ **cups flour**
1 **teaspoon soda**
1 **teaspoon salt**
1 **teaspoon vanilla**

Mix together in the order given. Bake in 1 large (9"x5") or 2 small (8"x4") greased and floured loaf pans at 350F for about 45 minutes for small pans and 60 minutes for a large pan, or until a toothpick inserted in the center comes out clean.

JOYCE LEENSVAART

A Zondervan Daughter Remembers

by Joanne Zondervan Boer, daughter of co-founder Bernard Zondervan and Wilma Zondervan Teggelaar

At our house, almost without fail, dinner was at 5:15 P.M. My mom is a super cook. Meat and potatoes were the order of the day, as per my Dad's and my brother Bernie Jr.'s taste. For our devotions after dinner, we read the Bible straight through. It took us a year or two, but we didn't miss a verse. Reading the genealogies could be a real test of self-control because the pronunciations were sometimes so funny.

Saturday mornings were spent baking. The more Mom baked, the more dishes I did. Chocolate chip cookies, date bread, and

Date Bread

Makes 2 loaves

2 cups dates
2 cups water
1 tablespoon margarine, softened
1 tablespoon molasses
1 egg
1 teaspoon vanilla
1 cup sugar
2¾ cups flour
2 teaspoons soda
¼ teaspoon salt
½ cup nuts, chopped

In a large saucepan simmer dates in water for 5 minutes. Set aside to cool. When mixture is cool, add remaining ingredients in order listed. Bake in 2 well greased 9"x5" loaf pans for about 45 to 60 minutes, or until a toothpick inserted in the middle comes out clean.

Wilma Zondervan Teggelaar

cake were musts every week. When weather permitted, Dad golfed, and by the time he got home we were finished in the kitchen. Then it was off to visit the grandparents, and afterward go out for hamburgers.

Speaking of hamburgers, my folks could put on the best outdoor hamburger fries. Dad did the grilling, complete with chef's apron and hat. Mom had a matching apron. She prepared the trimmings, and her potato salad was always raved about. Any size crowd was just fine.

On the rare occasions when Mom wasn't there when we came home for lunch, a note, a phone number, and prepared lunch were on the table waiting for us. No matter what she did during the day, when Dad got home, dinner was ready, and Mom looked great!

As for a dishwasher, no matter what we said, Dad claimed that with all the able bodies we certainly had enough human dishwashers. The fact of the matter was that my Dad

Boston Brown Bread

MAKES 2 loaves or 3 or 4 small round loaves

1¾ cups water
2 cups raisins
½ cup sugar
1 tablespoon butter
2½ cups flour
2 teaspoons soda
½ teaspoon salt
1 egg
¼ cup dark molasses
1 teaspoon vanilla
½ teaspoon almond extract
½ teaspoon lemon flavoring (optional)
1 cup chopped nuts (optional)

In a saucepan bring to a boil water, butter, sugar, and raisins. Boil ½ minute. Into a mixing bowl, sift or stir flour, soda, and salt. Add molasses, egg, flavorings, cooled mixture, and nuts. Stir until blended. Bake in 3 or 4 well greased empty 15 ounce size cans, or 2 greased 9"x5" loaf pans at 350F for about 50 to 60 minutes for loaf pans, less for cans, or until a toothpick inserted in the middle comes out clean. Cool 10 minutes in cans before carefully removing bread. Cool completely before wrapping and storing.

JOANNE BOER

always washed the dishes and I always dried. Except on Sunday, when my brother would pick up Dad and put him on the steps to go upstairs for a nap.

During this "time to do dishes" my Dad and I reviewed events, schedules, and all quizzing was done: Bible verses for Sunday school, catechism questions, spelling words, history dates—you name it—it was done over dishes. Dates and curfews weren't forgotten either. The status of Zondervan Publishing House things didn't go unmentioned. We covered the bases.

Family reunions were a big deal. The women made wonderful food and lots of it. Sports were varied—softball organized by Dad for all kids and adults, then lawn football for anyone willing to sustain the wear and tear. If we had to be inside, great Monopoly contests went on and on and on and on. Dad loved organizing all this stuff.

Birthdays were also big at

Hibernia Bread

"This recipe is delicious with bean soup for a hearty winter meal."

MAKES 2 round loaves

5 cups whole wheat flour
2½ cups unbleached flour
¼ cup sugar
2 teaspoons soda
1 teaspoon salt
1 cup shortening, softened
2 eggs, beaten
2¼ cups buttermilk, or milk soured with 1
  tablespoon vinegar per cup

In a mixing bowl combine dry ingredients and cut in shortening with a pastry blender or two knives. Make a well in the middle of mixture. In a separate bowl combine beaten eggs and buttermilk. Pour into well and stir lightly. Handling dough gently, turn out onto a floured surface and form into 2 round loaves. Place on a greased baking sheet. Cut a 1" deep cross in the top of each loaf. Bake at 350F until golden brown, about 50 minutes. (If oven is too hot loaves won't rise properly.)

LINDA FALLIN

our house. Dad would not let anyone forget his birthday (he even wrote his own birthday in his date book every year). No matter what the weather was like he'd ask, "Isn't it a wonderful day for a birthday?"

Generally we had dinner out for birthdays, and always we had to sing "Happy Birthday" no matter how formal the restaurant. The older we got the more we rebelled against this practice—tough tradition to break.

Christmas was special—great dinner, Christmas carols, the Christmas Story, and later, gifts. Mom would have everything done, and then Dad would always have to go downstairs and finish his wrapping. I can't remember a Christmas with my Dad that we didn't wait for him.

He always had a package under the tree tagged "To Bernie, From Bernie." And the last gifts given were always wrapped envelopes of cash for each of us tucked in the

Irish Soda Bread

MAKES 1 loaf

3 cups flour
1 teaspoon salt
1 teaspoon baking powder
1 teaspoon soda
2 tablespoons sugar
2 tablespoons butter or margarine
1½ cups buttermilk or milk soured with 1
**   tablespoon vinegar per cup**
1 cup raisins or dried currants
1 tablespoon caraway seed

Sift together first five ingredients. Cut in butter with pastry blender or 2 knives. Add remaining ingredients, stirring well. Knead about three minutes, or until smooth. Place in 8″ round pan or 9″x5″ loaf pan. Cut a cross about ¼ inch deep in center of loaf. Bake at 350F for 50 to 60 minutes. Serve hot.

JOANNE BOER

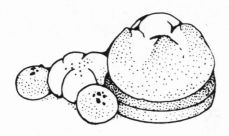

branches of the tree. The cash in the tree usually reflected the health of Zondervan Publishing House. Once he even gave my Mom a check and then told her he'd need it back for a while. ♥

1, 2, 3 Counting Banana Bread

MAKES 3 small round loaves, or one large one

1 stick of butter, softened
1 cup of brown sugar
1 teaspoon of baking soda
2 eggs
2 bananas, smashed up *real* well
2 cups of flour

1. Heat oven to 350F
2. Mix all ingredients together well
3. Grease 3 empty 15 ounce cans and dust them with flour

Fill each can half full and bake for about 45 minutes. Poke a knife or toothpick in the middle when you think it's done, and if it comes out clean, take the bread out of the oven. Remove from the cans right away and eat at least one piece while it's hot. It's very good hot with butter on it. (You can make this in a big 9"x5" loaf pan, but it isn't as much fun, and you only end up with one loaf instead of three.)

JANICE KEMPE

1, 2, 3 Counting Banana Bread

◄ *On those special days when my daughter, now six years old, wants to be just like me, we don our aprons and bake this family favorite. We have reduced the recipe to a system of 1s, 2s, and 3s to make it easy to remember, and in this case the simplicity of it seems to pay off. It doesn't matter if ingredients are measured precisely or added in the proper sequence, it just seems to work no matter what you do to it!*

Sometimes we have an extra treat by wrapping up one of the loaves and surprising a neighbor with a warm gift. It's never too early to help a child discover the unique joy of giving. ♥

JANICE KEMPE

Best Banana Bread Ever

"I have tried many banana bread recipes over the years, but when I found this one, I stopped looking."

This moist, delicious, loose textured bread breaks easily while warm, so handle it carefully. Since it is so moist you will need to avoid storing it in a completely airtight container (except, of course, when freezing) or it will become soggy.

MAKES 1 large loaf or 2 small ones

½ cup margarine or butter
1 cup sugar
2 eggs
½ to 1 teaspoon salt
3 large ripe bananas, mashed
1 teaspoon soda dissolved in ¼ cup warm
   water
1¾ cups flour
½ cup chopped nuts (optional)

Mix together butter or margarine and sugar. Add remaining ingredients in the order given, mixing well. Pour into one large 9"x5" or two small 8"x4" greased loaf pans. Bake at 350F for 10 minutes. Reduce heat to 300F and bake until done, about 50 more minutes.

OLIVIA & PAUL HILLMAN

Ursula's Cinnamon Topped Banana Bread

"Recipe doubles well, freezes well too."

MAKES 1 large or two small loaves

½ cup shortening
1 cup sugar
2 eggs
1 cup mashed banana (add water to fill cup if
    not quite enough banana)
2 cups flour
1 teaspoon soda
¼ teaspoon salt
⅓ cup hot water
cinnamon
sugar

Cream together sugar and shortening, add eggs and mashed banana, mix well. Sift together flour, soda and salt and stir into batter. Stir in hot water. Pour batter into 1 large 9"x5" or 2 small 8"x4" greased loaf pans. Sprinkle lightly with cinnamon and sugar. Bake at 350F for 50–60 minutes, or until a toothpick inserted in the middle comes out clean.

URSULA & PAUL VAN DUINEN

Sometimes we go around the table with each person saying something encouraging about the person on their left or right. ♥

RACHEL & LARRY CRABB

Easy Cinnamon Rolls

1 package refrigerator biscuits
¼ cup margarine or butter
½ cup sugar
½ to 1 teaspoon cinnamon
nuts, broken or chopped (optional)

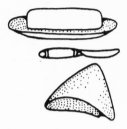

Preheat oven according to biscuit package instructions. Melt margarine or butter in round baking pan in heating oven while you cut biscuits in half, mix cinnamon with sugar, and set out nuts. Dip biscuits in melted margarine, then in cinnamon-sugar mixture. Place in pan, propping edge of pan on a table knife or potholder so melted margarine runs away from biscuits that have already been dipped. Sprinkle nuts between and around biscuits, if desired. Bake according to package instructions. Serve warm.

Variation: See Super Quick Coffee Cake in Cake section.

SUE MACDONALD

STRATAS, OVEN OMELETS, SOUFFLES, AND FRENCH TOAST

Dutch Baby 116
Cheese Pouf 117
Sunday Morning Casserole 118
Sandra's Breakfast Casserole 119
Bacon and Cheese Oven Omelet 119
Hall's Baked Omelet 120
Christmas Breakfast 121
Country Egg Soufflé 121
Chef Pinzon's Cheese Soufflé 122
Fritata 123
Oven Cinnamon French Toast 124

Dutch Baby

Interesting and impressive looking when it comes out of the oven and fun to watch baking through a glass oven door. As it bakes, a "cradle" is formed as the batter is pushed up out of the ends and sides of the pan. Later the "baby" appears in the middle. But when taken from the oven the "baby" quickly disappears (it falls in the middle).

SERVES 6

3 or 4 fresh peaches, peeled and sliced
1–2 tablespoons lemon juice
sugar, as desired, to sweeten peaches
6 eggs
1 cup flour
½ teaspoon salt
1 cup milk
¼ cup butter, melted
sour cream or whipping cream
nutmeg

Sprinkle peaches with sugar and lemon juice. Set aside. Beat eggs together until blended. Gradually add combined flour and salt, beating slightly after each addition. Stir in melted butter. Pour batter into a greased 9"x13" baking dish. Bake for 20 minutes at 450F. Reduce oven temperature to 350F and bake for 10 minutes more. Remove from oven and fill with peach slices. Top with sour cream or whipped cream and a sprinkle of nutmeg.

Variation:

This is also good without peaches and cream, served simply with butter and syrup.

DIANE HEAD

Our Family Devotions at breakfast were usually spent in company with Oswald Chambers, and his My Utmost for His Highest. *This was "heavy stuff" for four small boys, and my concentration as Mother was sometimes more directed to keeping them quiet than on the spiritual message of the day. One son later confessed that the advantage of Dad's absences when preaching, was that Mother seemed to read a shorter version—or none at all, which was probably sometimes true. The same son, however, now a father himself, even admits to taking Oswald Chambers with him on vacation.* ♥

E. JOAN & MAJOR THOMAS

Cheese Pouf

(pronounced "poof")

8 slices white bread
1 (8 ounce) package Old English cheese slices
¼ cup butter or margarine, melted
3 eggs
2 cups whole milk
1 teaspoon salt
½ teaspoon pepper
¾ teaspoon dry mustard

Tear 1 slice of bread and arrange over the bottom of a buttered shallow 2 quart baking dish. Tear 1 slice of cheese over bread. Continue layering with remaining bread and cheese. Pour melted butter over top layer. Beat together eggs, milk, salt, pepper and mustard. Pour over cheese and bread. Cover and refrigerate overnight. Bake, covered, at 350F for 30 minutes, uncover and bake another 30 minutes.

DEBBIE BARR

Grandfather's Saturday Breakfast

An idea I heard recently that sounded excellent was this: A grandfather kept up with each of his grandchildren by fixing a special Saturday breakfast for one each week and having a devotional time with them afterwards. ♥

VERNA ESTES

Sunday Morning Casserole

1 pound sausage
6 slices white bread, crusts removed
1 cup grated Cheddar cheese
3 eggs, beaten
1¼ cups milk
¾ cup light cream
½ teaspoon salt
pepper, to taste
1 tablespoon Worcestershire sauce

Brown sausage, drain well. Place slices of bread in the bottom of a baking dish. Spread cooked sausage over the bread and top with cheese. Mix together eggs, milk, cream, salt, pepper and Worcestershire sauce. Pour over the layered mixture. Cover and refrigerate until ready to bake. Bake, uncovered, at 350F for 30–40 minutes, or until firm.

PEGGY DARTY

Sunday Morning Casserole

◄ *In order to eliminate some of the chaos for a family of five, racing for showers, I consider my breakfast casserole an answer to prayer! The life-saving advantage to this casserole is the fact that it is best when prepared the night (or day) before. I simply prepare it, cover it with aluminum foil sometime Saturday when I'm already in the kitchen doing something else, then pop it in the refrigerator. On Sunday morning, as I stagger in to plug in the coffee, I also preheat the oven. Then, while we are arguing over showers it is bubbling away in the oven. The delicious taste of it goes a long way toward soothing us down into well-tempered individuals as we leave for church! I adore it!* ♥

PEGGY DARTY

Sandra's Breakfast Casserole

12 slices bread
butter, softened
2 cups grated cheese
1 onion, chopped
2 cups cooked sausage or ham chunks
5 eggs
3 cups milk
salt, to taste
pepper, to taste

Butter bread slices on both sides. Place 6 slices in the bottom of a 9"x13" baking pan. Cover with layers of cheese, onion, and meat. Top with remaining 6 slices of bread. Beat eggs, mix with milk, salt and pepper, and pour over mixture in pan. Cover and refrigerate overnight. Bake, uncovered, at 350F for 50 minutes.

SANDRA DRESCHER LEHMAN

Bacon and Cheese Oven Omelet

SERVES 5–6

12 slices bacon
6 slices processed cheese
6 eggs, beaten
1 cup milk

Cook bacon, drain. Curl 1 slice, chop 4 slices and leave the rest as whole slices. Cut cheese slices into halves and arrange in the bottom of a lightly buttered 9" pie pan. With a fork beat together eggs and milk, add chopped bacon. Pour over cheese and bake at 350F for 30 minutes. Arrange whole bacon slices on top of omelet around bacon curl. Bake 10 minutes longer. Let stand 5 minutes before cutting.

ANN & VERNON GROUNDS

Bacon and Cheese Oven Omelet

◄≪ *Our tradition for years has been a Christmas Breakfast (Brunch). We invite couples or singles who might be alone. We set it up for 10:00 A.M. but very often they stay most of the day.*

We start with fruit: cut up grapefruit and oranges, red and green maraschino cherries for color, sprinkled with coconut, if desired.

We have a marvelous German bakery, so I take my annual trip there for Stollen and Christmas Tree coffee cake. In addition, I make lots of muffins and serve real butter and homemade strawberry jam.

The egg dish has always been a bit of a problem, but this recipe was the answer. ♥

ANN & VERNON GROUNDS

Hall's Baked Omelet

"This is really versatile. Our favorite meat in it is Polish sausage sliced rather thin, but lots of it. Ham, sausage, or other meat is good, too. I'm giving directions for bacon because that includes a couple of extra steps. Great served with fruit and muffins or breads."

SERVES 8

8 slices bacon
4 green onions, sliced (I use minced onion
    when using meat other than bacon.)
8 eggs
1 cup milk
½ teaspoon salt
2½ cups (10 ounces) grated Monterey Jack
    cheese

Fry bacon and break into small pieces. Remove most of fat from pan. Brown onions in remaining fat. Beat eggs well, beat in milk and salt. Add cooked bacon and, if baking omelet immediately, add 2 cups of the cheese now and sprinkle remaining ½ cup over top when omelet is almost finished baking. If baking later, add all of cheese at this time. Pour into a greased 9"x13" baking dish. Cover and refrigerate until ready to bake. Or bake uncovered at 350F for 35–40 minutes. Cut in squares.

Note: recipe ingredients can be increased by half (e.g., 12 eggs, 1½ cups milk) and still fit into a 9"x13" baking dish.

SUE HALL

Breakfast

One of the most helpful hints that I ever received that helped me most in getting the morning started and through breakfast was to set the table the night before. And to set out the Postum, cereal, and other things that could be assembled the night before. ♥

ISABELLE BARKER

Christmas Breakfast

Serves 5 or 6

1 pound sausage
5 slices cubed white bread
5 ounces grated Cheddar cheese
5 eggs, slightly beaten
2 cups milk
1 teaspoon salt
½ teaspoon dry mustard

Saute sausage until no longer red. Drain fat. Layer bread, sausage and cheese in a buttered 9"x13" baking dish. Mix together eggs, milk, salt and mustard, and pour over ingredients in baking dish. (If using a multiple of recipe or a different sized dish, make sure baking dish is no more than ¾ full.) Cover and refrigerate overnight, if desired. Bake uncovered at 350F for 30 minutes, or until set.

Vonnie Palmitier

Christmas Breakfast

← *This recipe has been our traditional Christmas breakfast since being given to me by a neighbor in Indiana 20 years ago. Although the whole family loves it, they want it served only on Christmas morning.*

I make it the day before and then it's ready to pop in the oven while we open our Christmas gifts. Served with juice and a sour cream coffee cake, it's something to look forward to after the last present is opened. ♥

Vonnie Palmitier

Country Egg Soufflé

¾ pound bacon, cooked and crumbled
10 slices white bread, crusts removed
8 eggs, beaten
3 cups milk
1 cup grated Jack cheese
1 cup grated medium Cheddar cheese
1 tablespoon dried onion flakes
½ teaspoon salt

Cut bread into cubes and place in a buttered baking dish. Sprinkle onion flakes and crumbled bacon on bread cubes. Combine beaten eggs, milk, salt and cheese. Pour over mixture in baking dish. Cover with foil and refrigerate overnight. Bake uncovered at 350F for 30–40 minutes.

Carole Carlson

Chef Pinzon's Cheese Soufflé

"This looks great coming out of the oven. But serve it promptly as it tends to deflate as it cools. Still tastes great, but if looks count don't leave it sitting around before serving."

SERVES about 6

6 slices white bread
butter, softened
3 eggs
2 cups milk
¼ teaspoon dry mustard
¼ teaspoon salt
2 cups (9 ounces) grated sharp Cheddar
  cheese

Cut crusts off bread, lightly butter each slice, and cut into cubes. Put cubes in a buttered 2 quart baking dish. Beat eggs, beat in milk, mustard and salt. Pour over bread cubes. Sprinkle cheese over the top and press down. Cover and refrigerate 4 hours or overnight. Bake *uncovered* at 325F for 60 minutes.

WANDA PINZON

"Meals only have to be prepared one at a time." ♥
—*Donna Dayton's*
mother-in-law.

Sharing

My husband and I have learned to work together as a team to get needed tasks done. He picks up after meals and rinses dishes while I put away food and fill the dishwasher. We've also learned to work together on company breakfasts. He scrambles eggs and fries bacon superbly while I make the other breakfast preparations. ♥

DONNA & WILBUR DAYTON

Fritata

SERVES 9

¾ cup chopped, sliced or diced red or green
    pepper
1½ cups sliced mushrooms
1½ cups chopped, sliced or diced zucchini
¾ cup chopped, sliced or diced onion
6 eggs, beaten
¼ cup light cream
1 large clove garlic, minced
1 (8 ounce) package cream cheese, softened
1 teaspoon salt
¼ teaspoon pepper
1½ cups grated Cheddar cheese
2 cups cubed bread

In an electric blender blend beaten eggs, cream,
garlic, cream cheese, salt, and pepper. Remove
from blender and combine with peppers, mushrooms, zucchini, onion, grated cheese and bread
cubes. Pour into a greased 9"x9" baking dish or
springform pan. Bake at 350F for 45 minutes.
Remove from oven and let stand 10 minutes
before cutting. Cut in 9 3"x3" pieces if using a
square pan.

GLADYS HUNT

Fritata

◄ *This is my favorite luncheon
menu. And I do like having
people in for lunch. A good cup
of homemade soup and a tasty
open-face sandwich—or
something like this fritata with a
fruit salad. Lots of good
conversation enriches the idea-
bank and draws us together as
people with common concerns.* ♥

GLADYS HUNT

Oven Cinnamon French Toast

MAKES 6 slices (easily doubled or increased)

2 eggs, lightly beaten with a fork
½ teaspoon salt
1 tablespoon sugar
1 teaspoon cinnamon
¼ cup milk
6 slices bread

Preheat oven to 500F. Lightly beat together eggs, salt, sugar, cinnamon, and milk. Dip bread into egg mixture, lay on a well-greased cookie sheet, and bake at 500F about 5 minutes. Turn toast over. Bake 5 minutes more.

SUE HALL

Oven Cinnamon French Toast

With children in four different schools and schedules, weekend/holiday breakfasts are really special times together. As we do a lot of entertaining there is often more than just our family around the table in the morning. I like easy or do-ahead things so I can enjoy everyone too.

French toast is a favorite and we enjoy this method which allows a large batch to be done all at one time so everyone can sit down together. ♥

SUE HALL

LUNCH AND LIGHT SUPPER DISHES

Vietnamese Rice 127
Grandma's Macaroni and Cheese 128
Mickey's Macaroni Casserole 129
Crepes Marquis 130
Fettuccine Alfredo 131
Cheese Fondue 132
Hamburger Doo-Lollies 133
Chili Dogs 134
Olé Dogs 135
Mary Carroll's Whole Wheat Pizza 136
Easy Homemade Pizza 137
Mama Jeannie's Pizza 138
Susan Feldhake's Cornmeal Pizza
     Crust 139
Shelley Smith's Pizza 140
Frozen Bread Dough Pizza 141
Olivia's Pizza 142
Party Rye Pizza 143
Pizza Bread 144
Chili-Mac 145
Kendall's Chili 146
Latayne's Chili 147
Tim's Famous Chili 147
Johnny Cash's "Old Iron Pot" Family
     Style Chili 148
Open-Faced Sourdough Seafood
     Sandwiches 149

Pita Sandwiches 150
Broiled Baked Bean Sandwich 151
Corned Beef Party Buns 151
Tasty Ham Buns 152

Vietnamese Rice

Quick & Easy

"A very tasty and very *quick* meal."

SERVES 3 or 4

¼ cup oil
1 onion, chopped
¼–¾ pound meat, cooked or uncooked (bacon
   is very tasty), cut into small pieces or
   strips
1–2 cups leftover vegetables (green peppers,
   carrots, peas, broccoli, or other favorites)
3 cups cooked rice (brown is best)
1–2 tablespoons soy sauce
3 eggs, beaten
lettuce

In a large skillet or wok, in oil stir fry onion and meat together until onion is translucent and meat is thoroughly cooked, about 2 minutes. Add vegetables and stir fry 1 or 2 minutes more. Add rice, soy sauce and eggs. Over medium heat, stir continuously until egg is cooked. Serve hot over a bed of lettuce. Add more soy sauce if desired.

BILL VRIESEMA

I value thrift. Not stinginess or meanness, but thrift. Thrift means remembering the egg yolk in the refrigerator and using it up before it spoils or combining a little of several leftover vegetables to make a stir-fry dish while they are still fresh. ♥

GLADYS HUNT

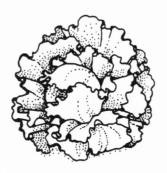

Grandma's Macaroni and Cheese

2 tablespoons margarine
2 tablespoons flour
1½ cups milk
1 (8 ounce) box Velveeta cheese, cut in pieces
1 can condensed tomato soup, undiluted
1 (8 ounce) package elbow macaroni, cooked
    and drained

Melt margarine in a saucepan. Remove from heat, stir flour into melted margarine. Slowly stir in milk. Return to stove and cook, stirring constantly, until thickened. Add cheese. Stir until melted. Stir in tomato soup. Combine with cooked macaroni in a greased baking dish. Bake at 350F for 30–45 minutes or until bubbly and lightly browned on top.

LEE DISTELBERG

Birthdays

When a family member has a birthday he or she is allowed to plan the dinner menu with all their favorite foods. This means we may have macaroni and cheese and rice at the same meal, or the desserts may have the same fruit in them. The rest of the family shares these foods with the birthday person. Then during dinner, my husband always tells the story of their birth—the kids know it by heart by now, but they love it!

Also, when they were small, they were permitted to choose their favorite activity on their birthday—bowling, skating, ball game—whatever. It was fun trying to guess what the person would choose to eat and do on his or her birthday. ♥

AILEEN & DAVID HANEY

Mickey's Macaroni Casserole

SERVES 8

1 (8 ounce) package macaroni, cooked and
    drained
½ cup mayonnaise
¼ cup chopped pimento
1 small onion, chopped
¼ cup diced green pepper
1 (10¾ ounce) can condensed cream of
    mushroom soup
½ cup milk
½ teaspoon salt
½ cup grated medium Cheddar or processed
    cheese
½ cup grated sharp Cheddar cheese

Combine cooked macaroni, mayonnaise, pimento, onion, and green pepper. Mix together
soup, milk, and salt. Add to macaroni mixture.
Mix together two kinds of cheese, add half of
macaroni mixture. Turn macaroni into a greased
1½ quart casserole. Sprinkle remaining cheese on
top. Cover and bake at 350F for about 20 minutes.

ISABELLE & KENNETH BARKER

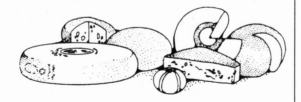

Crepes Marquis

Makes 9–10 crepes

Crepes:

3 eggs, beaten
⅔ cup flour
½ teaspoon salt
1 cup milk
¼ cup sugar

Filling:

8 slices bacon
½ cup chopped onion
½ cup chopped green pepper
½ cup chopped celery
1 (8 ounce) can sliced mushrooms
2 cups grated Cheddar cheese

Garnish:

catsup
additional grated Cheddar cheese

To prepare crepes, mix ingredients and let stand 30 minutes. For each crepe pour ¼ cup batter on a lightly greased skillet or griddle, or dip hot crepe pan in a shallow bowl of batter. Cook crepes on one side only.

To prepare filling, fry bacon until crisp, drain. Reserve 2 tablespoons bacon fat and saute celery, onion and pepper, until tender. Crumble bacon and combine with sauted vegetables, mushrooms and cheese, stirring lightly. Fill each crepe with ¼ cup of mixture. Roll. Garnish with catsup and/or cheese if desired. Place on a greased 10"x15"x1" baking pan and bake at 350F for 30 minutes.

Judith Markham

Crepes Marquis

◄ A New Year's Eve buffet was a family tradition in the German family in which I grew up. I've tried to carry that on in my own home, with our own personal touches, of course. One of my favorite buffet dishes is this one, which can be prepared ahead and refrigerated till ready to heat and serve (obviously not a German recipe!). ♥

Judith Markham

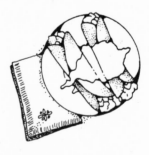

Fettuccine Alfredo

SERVES 4–5

1 cup heavy cream
3 tablespoons butter
⅔ cup freshly grated cheese (Parmesan,
   Asiago or caciocavallo—the classic recipe
   calls for Parmesan; I like to use half
   Asiago and half caciocavallo)
½ teaspoon salt
4–6 twists of freshly ground pepper
a pinch of nutmeg
12–16 ounces fettuccine noodles
additional grated cheese

In a heavy pan large enough to accommodate all the cooked noodles, put ½ cup of the cream and butter. Simmer until butter and cream thicken; usually this takes less than a minute. Turn off heat.

Cook noodles in salted boiling water, stirring to keep them from sticking together. Fettuccine should be cooked but still firm to the bite when it is done (al dente). Drain immediately and transfer to the pan containing cream and butter.

Turn heat on low, toss fettuccine to coat with cream-butter mixture. Add remaining cream and cheese, salt, pepper, and nutmeg. Toss fettuccine until well coated and serve with grated cheese on the side.

MARK HUNT

Cheese Fondue

Fondue Mixture:

2 tablespoons lemon juice
2 tablespoons butter
dash of Worcestershire sauce, if desired
1 (12 ounce) block Swiss, Emmenthal,
   Gruyère, mozzarella or Monterey Jack
   cheese, or ½ block of any 2 of the above
   cheeses
flour

Dipping possibilities:

(Cut any or all of the following into squares about ¾", i.e. bite-size. We usually have 3 items at a meal, about ¼ cup per serving.)

mushroom buttons (used whole)
brown bread
toasted white bread
Spam or similar canned meat
celery pieces
broccoli stems
green or red pepper
sweet onions

Cheese Fondue

◄《 *A fondue pot is handy, of course, but not essential. Any saucepan will do. As the fondue mixture cools and gets too thick, put it back on the stove a few minutes to warm again. A double boiler is even better; it stays hot longer.* ♥

Sandy Dengler

To prepare fondue, put lemon juice, butter and seasoning in fondue pot or pan and heat up. Cut cheese into small cubes, dust with flour to keep from sticking together, and drop them in the pot a handful at a time. Melt over low heat.

To serve, set pot in center of table. Each person dips morsels in the cheese, gives it a twist to coat, and lets it cool on his plate (at our house, the fork used to dip with is not the fork used to eat with). As the cheese thickens, it gets stringy—a never-ending source of amusement. This is especially true of mozzarella combinations. But a lot of laughter binds the family better than stern warnings. The fondue plus salad makes a generous meal.

Sandy Dengler

Hamburger Doo-Lollies

"A quick favorite of ours is Hamburger Doo-Lollies. I made up this recipe when Charles was in Veterinary School and we were living on a shoestring—actually, hamburger—budget. Now that we can have steaks and shrimp sometimes, we still enjoy this poor man's variation of pizza."

six slices white bread
about ½ pound ground beef
salt, to taste
1 onion, sliced
catsup
cheese, sliced (Cheddar, mozzarella, Swiss,
    any or all)

Taking small portions of raw ground beef at a time, spread thinly to the very edge of bread, being careful not to tear slices. Salt if desired. Fry meat side down in an ungreased iron skillet over medium heat. Arrange hamburgered slices, meat side up, on baking sheet. Add cheese and onion in slices. Crisscross with catsup. Bake at 350F 10–12 minutes, or until cheese is melting and catsup bubbly.

BRENDA KNIGHT GRAHAM

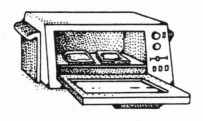

Mealtimes are together times at our house. With a veterinarian and a band member in the family, eating together is no small accomplishment, but we feel the closeness around the table is very important. Sometimes it means a lot of waiting for some of us, and juggling of time schedules. (I have written many a letter and sewed a lot of stitches after supper reached the "back burner" stage and the waiting began.)

We have our family devotion time at the breakfast table. People are usually pretty quiet that early in the morning and at least they look as if they are listening! At suppertime I like to "fix up," using best dishes sometimes, changing table decorations, occasionally turning plates upside down with a thought-provoker or special message or Bible verse for each

Chili Dogs

MAKES 32

3 tablespoons vegetable oil
1 cup finely chopped onion
½ cup chopped green pepper
1 clove garlic, crushed
2 pounds ground beef
3 (8 ounce) cans tomato sauce
2½ teaspoons chili powder
2 teaspoons salt
½ teaspoon pepper
¼ cup light molasses
2 (16 ounce) cans red kidney beans, drained
32 frankfurters
32 buns

Saute onion, green pepper, and garlic in oil. Add beef, cook until beef is no longer red, or until slightly browned. Add tomato sauce, chili powder, salt, pepper, and molasses and simmer, uncovered, for 15 minutes. Add kidney beans and heat well.

DAVID M. MARTIN

one underneath. Or I may ask some other member of the family to do this.

We have four cooks in our family, but so far no one has tried to root me out of my place as "chief cook and bottlewasher." Charles, my husband, is our outdoor cook, especially when it comes to frying fish. In our area fish fries are very popular, with either fresh pond fish or Gulf fish being used. My daughter Julie, fourteen, enjoys fishing with me at local ponds, but Charles cheerfully cleans and cooks our catch. The traditional favorite side dishes at a fish fry are cheese grits, cole slaw, hush puppies, pickles, and onions. By the way, Julie always has a grilled cheese sandwich at these times, because she hates to eat fish as much as she loves to catch them!

William, fifteen years old, is very fond of pizza and occasionally will cook his own special "from scratch with Bisquick" rendition. It is yummy with lots of cheese,

Olé Dogs

"Good with a green salad and a fresh fruit plate."

SERVES 4

4 corn tortillas
1 (16 ounce) can chili with beans
4 wieners
¼ cup grated Cheddar cheese
¼ cup chopped onion

Wrap tortillas in a paper towel and microwave on high for 30 seconds. Remove from oven and place 2 tablespoons of chili in the center of each tortilla, top with wieners and roll up. Place, seam side down, in a glass baking dish. Cover with remaining chili, cover, and microwave on high for 7–8 minutes. Remove from oven, sprinkle cheese and onions on top. Cover and let stand 5 minutes before serving.

MRS. JOHN CARPENTER

hamburger, and mushrooms, also pepper and onions. Once he made a beautiful blueberry pie with intricate latticework piecrust. We all thoroughly enjoyed it, but he's never wanted to make another one. Is that a smug smile he wears when he sees me produce my scrappy looking pies? Oh, well, he eats them heartily—that's all that matters! ♥

BRENDA KNIGHT GRAHAM

Mary Carroll's Whole Wheat Pizza

"This is a fun family recipe, as everyone can help with the mixing, chopping, and decorating of the pizzas."

MAKES 2 pizzas

Pizza Crust:

2 tablespoons or 3 packages dry yeast
1¼ cups very warm water (but not hot)
1 teaspoon honey
3 cups whole wheat flour
1 tablespoon nutritional yeast (optional)
¾ teaspoon vegetable salt, or salt
¼ cup safflower oil

Sauce:

1 (16 ounce) can tomato sauce
1 (6 ounce) can tomato paste
2–3 teaspoons Italian seasoning
½ teaspoon pepper
½ cup chopped onion
1 clove garlic, minced
¼ cup water

Topping:

choice of or combinations of grated or sliced
    cheese: mozzarella, Cheddar, Swiss, etc.
sliced onions
sliced mushrooms
sliced peppers
pineapple chunks
grated Parmesan cheese

To prepare crust, sprinkle dry yeast over surface of water, mixing as you go. Add honey. Set aside for 5 minutes or more. Combine all dry ingredients. Add oil to dissolved yeast. Using a fork, combine wet and dry ingredients. (Eventu-

➤→

ally I use my hands to finish mixing and then to form a ball.) Knead until smooth. (If you have time, you can let it rise for 1–2 hours in an oiled bowl and knead it down again, but you can use it right away, too.) Divide dough into 2 balls. Roll out each ball onto a greased and floured cookie sheet, either with a rolling pin or press with hands.

To prepare sauce, mix together tomato sauce, tomato paste, Italian seasoning, pepper, chopped onion, minced garlic and water.

To assemble pizzas, spread sauce over dough on cookie sheets. Put on as many layers and kinds of cheese as desired. Add sliced onions, etc. as desired. Top with Parmesan. Bake at 450F for about 15 minutes.

Phyllis & James Hurley

Easy Homemade Pizza

"This is a fun recipe because you can improvise with almost anything your family enjoys—whatever you'd order at a pizza restaurant."

2 cups biscuit mix
½ cup water
2 tablespoons oil
canned sauce (Pizza Quick, Ragu, etc.)
½ pound grated cheese
salami or pepperoni slices
chopped onion
sliced black olives

With a fork mix together biscuit mix and water. Knead briefly on a floured surface. Place on a greased pizza pan, shaping to fit pan. Pinch edge of dough to make a slight rim. Spread oil over dough. Add remaining ingredients as desired. Bake at 425F for 20–25 minutes.

Debbie Barr

Since "family" in my case means just my husband, Darrell, and myself (plus an exuberant Labrador Retriever named Cassidy!), and since we are constantly on the go, our favorites tend to: (a) be quick and easy, (b) make more than one meal for us, (c) feed a crowd, or (d) all of the above! ♥

Debbie Barr

Mama Jeannie's Pizza

Mama Jeannie's Pizza Crust:

MAKES 1 thick or 2 thin crusts

1 cup warm water
1 package dry yeast
1½ teaspoons sugar
½ teaspoon salt
2 tablespoons oil
2½ cups flour

Dissolve yeast in warm water. Stir in sugar, salt and oil Add enough flour to form a stiff dough. Knead on floured surface for 5–10 minutes. Let rest 5 minutes. Cover 1 (for thick) or 2 (for thin) greased pizza pans with dough. Let rise in pan while preparing pizza fixin's.

Mama Jeannie's Pizza Fixin's:

For 1–2 pizzas:

1 (8 ounce) can herb flavored tomato sauce
Italian seasoning
sliced pepperoni
cooked sausage
cooked ground beef
green and black olives
mushrooms
bacon bits
12 ounces mozzarella cheese, grated
12 ounces Cheddar cheese, grated
1 (8 ounce) can grated Parmesan cheese

Spread tomato sauce over crust(s) in pan(s). Sprinkle with Italian seasoning. Add desired meat, cooked and drained well to remove excess grease. Sprinkle with olives, mushrooms, and bacon bits as desired. Combine cheeses and pile on top. Bake at 375F–475F for 15–25 minutes, or until browned to your taste.

JEANNIE & STEVE HARPER

Mama Jeannie's Pizzeria

On Friday Family Night we have Mama Jeannie's pizza— replete with checked tablecloths, candlelight, and menus for our guests from which to choose their favorite pizza.

This has been a family tradition (off and on) every Friday night for four years, ever since we moved to Wilmore, Kentucky—depending on whether we're dieting or not. We provide our own homemade menus, for the adults: á là theologica, and for the kids: á là favorite books, television programs, and special interests.

I must tell you where we got the inspiration for this in the first place . . . besides our love for pizza!

When Steve graduated from Duke University four years ago he interviewed at Fuller Theological Seminary in Pasadena, California. While we were there we ate in the

Susan Feldhake's Cornmeal Pizza Crust

MAKES 2

1¼ cups warm water
¼ cup yellow cornmeal
2 tablespoons sugar
2 cups flour
½ package dry yeast
½ teaspoon salt or garlic salt
3 tablespoons oil or melted shortening

Place water in a large mixing bowl. Stir in cornmeal, sugar, and half of flour. *Then* sprinkle yeast over the mixture. Stir well. Stir in oil and salt. Add enough flour to make a thick dough. Turn out on a floured surface and knead until smooth and elastic (about 5 minutes). Place in a greased bowl, cover, and let rise in a warm place until doubled. Divide dough in half, grease pizza pans, and with greased hands press out dough onto pan(s). Sometimes dusting the top of the dough with flour makes it easier. Prick dough all over with a fork to prevent air bubbles during baking. Let dough rise about 15 minutes, then bake at 350F until crust starts to turn slightly golden. Remove crust from oven, spread with sauce, toppings and cheese. May be returned to oven to finish baking to eat immediately, or may be topped and refrigerated to bake later, or may be topped and frozen.

SUSAN FELDHAKE

sandwich shop on campus. There they had numerous sandwiches from which to choose—á là theologica. Thus the idea was born to adapt it to pizza. So some of the items are entirely original, while others are á là Fuller. The kids' versions are absolutely original.

Our family has really enjoyed sharing Mama Jeannie's pizza with our friends and neighbors, and it has strengthened our family, if for no other reason than there's now more of us to love.

Menu

MAMA JEANNIE'S 'á là theologica''

The world's first theological pizzeria. We've taken the

Shelley Smith's Pizza

MAKES 2 pizzas

Dough:

1 package dry yeast
¼ cup warm water (105F–115F)
1 cup skim milk
2 tablespoons shortening
1 teaspoon salt
1 tablespoon sugar
3 cups flour

Sauce:

1 large onion, finely chopped
olive oil
2 (8 ounce) cans tomato sauce
½ teaspoon oregano
½ teaspoon basil
2 bay leaves
½ teaspoon garlic salt, or to taste
pepper, to taste

Topping:

pepperoni
ground pork, cooked
ground beef, cooked
green pepper
green olives
mushrooms
anchovies
bacon or ham
mozzarella cheese

Dissolve yeast in warm water, scald milk, add shortening, salt, and sugar. Cool to lukewarm. In a large bowl, combine yeast with milk. Add enough flour to make a stiff dough. Turn out on a floured surface and knead 5–10 minutes. Place dough in a greased bowl. Brush with olive oil or shortening. Cover with wax paper or plastic wrap,

➤→

fundamental pizza and transformed its conservative character into liberal creations while retaining its basic orthodoxy.

ST. PAUL PIZZA (it'll make a believer out of you). Deluxe: Cheese, pepperoni, mushrooms, olives, hamburger.

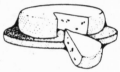

ST. FRANCIS PIZZA (a humble pizza). Plain cheese.

JOHN CALVIN PIZZA (made for "two lips"). Ingredients are predestined—no free choices. Cheese and hamburger.

JOHN WESLEY PIZZA (the perfect pizza). This has EVERYTHING but there's room for more. Deluxe with bacon.

FRANCIS ASBURY PIZZA (for the person "on the go"). ONE slice only: Cheese, olives, and mushrooms.

JONATHAN EDWARDS PIZZA (a pizza in the hands of

and a towel. Let rise in a warm place until doubled (about 1 hour). Punch down and let rise again until doubled. Punch down, and let rest five minutes. Divide in half and roll out into circles. Fit into oiled pizza pans (if making one pizza, freeze other half). Spread with sauce, top as desired, bake at 425F for about 15–20 minutes.

SHELLEY SMITH

Frozen Bread Dough Pizza

MAKES 4 pizzas

Crust: **3 loaves frozen bread dough**

Sauce: **1¾–2 (15 ounce) cans tomato sauce**

Topping:
2 pounds sausage, cooked and drained
1 large can mushrooms, drained
½ teaspoon thyme
1 teaspoon oregano
1 teaspoon garlic salt
½ teaspoon pepper
1 pound mozzarella cheese, grated
Parmesan cheese, to taste

Defrost bread dough in a large plastic bag (allowing room to expand) in refrigerator overnight or about 2 hours or more at room temperature. Divide thawed dough into 4 parts. Roll out on a floured surface and line 4 greased pizza pans or cookie sheets with dough. Spread with tomato sauce. Distribute cooked sausage and mushrooms over pizzas. Combine thyme, oregano, garlic salt and pepper and sprinkle over pizzas. Add mozzarella and Parmesan. Bake at 400F for about 10 minutes, or until done. To freeze, cover top of cooled pizza with plastic wrap, then wrap with foil.

JOANNE BOER

an angry oven). Well-done. Hamburger and bacon bits.
RUDOLF BULTMANN PIZZA (don't "myth" this one!). A liberal assortment of ingredients.

C. S. LEWIS PIZZA (the mere pizza). Cheese and pepperoni.
ALBERT SCHWEITZER PIZZA (the quest for the historical pizza). A prize-winning pizza for the missionary minded. Olives only.
Mama Jeannie's Children's Menu features characters from a favorite TV Program for young children. You can be inventive and develop your own menu around the interests of your guests and appropriate to their ages.
Mama Jeannie illustrates her Children's Menu with line drawings of characters from the program. Pizza choices are presented as the favorite of each

Olivia's Pizza

"This pizza recipe is one that our family has enjoyed for many years. It requires a little time but is well worth the effort and can be made and frozen for later use."

MAKES 2 pizzas

Crust:

1 package dry yeast
1 cup warm water
2 teaspoons sugar
3¼ cups flour (approximately)
1 tablespoon oil
1½ teaspoons salt
1 egg

Sauce:

1 (8 ounce) can tomato sauce
1 (6 ounce) can tomato paste
⅛ teaspoon garlic powder
⅛ teaspoon red pepper
½ cup finely chopped onions

Toppings:

¼ pound ground beef, cooked and drained
3 ounces grated Cheddar cheese
2 (4 ounce) cans mushrooms (optional)
8 ounces mozzarella cheese, grated
2 teaspoons oregano
3 ounces pepperoni, sliced
Parmesan cheese, as desired

Dissolve yeast in warm water in a large bowl. Add sugar and 1½ cups of the flour. Beat well with a large spoon. Add oil, salt, egg and more flour, as needed, to make a soft, workable dough. Knead 5–10 minutes, until smooth. Place in a greased bowl, turning once to grease top of dough, cover and let rise in a warm place until doubled. Punch down and let rest 5 minutes.

➤→

character and includes his or her comments:

"Hello, my favorite shape is a triangle because it reminds me of my favorite food . . . Birdseed Pizza! Do you want a slice?" Cheese, bacon bits, and poppy seeds.

"Greetings. My favorite person in the neighborhood is the cook. Do you know why? Because she makes pizzas and I love to count them. How many pieces will you have? 1 . . . 2 . . . 3 . . . 4 . . . 5 . . . 6 . . ." Cheese, hamburger, mushrooms, olives, pepperoni, and bacon bits.

"Hi! It's time for your favorite show—THE PIZZA GAME. Can you guess what is on your slice of pizza?" Hamburger and bacon bits.

The menu ends with garbage pizza that contains "leftovers" of

Divide in half and roll or press with hands to fit pizza pans.

Mix sauce ingredients together. Spread sauce over dough. Place toppings over sauce in the order listed above. Bake at 375F for 15 minutes or until done. If frozen, bake at 400F for 20 minutes.

Olivia & Paul Hillman

Party Rye Pizza

"This is a favorite for a group of hungry teenagers."

1 pound bulk sausage (hot flavored)
1 pound Velveeta cheese
1 tablespoon Worcestershire sauce
2 tablespoons catsup
a pinch of oregano
dash of pepper
party rye bread

Brown sausage, drain well. Cut cheese into pieces and add to pan with cooked sausage. Stir until melted. Add Worcestershire sauce, catsup, oregano and pepper. Spread on party rye bread slices. Bake on a cookie sheet at 425F for 8–10 minutes.

Loretta R. Wilson

all ingredients.

Some other menu possibilities are:

DINOSAUR PIZZAS featuring:

TYRANNOSAURUS REX PIZZA (for the meat eaters with a tremendous appetite). Sausage, pepperoni, and ground beef.

PTERODACTYL PIZZA (the easy-flying pizza). Light and crispy crust, lightly topped with choice of toppings.

BRONTOSAURUS PIZZA (the big guy). Double everything. ♥

Jeannie & Steve Harper

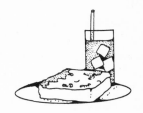

Pizza Bread

"Teenagers love this."

1 loaf unsliced Italian or French bread
1 pound ground beef (chuck)
¼ cup finely chopped onion
¼ – ½ cup catsup
2 tablespoons water

Slice bread in half lengthwise. Place plastic wrap between slices and wrap for freezer or wrap them separately, and freeze. (Bread must be frozen to prepare this.) When ready to prepare, mix ground beef, chopped onion, catsup and water together thoroughly. Spread mixture thinly (no more than ¼" thick) over cut side of frozen bread. Spread completely out to edges of bread. Broil in oven until done (meat will be browned).

Variations: After it is broiled, top with grated cheese (Cheddar, mozzarella, Parmesan, etc.) and return to broiler to melt. Sprinkle with pizza seasoning, basil, oregano, garlic salt, etc. Add chopped parsley, celery, chili or bell peppers, olives, etc. to meat mixture.

Use instead of or in addition to catsup: steak sauce, barbecue sauce, taco sauce, spaghetti sauce, chili sauce. Just make sure mixture is diluted enough to spread thinly.

Melba Petersen

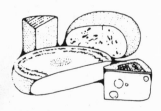

Chili-Mac

2 medium onions, chopped
oil
1 pound ground beef
2 (8 ounce) cans tomato sauce
salt, to taste
chili powder, to taste
2 cans solid packed tomatoes
2 cans red kidney beans
¼ of a (1 pound) package spaghetti, cooked
    and drained

In a large pot saute onions in oil until tender. Add ground beef and cook until browned. Remove excess fat. Add tomatoes, beans and sauce. Simmer for 1 hour. Add cooked spaghetti. Season to taste with salt and chili powder. Serve with cheese sauce and chopped green onions.

Cheese Sauce:

sharp Cheddar cheese, grated
sour cream
garlic salt, to taste

Combine cheese and sour cream. Warm slowly over low heat, just enough to melt cheese. Sprinkle on a little garlic salt.

SHIRLEY & PAT BOONE

Through the years of raising five children I've tried to make birthdays special by letting the honoree choose his own gift and the menu for the birthday dinner. Where the menu is concerned there are no limitations and I've prepared some pretty strange meals. ♥

EDA STERTZ

Kendall's Chili

"Following instructions in the order given is very important."

SERVES 10–12

5 strips bacon, cut in small pieces
3 large green peppers, coarsely chopped
3 large onions, coarsely chopped
1 tablespoon oil, if needed
½ clove garlic, crushed
½ teaspoon salt
½ teaspoon pepper
2 tablespoons sugar
3 pounds ground beef (chuck)
1 teaspoon chili powder
2 tablespoons Worcestershire sauce
2 (6 ounce) cans tomato puree
3 (8 ounce) cans tomato sauce
2 (24 ounce) cans dark red kidney beans
2 (16 ounce) cans great northern beans
32 ounces tomato juice
4 ounces chopped olives

In a large pot or Dutch oven, fry bacon until done but not crispy. Add chopped green pepper and onion and saute until tender, adding oil if needed. Then add garlic, salt, pepper, and sugar. Add ground beef gradually, to keep lump-free. Cook until excess fat can be removed. Remove fat. Sprinkle on chili powder and add Worcestershire sauce. Stir in tomato puree and tomato sauce. Add beans, tomato juice and olives. Bring to a boil. Reduce heat and simmer 1 hour.

MRS. R. T. KENDALL

Latayne's Chili

1 pound ground beef
1 can tomatoes with chilis
1 can tomato sauce
1 tablespoon chili powder
1 medium onion, chopped
1 can pinto beans
salt, to taste
pepper, to taste

Brown ground beef. Remove fat. Add remaining ingredients. Simmer 1 hour.

LATAYNE SCOTT

Tim's Famous Chili

Quick & Easy

2 pounds lean ground round, fried medium,
    fat removed
salt, to taste
pepper, to taste
1 can condensed tomato soup
1 can whole tomatoes, cut into bite-size pieces
chili powder, to taste

Cook for 10 minutes and serve piping hot!

TIM LaHAYE

Entertaining

Another social time we had recently around food, involved my nine-year-old son's slumber party. We invited the children to come between 8:30 and 9:00 in the evening and at the same time invited the parents to come along and enjoy some chili with us and the kids. It was a great time for us to become acquainted with the parents of Carlton's friends in an informal and relaxing way. For a snack to go along with the chili, I fixed chips and cheese—tortilla chips with grated Cheddar cheese spread on top and placed in the oven for a few minutes. ♥

RUTH TUCKER

Johnny Cash's "Old Iron Pot" Family Style Chili

This chili offers the height of flexibility—and hazard—because you have to guess and experiment with several of the herbs and seasonings. Johnny doesn't give the amounts because he doesn't measure them.

"SERVES 12 people 3 helpings each."

5 pounds sirloin steak
shortening
3 packages McCormick's, Schilling, Lawry's or
      any good chili seasoning mix
Mexene chili powder
Spice Island chili con carne seasoning
cumin
thyme
sage leaves
chopped raw onions
chopped chili peppers
3–4 cans red kidney beans
3–4 cans whole tomatoes
1 (6 ounce) can tomato paste
garlic powder
onion powder
2 tablespoons sugar
salt, to taste

Chop steak and cook in a small amount of shortening to medium doneness. Add packages of chili seasoning mix and cook 5 minutes. Add remaining ingredients. Mix and taste. If it's too hot add more tomatoes. Simmer on low for 20 minutes, adding water if too thick.

Serve with soda crackers and Pepsi or Coke.

Johnny says: "It will be better tomorrow if properly taken care of overnight."

JOHNNY CASH

Open-Faced Sourdough Seafood Sandwiches

MAKES 8 sandwiches

1 cup crab or shrimp, cooked (or a combination of the two)
¼ cup diced celery
2 teaspoons finely chopped green onion or chives
1 cup (4 ounces) grated Cheddar cheese
3 scant tablespoons mayonnaise
salt and pepper, to taste
4 whole (8 halves) sourdough English muffins

Split and toast muffins. Combine crab or shrimp, celery, onion, and cheese. Add mayonnaise and a dash of salt and pepper if desired, blend. Spoon equally on muffin halves. Place in a glass baking dish that has been lined with a paper towel and microwave on high 1 minute, uncovered. Turn ¼ turn and cook an additional ½–1 minute. Check to see if filling is warm and cheese is melted. If they need more time zap them 15 seconds at a time, taking care not to overcook as overcooking will toughen the muffins.

Variation:

Salmon sandwiches: Substitute cooked (canned works well) salmon for the shellfish. "With salmon I often add a chopped dill pickle when I mix the filling."

JOHN CARPENTER

Saturday Night Hamburgers

I can tell you what I had practically every Saturday night when I was growing up. Back then I thought everyone in the world had the same custom. Now, as a mother, I realize what a relief it was for my mother not to have to plan a menu one night a week.

Saturday Night Hamburgers
Real Buns (Other days of the week we got plain bread.)
Potato Chips
Celery
Dill Pickles
Water
Ice Cream

We hardly ever went away on Saturday night because that was the night to study your Sunday School lesson and to wash hair. Without hamburgers, we barely knew to go to church the next day! And it was one menu no one ever complained about. ♥

MELODIE DAVIS

Pita Sandwiches

"My daughters love this."

SERVES 4 generously

¾ **pound ground beef**
1 **tablespoon oil**
1 **(10 ounce) package frozen Italian vegetables**
2 **tablespoons water**
½ **cup (2 ounces) feta cheese, in chunks (or**
   blue cheese, crumbled)
2 **tablespoons chopped fresh parsley**
4 **medium pita bread rounds, cut in half to**
   make 8 pockets
yogurt dressing or sour cream

Brown ground beef in oil in a large skillet. Drain off all except 1 tablespoon of fat. Add vegetables and water. Bring to a full boil over medium heat, separating and breaking apart frozen vegetables with a fork. (I cut the vegetables up with the spatula as they cook.) Reduce heat. Cover and simmer for 2 minutes. Remove from heat and stir in cheese and parsley. Serve with dressing in warmed pita bread pockets.

CAROLYN & ROBERT DE VRIES

Working Mothers' Easy Menu

When I get home from work and don't know what to fix, this is what my family likes, especially on cold nights.

I make small pancakes (from mix), bacon, fried eggs, sliced cheese. We stack these together on our plates as follows: pancake, egg, cheese, bacon, pancake. Top with butter and syrup. It tastes kind of like a homemade Egg McMuffin. Serve with juice or milk, carrot sticks to round out the nutrition, and applesauce for dessert. ♥

MELODIE DAVIS

Broiled Baked Bean Sandwich

slices of bread
canned pork and beans, drained
grated cheese of your choice
bacon strips, cut into small pieces
catsup
prepared mustard

Arrange slices of bread on cookie sheet. Spread pork and beans on each slice of bread, sprinkle with cheese, arrange bacon pieces on top, and dot with catsup and mustard. Broil slowly so bacon cooks and cheese melts, about 15 minutes.

BETTY & JAMES BUICK

Corned Beef Party Buns

1 can corned beef
1 package onion soup mix
1 pint sour cream
potato rolls or small hamburger buns

Combine corned beef, soup mix, and sour cream. Spread on potato rolls or hamburger buns. Wrap each in aluminum foil and heat in oven for 15 minutes at 350F.

CHERYL ROSE
SHIRLEY SCHOLTEN

Tasty Ham Buns

1 cup butter, melted
½ cup prepared mustard
¼ cup minced onion
¼ cup poppy seeds
small potato rolls
ham slices
Swiss cheese slices

Combine melted butter, mustard, minced onion, and poppy seeds. Split potato rolls, spread with mixture and top with ham and Swiss cheese. Put halves together, wrap individually in aluminum foil, and heat in oven for 15 minutes at 350F.

CHERYL ROSE

CHICKEN

Almond Chicken 154
Oriental Chicken 155
Goombay Walnut Chicken 156
Indonesian Stir-Fry 157
Chicken Paprikash 158
Parmesan Chicken Breasts 158
Pan Chicken 159
Chicken Enchiladas in Green Sauce 160
Chicken Enchiladas Rancheros 161
Pastel de Chocolo 162
Chicken Adobo 163
Oven Barbecued Chicken 163
Sweet and Sour Chicken 164
Sweet and Sour Chicken Wings 165
Popover Chicken 166
Stuffed Breast of Chicken 167
Fosmire's Favorite Chicken Kiev 168
Chicken and Mushrooms in Madeira
      Sauce 169
Chicken Marengo 170
Chilled Rock Cornish Game Hens 170
Microwave Crispy Chicken 171
Moist and Crispy Chicken 172
Can Can Chicken 172
Bonnie's Easy Baked Chicken 173
Special Baked Chicken 173
Easy Chicken Divan I 174
Easy Chicken Divan II 175
Hot Chicken Salad Casserole 176

Almond Chicken

**4 chicken breasts (or more if you want it
    meatier)**
1 egg white
1 tablespoon soy sauce
1 tablespoon cornstarch
3 slices of fresh ginger root
3 green onions
2 medium green peppers
2 dried red peppers
½ cup oil
1 cup whole blanched almonds

Sauce:

2 tablespoons soy sauce
1½ teaspoons cornstarch
½ teaspoon salt (optional)
1 teaspoon sugar

Bone and skin chicken, saving bones and skin
to make broth for other use. Cut meat into 1"
cubes. Mix together egg white, soy sauce and 1
tablespoon of the cornstarch. Pour over chicken
and set aside for about 30 minutes. Meanwhile,
prepare other ingredients.

Chop ginger into slivers, cut green onions in 1"
pieces, cut green peppers into 1" squares and
crumble dried peppers. Mix sauce ingredients
together and set aside.

In a large skillet or wok, stir fry almonds in oil
until lightly browned. Remove almonds with a
slotted spoon and set aside. Add chicken to oil
and stir fry for 3–4 minutes. Remove chicken and
keep warm.

Remove all but about 2 tablespoons of oil from
skillet or wok. Add ginger and green onion, stir
fry for a few seconds. Add green pepper and cook
for 2 more minutes. Add chicken, almonds and
red pepper to the pan. Add sauce mixture. Cook
until bubbling and thickened. Serve over hot rice.

➤➤

Almond Chicken

◄⧯ *I buy whole chickens. Cut off
the breasts to make a Chinese
chicken-almond dish. The wings,
back, neck, liver, gizzard and
legs go into a big pot to simmer
for broth. The legs are served
for the first meal, the chicken-
almond for another day. And
the meat cleaned off the bones is
refrigerated while the rest of the
broth simmers with vegetables
for a good soup, with the meat
pieces added last. How thrifty I
feel with all that nourishment
coming from a couple of
chickens—low in cost,
delicious!* ♥

GLADYS HUNT

Variation: Substitute an equal amount of Chinese pea pods for green peppers. Add water chestnuts, if desired.

GLADYS HUNT

Oriental Chicken

SERVES 4

2 tablespoons cornstarch
¼ cup soy sauce
2 cups bouillon or broth
1 tablespoon oil
½ cup thinly sliced celery
¼ cup green pepper, cut in small pieces
¼ cup slivered carrots
½ (20 ounce) bag frozen oriental style
**   vegetables**
2 cups cooked chicken, cubed
½ can sliced water chestnuts

Blend together cornstarch, soy sauce and bouillon. Set aside. Saute or stir fry celery, green pepper and carrots in oil until celery is translucent. Add frozen oriental-style vegetables and continue cooking until vegetables are crisp-tender. Add bouillon mixture, cook, and stir until thickened. Add chicken and water chestnuts and simmer until heated through. Serve over rice.

DOROTHY YOUNG

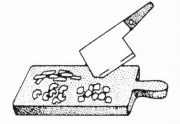

Goombay Walnut Chicken

2 whole chicken breasts
3 tablespoons soy sauce
2 teaspoons cornstarch
2 tablespoons dry sherry
½ teaspoon sugar
½ teaspoon salt
½ teaspoon crushed red pepper (optional)
2 tablespoons cooking oil
2 medium green peppers, cut in ¾" squares
4 green onions, bias sliced in 1" lengths
1 cup walnut halves

Skin and bone chicken, cut into 1" pieces, set aside. Stir soy sauce into cornstarch, stir in sherry, sugar, salt, and red pepper, if desired. Set aside.

Preheat wok, add cooking oil. Stir fry peppers and onions 2 minutes or until crisp-tender. Remove. Add walnuts to wok, adding more oil, if necessary. Stir fry 1 minute. Remove. Add chicken to wok. Stir fry 2 minutes. Add soy sauce mixture. Cook and stir until bubbly. Add vegetables and walnuts. Cover, cook 1 minute. Serve over hot rice.

Variations: Mushrooms, carrots and zucchini can also be used.

DAVID FOSTER & MARTHA MANIKAS-FOSTER

David and I are big on chicken—not only because it's relatively inexpensive, but because it's a part of our effort to lessen the amount of red meat we eat. We add ground turkey to spaghetti sauce and the like. ♥

MARTHA MANIKAS-FOSTER

Indonesian Stir-Fry

2 or 3 tablespoons peanut or sesame oil
2 or 3 tablespoons Ketjap Manis* (Indonesian
   soy sauce)
2 or 3 tablespoons sherry
1 clove garlic, chopped
2 slices fresh ginger root, chopped
1 pound skinned and deboned chicken breast,
   cut in ¾" cubes
1 cup raw blanched peanuts
1 cup diagonally sliced carrots
1 cup diagonally sliced celery
1 bunch green onions, sliced
1 green pepper, seeded and cut in 1" squares
6–8 radishes, sliced
1 bunch fresh broccoli, tops only
½ medium head cauliflower, broken into
   flowerets
1 package frozen snow peas, or 1 cup fresh

Heat electric wok to 400F. Add oil, soy sauce and sherry. Add garlic and ginger and cook a few moments before adding chicken. Cook chicken about 3 minutes, then add raw peanuts and carrots. Add celery, onions, peppers and radishes. Cook about 5 minutes. Add broccoli, cauliflower and snow peas. Cook briefly. Serve with rice.

Ketjap Manis, Indonesian soy sauce, can be purchased at food specialty shops and Dutch import stores. If unavailable substitute an equal amount of Sweet Soya Sauce: Boil together ½ cup soy sauce and 1 cup brown sugar. Store in a jar in the refrigerator, where it will keep for many months.

RUTH & ED VAN DER MAAS

Chicken Paprikash

1 large onion, chopped
¼ cup oil
1 tablespoon paprika
2 teaspoons salt
4 pounds chicken, cut up
1½ cups water
1 cup sour cream

Saute onion in oil. Add paprika. One minute later add chicken and salt. Brown meat for 10 minutes. Add water, cover, and simmer until tender. Remove chicken pieces and keep warm. Add sour cream to pan juices and mix well. If desired, thicken with 1 or 2 tablespoons flour. Put chicken pieces back into gravy. Serve.

JULIE & KALMAN TOTH

Parmesan Chicken Breasts

8 chicken breast halves, skins and bones
    removed
½ cup butter
1 cup bread crumbs
1 cup grated Parmesan cheese
½ teaspoon garlic powder
1 teaspoon salt

Place butter in a glass baking dish and melt in oven as you preheat to 350F. Mix together bread crumbs, Parmesan, garlic powder and salt. Coat chicken pieces in melted butter, then in crumb mixture and place in baking dish. Bake 60 minutes. *Do not turn chicken over* during baking.

M. G. BOEHMS

Pan Chicken

SERVES 4

**2 boxes frozen chicken, or 6 chicken breast
    halves, or 1 whole chicken, cut up**
2 tablespoons butter
1 clove garlic, minced
salt, to taste
pepper, to taste
1 tablespoon lemon juice
1 teaspoon sugar
1 onion, sliced
3–4 carrots, whole
4 medium potatoes, quartered (optional)

Remove skin from chicken. In a heavy skillet brown chicken pieces in butter and garlic. If using white meat, leave meat side down. Sprinkle with salt, pepper, lemon juice and sugar. Add water to cover chicken. Add onion and carrots. Cover skillet and simmer 1½ hours, adding water, if necessary, to keep ingredients moist. Add potatoes, if desired, after 1 hour. Near end of cooking time allow pan liquid to evaporate until it forms a rich sauce—almost dry, and coats chicken. To serve, turn chicken meat side up and garnish with pan juice and vegetables.

Variation: Saute mushrooms with garlic in butter and spoon over chicken when served.

GLADIS DePREE

Our family consists of Larry, Rachel, and two teenaged boys, Kep (15), and Ken (13); however, it's rarely just the four of us at meal time. We think we have fun but I checked it out with regular dinner guests.

David and Doug say no meal at our house is ever complete without a game of Authors *or another table game.*

Ruthie, Dan, Jo Nell, Becky, and Tom say they have learned much about various Bible characters at our meal table from playing the following game: One person picks a Bible character. The other players ask yes or no questions in order to find out who the character is. (Our boys have searched the Scriptures to find obscure names to use during this time.) ♥

RACHEL & LARRY CRABB

Chicken Enchiladas in Green Sauce

MAKES 24 enchiladas in two 9"x13" casseroles.

6 whole chicken breasts
1 can tomatillos (found in specialty food
    section in your supermarket)
3 ripe avocados, peeled and diced
1 can green chilis, diced
¼ onion, chopped
¼ cup water (or juice from tomatillos, for
    added spiciness)
3 cloves garlic
salt, to taste
pepper, to taste
4 cups sour cream
2–3 tablespoons cooking oil
24 corn tortillas
1 cup grated cheddar or Monterey Jack cheese

Cook chicken breasts in salted water. When tender remove, cool, bone, and shred chicken. Reserve ⅓ cup broth. In a blender or food processor, combine tomatillos, avocados, chilis, onion, water or juice, garlic, salt, and pepper. Blend until smooth. Turn into a large saucepan. Add sour cream and chicken broth. Blend and heat. (Do not boil.)

In a skillet heat oil and cook tortillas briefly, one at a time, to soften. Drain on paper towels.

Salt chicken to taste and place some in each tortilla. Arrange 12 tortillas (rolled up and secured with a toothpick) in each casserole. Cover with sauce and a layer of cheese. Place in a preheated 400F oven. Immediately reduce to 300F and bake for 15 minutes.

DIANE HEAD

Chicken Enchiladas in Green Sauce

◂◂ *When expecting my daughter Melinda (who is now 11), rather than craving pickles and ice cream in the middle of the night, I yearned for a delicious cheese and chicken enchilada smothered in a spicy green sauce from a nearby Mexican restaurant. Fortunately, my husband indulged my cravings and would either deliver me to the restaurant—or deliver the enchilada to me. By the time I was expecting daughter number two, Amy, the restaurant changed owners and recipes. Happily, I came across an identical-tasting recipe for enchiladas which carried me through my pregnancy. The following is now a favorite of the whole family—Melinda and Amy especially! (Hmmm, I wonder why . . .)* ♥

DIANE HEAD

Chicken Enchiladas Rancheros

MAKES 24 enchiladas in two 9"x13" casseroles

24 corn tortillas
3 tablespoons corn oil
2 large onions, diced
2 green peppers, diced
4–5 cups cooked chicken (or turkey), diced
1 (7 ounce) can green chili peppers, diced
1 cup slivered almonds
½ cup raisins
4½ cups canned or bottled red chili sauce or
    enchilada sauce
4 cups grated Monterey Jack cheese (about 1
    pound)
2 cups sour cream
2 cups chopped green onion

Soften tortillas by steaming; or sprinkle them with water, wrap in foil, and heat in a 350F oven until softened. Heat corn oil in a large skillet; add chopped onion and green pepper. Saute until translucent. Add chicken or turkey, diced chilis, ½ cup of the chili or enchilada sauce, almonds, and raisins. Toss to combine, remove from heat, and set aside.

Oil two 9"x13" baking dishes. Pour additional ½ cup of sauce onto bottom of each dish, spreading into a thin film. Spoon chicken filling down center of each *softened* tortilla and roll up. Lay filled tortillas seam-side-down in baking dish, 12 in each dish. Divide remaining sauce and pour over enchiladas. (Be sure to coat edges to keep them soft.) Top with grated cheese.

Bake in a preheated 350F oven for 25–30 minutes, or until heated through. Sauce and cheese should be bubbly, but not brown or dry. Serve enchiladas warm from the oven, topped with sour cream and chopped green onions.

JOHN BOYKIN

Pastel de Chocolo

(Chilean Corn-Chicken Casserole)

"This is a typical 'special' dish from Chile—which is absolutely delicious—but I don't know how many North Americans will try it when they read the ingredients."

1 chicken, cut up
3 tablespoons oil
1 large onion, chopped
½ pound ground beef
1 cup milk
¼ teaspoon basil
1 clove garlic, crushed
2 cups fresh or frozen corn kernels
¼ teaspoon pepper
1–1½ teaspoons salt
¼ cup raisins, soaked in ¼ cup water for 15
   minutes, then drained
½ cup chopped black olives
1 hard boiled egg, chopped (optional)
1 tablespoon sugar

In a skillet brown chicken in oil. As pieces brown, transfer to an ovenproof casserole. Bake, covered, at 350F while preparing remaining ingredients.

In oil in skillet saute onion until translucent. Add ground beef and cook until browned. In a saucepan simmer milk with basil and crushed garlic clove for 5 minutes, then remove garlic. When meat is browned, add milk, corn, salt and pepper to skillet. Stir in browned bits from pan. Bring to a simmer. Remove chicken casserole from oven. Add raisins, olives and chopped egg to chicken. Pour contents of skillet over all. Sprinkle with sugar. Return to oven and bake uncovered until chicken is tender and top lightly browned.

KAREN KLETZING

Our shopping is quite different in Chile. They have an open-air market where I go once a month with the Bishop's wife (because she has a car) and buy 4 cases of milk. The milk is superpasteurized so you don't have to refrigerate it. We also buy vegetables and fruit. Avocados are very cheap here and are smashed and eaten on bread for the evening meal. The main meal is at about 1:30 in the afternoon. All the shops close for a three hour siesta and everyone goes home to eat. Around 6:00 or 7:00 there is a lighter meal of bread and palta (avocado) or Chilean hot dogs with mayonnaise, tomato sauce

Chicken Adobo

4 chicken breasts, skinned
1 clove garlic, chopped
¼ cup vinegar
¼ cup soy sauce
salt, to taste
pepper, to taste

Marinate chicken breasts in mixture of remaining ingredients. Bake, covered with foil, at 375F for 45–60 minutes, or barbecue outside on grill.

LATAYNE SCOTT

Oven Barbecued Chicken

12 pieces chicken or 2 chickens, cut up
½ cup catsup
1 cup water
¼ cup oil
1 tablespoon lemon juice
1 tablespoon Worcestershire sauce
1 teaspoon liquid smoke
½ teaspoon onion salt
½ teaspoon salt
½ teaspoon chili powder

Lay chicken pieces flat in a baking pan. Combine remaining ingredients and pour over chicken. Bake at 350F for 1 hour or until chicken is tender, turning chicken 2 or 3 times during baking.

LATAYNE SCOTT

and palta. The richer families eat another big meal at 8:00 or 8:30.

There is a new supermarket only four blocks away, but on the way home that seems far without a car. We walk an average of one and a half miles a day so we've each lost about twelve pounds even though we consume a large amount of bread—all white, but with different names and sizes. There are "bread stores" in every neighborhood. Bread is bought every day so it can be eaten fresh. Paper towels and facial tissues we don't buy—they run $3–$4. There are certain things that can't be bought, maple syrup for one; we use honey syrup on our pancakes. There's only one kind of cold cereal—American cereal, which only exists in specialty shops is 600–700 pesos (about $8). A jar of decaffeinated coffee is $10.

On the way home from the supermarket we give our change to regular beggars—a blind young man who jingles his cup

Sweet and Sour Chicken

SERVES 8

8 chicken breast halves, boned
salt, to taste
pepper, to taste
½ cup flour
⅓ cup shortening or oil

Sauce:

1 cup sugar
¼ teaspoon ginger
½ cup white vinegar
1 tablespoon soy sauce
1 chicken bouillon cube
2 tablespoons constarch

Topping:

1 green pepper, sliced
1 (20 ounce) can sliced pineapple, drained

Salt and pepper chicken breasts as desired, dredge in flour and, in a skillet, brown in hot shortening. While chicken is cooking prepare sauce. In a small saucepan, mix together sugar, ginger and cornstarch, stir in vinegar and soy sauce. Crumble and add bouillon cube. Bring to a boil, remove from heat.

When chicken is browned remove from skillet and place in a glass baking dish. Cover with sauce. Bake uncovered at 350F for 30 minutes. Top with sliced green pepper and sliced pineapple. Return to oven and bake 10 minutes longer.

REA & ALAN JOHNSON

as he walks, an old woman, a man without legs on a little board with wheels and a woman with 2 young children. It is a vivid reminder of how fortunate we are to be able to buy things at the store.

We can buy fish from a door to door fish salesman. We boil all our water because there's lots of typhoid here. The water is purified but not as much as ours in the States.

All the ovens must be lit with matches and are still not likely to light right away. (I've said that if I could light one with my foot I'd never have to shave my legs—because they blow up!) We do have a blender from the States which we use with a transformer because the electrical current is different here.

Each of our two children prays before meals, and the two year old takes requests if someone is sick or hurt. Then we sing "Praise God from Whom All Blessings Float" (my five year old's version) or "I

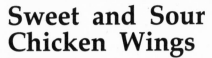

Sweet and Sour Chicken Wings

2 pounds chicken wings
salt, to taste
pepper, to taste
garlic salt, to taste
beaten egg
cornstarch
oil
1 cup sugar
1 cup vinegar
6 tablespoons catsup
2 tablespoons soy sauce
1 teaspoon salt
½ cup chicken stock, bouillon or water

Remove flippers from chicken wings. Season lightly with salt, pepper and garlic salt. Dip in beaten egg, roll in cornstarch and brown in a skillet in hot oil. Transfer wings to a baking dish. Mix together sugar, vinegar, catsup, soy sauce, salt and chicken stock. Pour over chicken. Bake uncovered at 350F for 30 minutes or until tender, turning once during baking. Serve over rice.

Variation: Substitute chicken parts or shrimp for the wings.

LATAYNE SCOTT

have the joy, joy, joy down in my heart." After the meal we choose verses from a colored box of little verse cards (we have them in Spanish and English). Then we put prayers on a heart-shaped prayer pillow a friend made for us. The prayers are written on little slips of paper which we stick on the pillow with pins. When the prayers are answered we take them off the pillow. Our longest remaining prayer is for the return of three trunks we lost in Miami when we came to Chile in August.

After the meal we light the calefont (water heater), which has also blown up. Ours is very old so my husband has rigged up a tray to catch the ashes (since it sits right over my dishes). ♥

KAREN KLETZING

Popover Chicken

SERVES 4–6

6–8 pieces chicken (If using chicken breasts, cut into fourths.)
salt
pepper
flour
¼ cup cooking oil

Popover batter:

5 large eggs
2 cups milk
2 cups sifted flour
1 teaspoon salt

Lightly salt and pepper chicken, dust with flour. In a skillet, brown chicken on all sides, remove and drain on paper towels. While chicken is browning, lightly beat eggs with an electric mixer, then beat in milk, flour and salt until smooth. Do not overbeat. Pour into a well buttered oblong baking dish with sides that are at least 2″ high. Preheat oven to 425F. Arrange browned chicken pieces on top of batter. Bake at 425F for 25 minutes. Change oven temperature control to 325F and bake for 15 minutes. *Do not open oven door during baking.* Make gravy in skillet used to brown chicken.

MRS. CHARLES W. COLSON

Stuffed Breast of Chicken

SERVES 4

4 chicken breasts, bones removed
1 (4½ ounce) can mushrooms, finely chopped
¼ cup finely chopped celery
1 tablespoon chopped parsley
¼ cup oil
½ cup flour
1 teaspoon salt
⅛ teaspoon pepper
1 cup thinly sliced onion
¼ teaspoon basil, crumbled
¼ cup corn syrup
½ cup water

Preheat oven to 350F. Cut chicken breasts in half and slit thick portion of each piece to form a pocket. In a large frying pan saute mushrooms, celery and parsley in 1 tablespoon of the oil until celery is tender. Spoon mixture into pocket of each chicken breast and pinch edge together to seal. Carefully coat chicken with flour seasoned with salt and pepper. Heat remaining oil in frying pan and brown chicken breasts on both sides. When browned, arrange chicken in a baking dish. To frying pan add onion and fry until slightly brown or golden brown. Top chicken breasts with onion and sprinkle with basil. Spoon 1 tablespoon corn syrup over each chicken breast. Add water to frying pan to clean pan, then pour over the chicken. Bake uncovered at 350F for 30–40 minutes or until chicken is tender. Baste occasionally with liquid in baking dish.

HELEN ENNS

Handy Hint for Summer
Barbecue

When barbecuing chicken, the outside is sometimes done before the meat close to the bone. Try microwaving the chicken pieces for about 10-15 minutes before basting with sauce and putting them on the grill. We find this very effective. For amounts larger than one pound increase microwave time accordingly. ♥

MARTIN & SHERRY SINGER

Fosmire's Favorite Chicken Kiev

SERVES 4–6

8 chicken breast halves, skinned and boned
salt, to taste
1 tablespoon chopped green onions or chives
1 tablespoon chopped fresh parsley
½ cup butter (1 stick), chilled
flour
1 egg, beaten
fine dry bread crumbs, or cornflake crumbs
oil for deep frying
fresh parsley and lemon slices for garnish

When removing skin and bones, don't tear the meat—each half should be all in one piece (can also use boneless chicken breasts to save time—but not money).

Place each piece of chicken, boned side up, between two pieces of plastic wrap. Working out from center, pound with a wooden mallet (or suitable substitute) to form cutlets not quite ¼" thick.

Peel off plastic wrap. Sprinkle meat with salt, green onions or chives and parsley. Cut stick of chilled butter lengthwise into 8 sticks.

Place small stick of butter near end on cutlet. Roll as for jellyroll, tucking in sides of meat. Press to seal well. Dust with flour; dip in beaten egg; roll in fine dry bread crumbs or corn flake crumbs.

Chill rolls of chicken thoroughly, at least 1 hour. Fry in deep, hot fat (340F) about 5 minutes or until golden brown. Serve on a platter garnished with fresh parsley and lemon slices.

BEA FOSMIRE

Fosmire's Favorite Chicken Kiev

◄≪ *Whenever the children saw me making Chicken Kiev they knew company was coming. It became a favorite dish in our family and was the most requested entree on special days such as birthdays.* ♥

BEA FOSMIRE

CHIVES

Chicken and Mushrooms in Madeira Sauce

"Good with rice and salad."

3 whole chicken breasts, skinned and boned
¼ cup plus 1 tablespoon butter
salt, to taste
pepper, to taste
3 cups sliced fresh mushrooms
3 tablespoons chopped shallots
3 tablespoons lemon juice
1 tablespoon flour
¾ cup heavy cream
¾ cup Madeira wine
1 cup grated Swiss cheese

Saute chicken breasts (cut in half to make 6) in ¼ cup of the butter until tender and brown. Transfer to a casserole dish and season with salt and pepper. Add remaining tablespoon of butter to skillet and add shallots. Saute until translucent. Toss the mushrooms with lemon juice and add to shallots. Cook 5 minutes or until mushrooms give up their liquid. Add flour and stir constantly to prevent it from burning. Add Madeira, then heavy cream. Cook, stirring constantly, until the sauce thickens. Add cheese and stir until melted. Pour sauce over chicken and cover. Bake at 400F for 20 minutes.

MARTHA MANIKAS-FOSTER

Chicken Marengo

1 chicken, cut up (about 3 pounds)
salt
pepper
flour
¼ cup butter or margarine
¼ cup olive oil
1 clove garlic, chopped
2 teaspoons flour
1 (1 pound) can tomatoes
1 cup dry white wine
½ cup sliced fresh mushrooms, or 1 (6 ounce)
   can
chives, for garnish

Sprinkle chicken with salt and pepper. Roll in flour. Heat butter and oil in a large skillet. Add garlic and chicken and brown on all sides. Place pieces in a single layer in a shallow baking dish. Stir flour into pan drippings. Add tomatoes and wine. Stir briskly until sauce bubbles and thickens. Add mushrooms. Pour sauce over chicken. Bake at 350F for 40–45 minutes, or until chicken is tender. Serve sprinkled with finely chopped chives.

MARTHA MANIKAS-FOSTER

Chilled Rock Cornish Game Hens

SERVES 2

2 Rock Cornish game hens, thawed
salt
pepper

Basting sauce:

¼ cup butter, melted
¼ cup dry vermouth or other dry white wine

Chilled Rock Cornish Game Hens

◄◄ *Because we live near a beautiful, unspoiled stretch of beach we have an easily accessible picnic spot. The following "movable feast" is a simple but elegant picnic we and our guests have enjoyed:*

Chilled Rock Cornish
Game Hens
Crusty French Bread with
Boursin cheese spread
Fresh Raw Vegetables and
Dip
Pears and Chocolates
(Chocolate mints placed in a cooler are easy to serve even on a hot day.)

I like to serve this meal on clear glass plates which are chilled in the same cooler in which we pack the food. ♥

MARTHA STOUT

➤➤

½ teaspoon garlic salt
½ teaspoon onion salt

Rub cavities of thawed hens with salt and pepper. Place breast side up on a rack in a shallow roasting pan. Roast at 350F approximately 60 minutes. Combine basting sauce ingredients and baste hens 3 or 4 times while roasting. Chill hens thoroughly before serving. Keep refrigerated.

MARTHA STOUT

Microwave Crispy Chicken

~M

3 pounds chicken pieces (I usually use
    quartered breasts.)
1 cup cornflake crumbs
½ teaspoon onion salt
½ teaspoon garlic salt
1 teaspoon paprika
a pinch of oregano or poultry seasoning
    (optional)
½ cup skim milk

Remove skin from chicken pieces, rinse and drain. In a plastic bag combine cornflake crumbs, salt, garlic salt, paprika and oregano or poultry seasoning, if desired. Dip chicken pieces (usually 2 at a time) in milk and shake in the crumb bag to coat. Arrange chicken pieces in baking dish with large parts to the outside, wings, legs, and small parts in the center. Sprinkle leftover crumbs over chicken. Cover loosely with plastic wrap. Cook in microwave oven on high 18–20 minutes, rotating ¼ turn once, until chicken is tender.

JOHN CARPENTER

College Food

When I transferred from a local college to the University of Michigan during my sophomore year, I was looking forward to living in the dorm—but I was afraid that I would starve there. Growing up with a mother who is an excellent cook and who almost puritanically avoids convenience foods, I had become quite picky. I ate a wide variety of foods—by the time I was in college I had tried everything from guacamole to pig's lungs and snails, and had liked most of what I had tried—but a can of Spaghetti-Os filled me with revulsion, and my fear and loathing of institutional food was one of the main reasons I had decided to live at home during my first three semesters of college.

The food in the dorm cafeteria turned out to be better than I had expected, but no breakfast was served and the quality varied, so I often found myself hungry with little time or money to spend at a restaurant. I discovered I could stave off hunger for hours at a time (as opposed to the short-term satisfaction of candy or junk food) by eating uncooked quick

Moist and Crispy Chicken

3 cups Rice Krispies, crushed
1 teaspoon paprika
½ teaspoon salt
¼ teaspoon pepper
1 broiler/fryer chicken, cut in pieces
½ cup mayonnaise

Place crushed Rice Krispies, paprika, salt, and pepper in a large plastic food bag. Shake to blend well. Brush chicken on all sides with mayonnaise. Place one piece of chicken in the bag at a time. Shake until well coated. Place on rack in broiler pan. Bake at 425F for 45 minutes or until brown and tender.

DOROTHY HALVERSON

Can Can Chicken

"Easy meal when your family wants supper five minutes after you get home."

Serves 4–6

1 can condensed cream of chicken soup
1 can condensed cream of celery soup
1 soup can water
1⅓ cups minute rice
1½ cups cut up cooked chicken
2 cans chow mein noodles

Place all ingredients except chow mein noodles in a large saucepan. Bring to a boil, cover and simmer 7 minutes. Stir well. Serve over chow mein noodles.

MARY & KEN REGAN

oats mixed with a little pineapple juice, so I always kept a container of rolled oats and small cans of pineapple juice in my chest of drawers. My taste for this sticky pineapple gruel diminished after a semester of heavy consumption; it was a good thing that I was able to increase my food budget the next fall and buy more traditional foods for snacks, resorting to the oats and juice only when I was too busy or too lazy to go to the store.

Sometimes several days would go by during which none of the main dishes in the cafeteria appealed to me and I would subsist almost entirely on the excellent granola that was available at every meal. After a couple of days of granola-eating, though, the roof of my mouth would become raw and for some reason I would develop a sore throat, as well as other unsavory symptoms whose cause was more obvious. When the food in the cafeteria was good, I ate everything I could hold, which was a lot, since I had developed an enormous capacity for food as a tall teenager. Having always been a slow

Bonnie's Easy Baked Chicken

"Chicken will be extremely tender and covered with an already thickened, delicious gravy."

1 frying chicken, cut up
1–2 cans condensed golden mushroom soup
1 envelope Shake & Bake
⅓ cup cooking wine

Wash and pat chicken dry. Place, spread out, in baking pan or roaster. Cover with soup, using two cans if one doesn't cover all of the chicken. Sprinkle Shake & Bake over soup. Sprinkle cooking wine over Shake & Bake. Cover and bake at 325F for 2 hours.

BONNIE & HADDON ROBINSON

Special Baked Chicken

SERVES 6

1 (3 ounce) package sliced dried beef
3 large chicken breasts, skinned and halved
6 slices bacon
rosemary (optional)
1 can condensed cream of mushroom soup
1 cup sour cream

Run cold water over dried beef. Drain and arrange in the bottom of a 9"x13"x2" baking dish. Place halved chicken breasts over beef. Top each with a slice of bacon. Sprinkle a little rosemary on each, if desired. Bake uncovered at 350F for 30 minutes. Combine soup and sour cream, pour over chicken and bake for 40–50 minutes or more, depending on the size of the chicken.

BERTHA G. & RICHARD S. TAYLOR

eater, I would often spend an hour or so in the cafeteria when the pickings were good, eating dinner with two or three different groups of friends as they rushed through their much smaller meals, replenishing my tray several times during the meal. When the food was not up to my exacting standards, I would change from glutton to ascetic, perhaps eating a bagel, a salad, and a glass of orange juice for supper.

When I got really hungry I would take an extra weekend trip home, calling my mother in advance to let her know which foods I craved most. I enjoyed seeing my family, of course, but the food waiting for me at home was an added incentive to make the two-hour trip between Ann Arbor and Grand Rapids. After a weekend spent stocking up on calories I would return to school with a cake or some homemade granola, ready for dry spells in the cafeteria.

During my senior year I lived in an apartment in the basement of the dorm and was able to make my own food, so my eating habits became much more stable. However, I had

Easy Chicken Divan I

Smaller Recipe

2 (10 ounce) packages frozen broccoli spears
2–3 cups sliced cooked chicken (about 3
     breasts, cooked and boned)
2 cans condensed cream of chicken soup
½–1 cup mayonnaise
1–6 teaspoons lemon juice
¼–1½ teaspoons curry powder (depending on
     your taste)
½–1 cup grated Cheddar cheese

Either partially cook and drain broccoli, or leave uncooked. Arrange broccoli spears in a greased 9"x13" casserole dish with the heads to the outside of the dish. Place chicken on top of broccoli in the center of the dish. Combine soup, mayonnaise, lemon juice and curry and pour over chicken. Sprinkle cheese on top. Bake at 350F for 25 minutes to 1 hour. Trim with pimento strips, if desired.

Variation: Top with 1 cup fresh bread crumbs mixed with ¼ cup melted butter or margarine. Sprinkle with slivered almonds.

Mrs. Walter Henrichsen
Dena Korfker
Barbara & Gary Dausey

become used to eating as much as I could hold when the food was good, and since I am a good cook, the food was always good and I was always eating. Swimming, lifting weights, and walking about the university's sprawling campus kept me from gaining more than a few unnoticeable pounds. I often would eat the same dish at each meal for three or four days in a row, which helped to curb my appetite some. Since I usually just cooked for myself, the batches were always too large to consume at one or two sittings, but since this saved a lot of time I didn't bother to reduce my recipes by more than half.

Some foods seemed particularly well suited to my needs. Spaghetti, tacos, pizza, and rice dishes were all easy to fix and flavorful enough to be bearable for several days in a row. Bread also fit my diet and schedule well. It takes a lot less effort to make bread than most people think. They don't want to wait for it to rise, but the short and widely spaced steps in preparing bread make perfect breaks in a long afternoon or evening of studying.

Easy Chicken Divan II

Larger recipe

6–7 chicken breasts, skinned, cooked, and
    boned
2 (10 ounce) packages frozen broccoli spears,
    thawed
1⅓ cups mayonnaise
1 teaspoon curry powder, or to taste
3½ tablespoons lemon juice
3 cans condensed cream of mushroom soup
¼ cup sherry (optional)
1 (4 ounce) can mushrooms, or ½ cup fresh
    mushrooms, sliced and sauteed in butter
1 small can whole water chestnuts, sliced
1 cup grated Cheddar cheese
1 cup crushed stuffing mix, or Italian bread
    crumbs
2 tablespoons melted butter

Cut chicken breasts in large strips or large
pieces. Do not cook broccoli. Mix together mayonnaise, curry powder, lemon juice, condensed soup
and sherry until smooth.

In a 9"x13" baking dish layer half the sauce
mixture, sliced water chestnuts and half the
cheese. Next arrange all the chicken over ingredients in pan, then all the broccoli. Next, add in
layers remaining sliced water chestnuts, sauce and
cheese. Toss crushed stuffing mix or bread crumbs
with melted butter and sprinkle over dish. Bake
uncovered at 350F for 1 hour.

WILMA ZONDERVAN TEGGELAAR

*When the bread was baking I
always seemed to have visitors—
girls especially, for some reason.
They would walk past my
isolated basement apartment and
come in when they caught the
scent of fresh bread through my
open door. They were so
impressed that I made bread
from scratch that it was a little
scary. I told them it was easy,
which they seemed to interpret
as heroic modesty, and as they
ate piece after piece of hot bread,
oohing and aahing and telling
me what a great cook I was, I
wondered what it would be like
to be married to them. If the
simple task of making bread
seemed so enormous to them,
what kind of convenience-food
swill would they try to serve
me? Would I be forced to do all
the cooking or spend all my
money in restaurants? It never
came to that, though in one or
two cases I'm a little sad it
didn't.*

*After I graduated from college
I spent a few months at home
during which I did little else
than read, watch television, and
swim in the pool, silently
repeating to myself all the while
different versions of the same*

Hot Chicken Salad Casserole

"A special company dish. Well worth the expense of the ingredients. Serve with Cranberry Jell."

SERVES 4–6

2 tablespoons fresh lemon juice
1 cup mayonnaise
2 cups cubed cooked chicken breasts
2 cups diced celery
½ cup sliced almonds, browned in a teaspoon
   of butter
½ teaspoon salt
2 teaspoons grated onion
½ cup grated Cheddar cheese
1–2 cups crushed sour cream flavored, or
   green onion and sour cream flavored,
   potato chips

Combine lemon juice and mayonnaise. Mix with chicken, celery, almonds, salt and onion. Place in a greased flat 9"x9" casserole. Top with cheese and then with crushed potato chips. Bake at 350F for 30 minutes.

DORIS RIKKERS
ARDETH & RON BOSMAN

question: What next? I still had the feast-and-famine eating habits that had kept me healthy when I depended on the cafeteria for food, but now the food was plentiful, and if someone else wasn't cooking I had lots of time to cook, so it was always feast and never famine. With no classes to walk to my calories had nowhere to go. When it became difficult for me to button the top of my pants, I decided to start eating until I was full, and no more.

My food experiences in college taught me how to adapt my diet to different eating situations. If my first choice is not available or time or money is short, I can fall back on cheap, ready-to-eat staples that I know will keep me healthy and satisfied: milk, fresh fruits and vegetables, and bread, rice or oatmeal. If I have access to a kitchen but little time to cook, I've learned that simple food made from scratch is inexpensive and far more satisfying than more complicated convenience foods that cost more and take almost as much time to fix. I'm a far more resourceful eater than I was before I went away to college, and when the cupboards really are bare, there's always pineapple-oatmeal mush. ♥

DAVID GUNDRY

PORK

Sweet and Sour Pork 178
Outdoor California Glazed Ribs 179
Peach Glazed Spareribs 180
Sarma 181
Tourtiere 182
Pork Chops and Orange Rice 183
Herbed Chops and Rice 184
Pork Chops Southern Style 185
Tropic Chops 186
Kraut 'N' Pork Chops 186
Ham-Broccoli Casserole 187

Sweet and Sour Pork

SERVES 4

1 pound lean boneless pork, cut in ¾" cubes
half of a red pepper, cut in large pieces
half of a green pepper, cut in large pieces
4 green onions, chopped
2 apples, peeled and quartered
oil for deep frying

Marinade:

3 tablespoons plus 2 teaspoons soy sauce
4 teaspoons dry sherry
pinch of monosodium glutamate (optional)
1 teaspoon very finely chopped fresh ginger

Batter:

¼ cup flour
¼ cup cornstarch
pinch of salt
2 eggs, beaten

Sauce:

1 rounded tablespoon brown sugar
2 tablespoons plus 1½ teaspoons vinegar
4 teaspoons soy sauce
4 teaspoons cornstarch

Mix marinade ingredients. Add pork, cover, and marinate in refrigerator 2 hours.

Combine flour, cornstarch, and salt in a bowl. Gradually beat in eggs until smooth. Coat pork with batter and fry in deep fat until light golden brown. Drain and keep hot.

In a saucepan mix sauce ingredients and bring to a boil. Add green and red pepper, onion, and apples. Simmer 5 to 7 minutes. Combine with pork and serve immediately with rice.

EDA STERTZ

Outdoor California Glazed Ribs

"This recipe always draws raves. It's easy yet showy, and the sauce is also good on ham steak or pork chops."

SERVES 4

Sauce:

1 cup catsup
½ cup soy sauce
½ cup honey
2 teaspoons garlic powder
½ cup water

Ribs:

4–5 pounds lean pork ribs
½ cup vinegar
water, to cover ribs

Combine catsup, soy sauce, honey, garlic powder and water in saucepan and simmer 1 hour. Remove from heat and allow to cool ½ hour before basting ribs.

In a large pot simmer ribs in vinegar water until meat is tender, about 45 minutes. Remove ribs and drain on paper towels.

Cook ribs on grill over very low heat, basting with sauce and turning frequently until well browned.

JO BERRY

Mealtime Stories

My personal recollections of mealtime in the home of my rather strict Victorian grandmother, were in the atmosphere of the idea that "children should be seen, but not heard." In order to improve our deportment, we children sat upright on stools without backs at the table, while the adults enjoyed the comfort of padded, comfortable chairs. Our silverware was not silver, as was that of the adults, but of inferior quality!

Grandmother was particularly strict about not eating between meals. One day, being very

Peach Glazed Spareribs

4 pounds spareribs
1 (16 ounce) can sliced peaches
½ cup brown sugar
¼ cup catsup
¼ cup vinegar
2 tablespoons soy sauce
1 clove garlic
1 teaspoon salt
1 teaspoon ginger
pepper, to taste

Bake ribs uncovered at 325F for 1 hour. While ribs are baking prepare sauce: puree peaches in an electric blender. Add remaining ingredients and blend. Pour sauce over ribs and bake an additional 45 minutes, or until done.

Lee Distelberg

hungry, I persuaded the hired cook to give me one of her freshly baked and well buttered biscuits (scones, to the English), with sugar lavishly shaken on top. This I took to the vegetable garden, covered it with freshly shelled, sweet garden peas, and hid behind a hedge to eat. Just as I raised the delicious morsel to my mouth, Grandmother came by! With scarcely a word, she removed the scone from my hand and disappeared down the garden path. I discovered later that it had been carefully placed on the dining room table at my allotted position in order that all the world would see my misdeed, and that I might forfeit the evening meal of poached, fresh salmon and other good things which the rest of the family would enjoy. As far as I remember, I think I learned my lesson, and eventually established peace with Grandmother.

At mealtimes now with three little grandsons, I find they enjoy hearing funny anecdotes about my childhood. Sometimes

Sarma (Serbian Cabbage Rolls)

"My husband's family is Serbian. One of their favorite ethnic dishes is Sarma, which I had to learn to cook before George would agree to marry me. At our home we serve it on special occasions, such as George's birthday and Christmas Eve. It freezes well and reheats well in the microwave at 80% power to 150F."

1 large head cabbage
3 pounds lean ground pork loin
¾ cup white long grain uncooked rice
1 medium onion, finely chopped
3 (1 pound 13 ounce) cans sauerkraut,
     including liquid
1 ham hock

Soak cabbage in the sink in extremely hot water until whole leaves come off easily. While cabbage is wilting, combine ground pork, rice and onion in a large mixing bowl, then form the mixture into 16–18 medium-sized meatballs. Wrap meatballs in cabbage leaves. Line the bottom of a large, heavy Dutch oven (8–10 quart size) with cabbage leaves. Add a layer of sauerkraut, using 1 can. Place ham hock on sauerkraut, in the center, and surround it with half of the cabbage rolls. Cover with another layer of sauerkraut, using second can. Arrange remaining cabbage rolls on sauerkraut and cover with remaining can of sauerkraut. Add any remaining sauerkraut liquid and water to within 2" of the top of the pot. Cover tightly and bring to a boil. Reduce heat and simmer on low heat for 6–8 hours.

. Serve with baked potatoes and fruit. "We mash the potato together with a cabbage roll, then top it with sauerkraut and ham pieces. If you wish, you can serve additional ham slices."

Jo Berry

my daughter-in-law and I take turns recounting some intriguing tale about our own childhoods, but only on condition that at the same time dinner is fast disappearing from their plates. ♥

E. Joan & Major Thomas

Tourtiere

SERVES 6

1½ pounds ground pork, or pork and beef
    combined
1 large onion, finely chopped
1 cup finely chopped celery
1 garlic clove, minced
½ teaspoon cinnamon
¼ teaspoon allspice
¼ teaspoon sage
¼ teaspoon savory
1 bay leaf
2 medium potatoes, peeled and grated
½ cup water
1 tablespoon flour
rich pastry for a 9" double crust
1 egg, beaten

Brown meat in a large frying pan. Remove meat
and pour off fat except for about 2 tablespoons. To
the fat in frying pan add onion, celery, and garlic.
Cook until vegetables are tender. Add meat to
vegetables and stir in cinnamon, allspice, sage,
and savory. Add grated potatoes, water, and bay
leaf. Cover frying pan tightly and simmer gently
for about 40 minutes. Remove bay leaf. Sprinkle
flour over mixture and cook, stirring constantly,
until thickened. Remove from heat and set aside
to cool.

Prepare pastry. Using half of pastry for bottom
crust, line a 9" pie pan. Brush pastry in pan with
egg mixed with a few drops of water reserving
part of mixture for top crust. Bake at 400F for 5
minutes. Remove from oven and fill with meat
mixture. Cover with upper crust that has been
perforated to form a pretty design. Brush top with
remaining egg mixture. Bake at 450F for 10
minutes. Reduce heat to 350F and bake for 10–15
minutes longer. Serve hot.

PRISCILLA & W. STANFORD REID

SAGE

Tourtiere

◄ ≪ *This traditional French
Canadian meat pie was
originally a delicacy for the
Seigneur's table, made with
pigeon or dove. Later, other
meats were substituted and it
became a festive dish for all
Quebecois as well as for many
others.* ♥

PRISCILLA & W. STANFORD REID

Pork Chops and Orange Rice

SERVES 6

6 pork chops*
salt
pepper
1⅓ cups uncooked Minute Rice
1 cup orange juice
1 can chicken with rice soup, undiluted

Brown pork chops. Season with salt and pepper to taste. Place rice in bottom of flat baking dish. Pour orange juice over rice. Place pork chops on rice. Pour soup over all, cover and bake at 350F for 45 minutes. Uncover, bake 10 minutes more.

*"I've often substituted pork steaks (it's cheaper) and the recipe is still great. Also great with chicken. This recipe can be easily cut in half to serve 2–3. (I've been doing it that way for 12 years.)"

DORIS RIKKERS

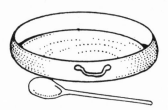

Brunswick Stew for the Intrepid

Editor's Note: I am absolutely willing to trust Brenda and Charles Graham on this recipe, having no desire at all to test it. But perhaps someone else would love to make a large batch of Brunswick Stew. If so, here it is. If not, it still makes an interesting story.

On a cold day in February (yes, it does get cold in south Georgia!) you may find us preparing to make our annual batch of Brunswick Stew. It is definitely a joint effort between Charles and me. A few times I have, with my eyes closed, placed the hog's head in boiling water, but somehow I always get a glimpse of the floppy ears and the still eyes, so if at all

Herbed Chops and Rice

6 pork chops
1 onion
1½ cups uncooked rice
salt, to taste
pepper, to taste
½ of (10 ounce) package frozen peas
   (optional)
1½ cups boiling water
1 can condensed golden mushroom soup
boiling water
½ teaspoon thyme
½ teaspoon marjoram

THYME

Brown pork chops while preparing the following: slice onion, separate into rings, and set aside. Place rice in a well greased baking pan 9"x13" or larger. Sprinkle with salt and pepper, and peas, if desired. Pour 1½ cups boiling water over rice. Place browned pork chops on top of rice. Blend soup with enough boiling water to make 2 cups liquid. Pour over pork chops. Arrange onion rings over ingredients in pan. Sprinkle with thyme and marjoram. Cover tightly and bake at 350F for 60 minutes.

BARBARA BUSH

possible we plan this event to coincide with Charles' time off. He has to be the one who removes the meat from the head! Cooking the meats and taking it off the bones takes most of one day. Then I usually cook the stew most of the next day. The finished product is one of the few dishes that our whole family likes. It is delicious with freshly baked yeast bread and butter, accompanied with a tossed salad. We enjoy sharing our stew with friends, and we freeze the remainder in pints and quarts for quick meals later. Here is our recipe, though it may vary some from one year to the next:

Brunswick Stew

   1 hog's head
   5 lbs. pork roast
   ham hocks, pig's feet, etc.
   2 chickens
   4 cans whole kernel corn
   3 cans tomatoes
   2 cans herb seasoned tomato
sauce
   3 cans lima beans or 1
package dried limas, cooked

Pork Chops Southern Style

5 pork chops
2 tablespoons flour
2 tablespoons lard or shortening
1 tablespoon chopped green pepper
1 tablespoon Worcestershire sauce
1 cup water
½ cup tomato sauce (or rich cream sauce)
¾ cup whole kernel corn
salt
pepper
celery salt
onion salt or dried onion flakes

Dredge chops in flour and brown on both sides in hot lard. Place in a buttered baking dish. Remove part of drippings from the pan in which chops were browned. In that pan heat green pepper, Worcestershire sauce, water, corn and tomato sauce to boiling. Pour over chops in baking dish and sprinkle lightly with salt, pepper, celery salt and onion salt or flakes, to taste. Cover and bake at 350F for about 60 minutes. Serve with applesauce.

JOYCE LEENSVART

salt and pepper to taste
1 or 2 cups chopped onion, if desired

Cook all meats and remove from bones. Chop finely. Place all ingredients in a large pot, bring to a boil on medium heat, stirring occasionally. Cover and simmer most of a day or until stew changes color. ♥

CHARLES & BRENDA KNIGHT GRAHAM

Tropic Chops

"Always a favorite, fruity treat—and so easy to make. This was shared with us by a friend from India."

SERVES 4

4 pork chops
1 medium can fruit cocktail, undrained
1 can condensed cream of mushroom soup

In a skillet cook pork chops until done. Add fruit cocktail, including juice, and soup. Cover and simmer 15 minutes. Serve over rice.

JUDY & BILL VRIESEMA

Kraut 'n' Pork Chops

SERVES 6

6 (½" thick) pork chops, or lamb chops
salt
pepper
shortening
1 (16 ounce) can sauerkraut, drained (for a milder flavor rinse sauerkraut with water and drain)
1 cup catsup
1 tablespoon brown sugar

Lightly sprinkle salt and pepper on pork chops. In a skillet brown lightly on both sides in hot shortening. Mix sauerkraut with catsup. Arrange a mound of the mixture on top of each chop. Sprinkle with brown sugar. Cover and cook over low heat for 40–50 minutes or until chops are tender. Baste with pan juices several times during cooking. Lift chops and sauerkraut carefully onto hot platter to serve.

HELEN ENNS

The most successful stories we had in our family story hour when we lived in India were of a "certain family" (ours) and of the things that happened that very day, or of the way they should have happened. Everyone always kept a straight face, but all eyes twinkled. Once I told this story, knowing one son would catch on: "Do you know what? Today the popcorn man came to school at recess. The

Ham-Broccoli Casserole

SERVES 2–4

1 (10 ounce) package frozen broccoli or 1
   small bunch fresh brocolli cooked until
   barely tender
1 (10¾ ounce) can condensed cream of
   mushroom or Cheddar cheese soup
1 (10 ounce) can flaked ham or 1 cup finely
   chopped cooked ham
1 cup cooked rice or *uncooked* Minute Rice
½ cup sour cream
grated Cheddar cheese, bread crumbs and/or
   buttered stuffing crumbs

Cook broccoli and drain. Place in a greased casserole. Mix remaining ingredients together and spoon over broccoli. Top with cheese, bread crumbs, and/or stuffing crumbs. Bake at 350F for 30–35 minutes.

Variation: substitute chicken for all or part of ham.

H. JUDITH AND ROLAND HARRISON
CHAR LUCAS

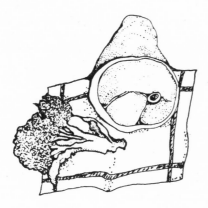

one little American boy in the school was sorry for all the Indian children who had no money to buy popcorn. They looked hungry, too. So the American boy ran to his home nearby and got all the money in his purse, but it wasn't enough. He emptied his mother's purse, too, and went back to school and passed the money around. The teacher saw that some of the children had big coins to spend and she knew they would never have that much money from home to use on popcorn, so she came to the American boy's mother with the rupees." My son was listening very intently to the story. Here he suddenly interrupted me to say, "That little boy should have asked his mother before he used her money!" What more can a mother ask than that her children learn their lessons the least painful way? ♥

ANNA B. MOW *(from* Preparing Your Child to Love God*)*

BEEF AND LAMB

Braised Short Ribs 191
Sweet and Sour Short Ribs of Beef 192
Mom's Saucy Meatballs 193
Barbecued Meatballs 194
Porcupine Beef Balls 195
Fried Greek Meatballs 196
Stuffed Cabbage 197
Salisbury Steak Supper 198
Dinner in a Skillet 198
Skillet Lasagna 199
Spaghetti and Vegetables 200
Topsy Turvey 201
Casserole Mexico 202
Creamy Beef Enchiladas 203
Mysaka 204
Beef Soong 205
Teriyaki Meatloaf 206
Pizza Meatloaf 207
Barbecue 207
Barbecued Beef 208
Golden Pot Roast 208
Return Engagement Beef Casserole 209
Beef-Mushroom Stew 210
Ethiopian Beef and Vegetable Alecha 211
Oxtail Pepper Stew 212
Hungarian Gulyás 213
Beef Stroganoff 214
Sherried Beef 215
Pigtails 215
Nystrom's Round Steak 216

Marinated Flank Steak I 216
Marinated Flank Steak II 217
Indonesian Dinner 218
Korean Skewered Beef 220
Irish Lamb Stew 221

Braised Short Ribs

SERVES 4

2 pounds beef short ribs
1 large clove garlic, cut in half
¼ cup flour
1 teaspoon salt
¼ teaspoon pepper
1 tablespoon paprika
¼ cup oil
1 (20 ounce) can tomatoes
1 cup hot water
1 large carrot, peeled and diced
1 medium onion, sliced
1 small bay leaf

Cut between ribs and trim off all excess fat. Rub all over with cut sides of garlic. Combine flour, salt, pepper, and paprika in a flat dish and roll ribs in mixture. Heat oil in a heavy saucepan or Dutch oven that can be put in oven. Add ribs and brown well on all sides. Lift out pieces as they are browned. Drain all except 2 tablespoons of fat from the pan. Sprinkle in any flour that was left from coating and let bubble up, stirring constantly. Remove from heat and add tomatoes and hot water all at once, stirring to blend. Return to heat and bring to a boil, stirring to blend. Add carrot, onion, bay leaf, and ribs. Cover tightly and bake at 325F about 2–2½ hours or until meat is tender.

HELEN ENNS

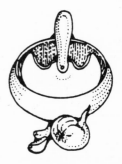

Sweet and Sour Short Ribs of Beef

3–5 pounds beef short ribs
½ cup flour
2 teaspoons salt
dash of pepper
1 onion, sliced
¾ cup catsup
2 tablespoons vinegar
2 tablespoons Worcestershire sauce
¼ cup soy sauce
½ cup sugar
¾ cup water

Coat ribs with mixture of salt and pepper. Arrange ribs side by side in a large casserole or roasting pan. Cover with sliced onion. Mix remaining ingredients and pour over ribs, cover and bake at 325F for 3 hours, removing cover for the last 30 minutes. Check occasionally while baking and add more water if needed.

SANDRA ZUIDERSMA

Mom's Saucy Meatballs

Meatballs:

1 pound ground beef
¼ cup chopped onion
¼ cup cracker crumbs
3–4 tablespoons skim milk
1 teaspoon salt
⅛ teaspoon pepper
¼ teaspoon poultry seasoning

Sauce:

1 can condensed cream of mushroom soup
¾ cup hot water

Mix all meatball ingredients together and form into walnut-size balls. Place on a rack or in a circle in a large pie plate and microwave on high 4 minutes. Drain off grease and put meatballs in a casserole. Mix cream of mushroom soup and water and pour over meatballs. Cover and cook on high power about 10 minutes, stirring and rotating ¼ turn halfway through cooking time. Meatballs should be tender and moist with a bubbly sauce. Let sit 4–5 minutes before serving. Garnish with chopped parsley if desired. Super with noodles or rice.

JOHN C. CARPENTER

The "Think Blessing"

Praying aloud in public is difficult for me. I think my reluctance to do so is related to memorized prayers. So I decided to teach my children to compose their own prayers, hoping they would be more spontaneous and confident when asked to pray in public.

Well, the first homemade prayer came out, "Thank you, God, for frogs." I found it difficult to keep my composure. I lectured to myself the value of frogs. I tried to picture them as cute creatures sitting on lily pads, but for the life of me I could only visualize a deep-throated, warty, scaly, bulgy-eyed, long-tongued flycatcher!

By trial and error I learned to guide my children in their

Barbecued Meatballs

Meatballs:

1½ pounds ground beef
2 eggs, beaten
1 teaspoon salt
⅓ cup milk
juice of 1 medium onion or 1 onion, finely
    chopped
about 1 cup quick oats

Sauce:

½ cup catsup
2 tablespoons brown sugar
2 tablespoons vinegar
½ teaspoon salt
2 teaspoons prepared mustard
2 teaspoons Worcestershire sauce
dash pepper
¼ teaspoon dill weed

To prepare meatballs mix together all meatball ingredients and form into walnut-size balls. Brown on all sides in a skillet in a small amount of oil or butter or place meatballs on a cookie sheet and bake at 450F until browned as desired. Place browned meatballs in a casserole or baking dish.

Mix together all sauce ingredients. Pour over meatballs and bake uncovered at 300F for 45–60 minutes, basting occasionally with sauce while baking.

WILMA ZONDERVAN TEGGELAAR

prayers by saying things such as: "When we're eating vegetables, it would be nice to thank God for vegetables and save the frog and worm prayer till you're outside." The oldest child understood. The second child had no problem either because he always copies his older brother.

As the years passed and our family grew, other problems arose. The baby always chimed in with squeals of delight at having folded her hands, which often drove the other three into hysterics. Finally, the clamor simmered down to just applause (a little enthusiasm before meals isn't too bad though!) and eventually graduated into hand folding and mumbling.

The children soon became so enthusiastic that it became a daily fight about who was going to say the blessing. They would rush to the table screaming, "First! First!" and the first to scream was "it." In our family, no one wants to be second. So prayer time at the table often

Porcupine Beef Balls

SERVES 10

1 cup uncooked rice
2 pounds ground beef
2 teaspoons salt
pepper, to taste
¼ cup minced onion
2 cans condensed tomato soup
2 cups hot water

Combine rice, beef, salt, pepper, and onion and shape into walnut-size balls. Brown in skillet, add tomato soup mixed with hot water, cover and cook 1½ hours over low heat.

Variation: Can be browned, then baked in the oven at 350F for 2 hours.

BETTY & JAMES BUICK

resulted in hurt feelings (usually in my hand), accusations of "she was first last," pouting, the children being sent to their bedrooms, then eventually one of them offering a half-hearted "duty" blessing.

So we developed a plan whereby each child was scheduled to give thanks the same day each week. I carefully explained that when one says the blessing, the others can be second, third, and so on if they wish, or the others can think a blessing.

They seemed to like the idea of thinking a blessing. I explained that God knows what we mean when we think it. We do not always have to pray aloud.

I was amazed at their response to the think blessing. And with one blessing rather than five, we were able to eat hot meals again.

This plan worked well for a while. Then one night, after putting the children to bed for the last time and turning out

Fried Greek Meatballs

"An easy and tasty Greek dish that can be eaten hot or cold."

2 pounds ground beef (or half beef and half lamb, or half beef and half pork)
1 cup chopped onion
1 tablespoon oil
2 cups moist, soft bread crumbs
2 eggs
2 tablespoons dried parsley flakes
¾ teaspoon dried mint leaves
¼ teaspoon oregano
1 tablespoon salt
½ teaspoon pepper
1 cup flour
1 cup butter or oil for frying

Saute onion in 1 tablespoon oil until brown. In a mixing bowl, place sauted onions, meat, and all other ingredients except flour and butter. Mix well by hand. Form into walnut-size balls and roll in flour. Fry in very hot butter or oil (butter is best) until brown on all sides. (I use an electric skillet for these.)

OLIVIA & PAUL HILLMAN

the light, I returned to the living room for my nightly deep sigh of relief.

After a few moments, the silence was interrupted by the patter of little feet. One of my dear children stood before me, her face glowing with a calm and satisfied smirk.

"What are you doing up?" I asked sternly.

She answered in all seriousness, "I can stay up. I thinked it."

I have become a little dense at my age, so I asked the inevitable, "You thinked what?"

"I thinked going to sleep, and God knows what I mean. So now I can stay up."

Oh well, who ever said parenting would be dull, anyway? ♥

YVONNE LEHMAN (reprinted from an article in Living with Children.)

MINT

Stuffed Cabbage

cabbage leaves (the inner leaves of white
    cabbage are best)
1 pound ground beef
1 cup rice, uncooked
¼ cup butter or margarine
1 (8 ounce) can tomato sauce
1½ teaspoons salt
1 teaspoon red pepper
½ teaspoon cinnamon
1 (16 ounce) can tomatoes
juice of 1 lemon

Soak cabbage leaves in scalding hot water for about 5 minutes. Blend beef, rice, butter, tomato sauce, salt, red pepper, and cinnamon together with hands. Place 2 heaping tablespoons of beef mixture on each cabbage leaf. Roll up firmly and secure with wooden toothpicks. Arrange cabbage rolls close together in a large skillet. Cover with tomatoes. Simmer, covered, for 1 hour. Add lemon juice. Simmer 30 minutes longer, or until rice is done.

DEBBIE BARR

Salisbury Steak Supper

SERVES 4

1 pound ground beef
salt and pepper, to taste
2 cans sliced potatoes
1 can onion soup

Form the beef into 4 large patties. Brown them in a heavy skillet. Salt and pepper patties. Place potatoes (including liquid) on patties. Pour onion soup over all. Cover, simmer for 30 minutes. Serve with a salad or vegetable.

DIANE BRUMMEL BLOEM

Dinner in a Skillet

1 pound ground beef
2 medium zucchinis
1 large tomato
½ cup onion
salt and pepper, to taste
½ cup grated cheese

Brown beef and drain all grease. Dice zucchini, tomato, and onion. Add to meat. Sprinkle with salt and pepper. Simmer until vegetables are tender. Top with cheese and serve.

OLIVIA & PAUL HILLMAN

Skillet Lasagna

"Fast and easy. Great for a busy cook."

1 pound ground beef
1 package dry spaghetti sauce mix
1 pound small curd cottage cheese
1 (16 ounce) can tomatoes
1 (8 ounce) can tomato sauce
1 tomato sauce can of water
3 cups flat egg noodles, uncooked
8 ounces mozarella cheese, grated

Brown ground beef. Drain off fat. Sprinkle half of spaghetti sauce mix over ground beef. Add in layers cottage cheese and tomatoes. Pour tomato sauce and water over all. Distribute noodles on top, making sure noodles get moistened with liquid. Sprinkle with remaining spaghetti mix. Bring to a boil. Cover and simmer 30 minutes. Sprinkle mozarella on top 5 minutes before serving.

Doris Rikkers

Quick Lasagne

Make your sauce and grate your cheese for "normal" lasagne, but DON'T COOK THE NOODLES! Add ¾ cup water to your sauce, and layer in a greased 9"x13" pan:
1. sauce first
2. uncooked noodles
3. cheese
4. uncooked noodles
5. cheese
6. sauce again
Cook covered at 375F for one hour. I'll often grate the cheese early in the morning and put the sauce (meat, tomatoes, spices) in the crock pot. I can go to work and then come home to a meal that's easy to put together: all I do is arrange the layers and stick it in the oven. ♥

Judy and Bill Vriesema

Spaghetti and Vegetables

SERVES 4

"Very good, has a unique, fresh taste."

2 strips bacon, diced
2 large carrots, cut lengthwise in matchlike
    strips
1 large onion, finely chopped
1 tablespoon water
1 small green pepper, chopped
1 tablespoon cooking oil
1 pound lean ground beef
1 (20 ounce) can tomatoes
2 cups cooked spaghetti (about 4 ounces
    uncooked)
½ teaspoon basil
1½ teaspoons salt
¼ teaspoon pepper

Fry bacon until crisp in large heavy skillet. Lift out with a slotted spoon and set aside. Add carrot strips, onion, and 1 tablespoon water to fat left in pan. Cover tightly (use aluminum foil if pan has no cover) and cook over highest heat 2 minutes. Add green pepper, cover again, and cook 1 minute more. Vegetables should be crisp-tender at this point—if they are not, add another table-spoon water, cover, and cook 1 minute more. Lift vegetables out with slotted spoon and set aside. Add 1 tablespoon oil to any drippings left in pan and add ground beef. Cook and stir until beef is lightly browned. Return vegetables to pan and add tomatoes, spaghetti, and seasoning. Blend lightly. Cover and simmer 10 minutes. Serve immediately, sprinkled with the crisp bacon bits.

HELEN ENNS

Topsy Turvey

"In the South we eat a lot of corn bread. This recipe is an interesting taste combination, with a meat sauce on corn bread."

1 pound ground beef
1 clove garlic, minced (liquid garlic may be
 used)
½ cup chopped green pepper
1 (6 ounce) can tomato paste
salt and pepper, to taste
6 slices tomato
1 large onion, separated into rings
corn bread batter, any recipe, or from a mix

Lightly brown garlic, meat, and green pepper. Add tomato paste, salt, and pepper. Simmer while preparing corn bread batter. In bottom of a black iron skillet arrange tomato slices inside onion rings. Cover with meat sauce. Pour corn bread batter over meat mixture. Bake at 425F for 20–25 minutes, or until brown. Invert on serving platter.

MARTHA MAUGHON

Sharing

Being newlyweds who still have to go to the laundromat each week, my husband, John, and I take turns each week with the washing and grocery shopping. Whoever is shopping drops the other off at the laundromat and picks him or her up again an hour later—both take about the same amount of time. So, if we don't like what the other person bought, or didn't buy, we can remedy the situation ourselves the following week. ♥

SANDRA DRESCHER LEHMAN

Casserole Mexico

1 pound ground beef
1 package taco seasoning mix
1 can whole kernel corn
1 can tomatoes
1 package corn bread mix

Brown ground beef. Add taco seasoning mix, corn, and tomatoes. Heat to boiling. Prepare corn bread mix batter according to package directions. Pour meat-vegetable mixture into a 2 quart casserole dish. Spread corn bread batter over the top. Bake at 400F until corn bread is fully done.

Variation: Omit corn bread mix and bake other ingredients until bubbly. Sprinkle grated cheese on top and return to oven until cheese melts and is lightly browned.

HARRIET & DERRALL KINARD

The New Me

I have to be honest with you in discussing recipes—I am not a creative cook. I often fantasize that a "new me" will wake up one morning. That a "new me" will be inspired to spend more time in the kitchen creating gourmet meals to delight my family (instead of the predictable, popular rotation of spaghetti, chili, tacos, chicken, and pizza which are "safe" with our three children); the "new me" will faithfully clip coupons AND USE THEM!! I will finance a family vacation with the money I save. I will also have some marvelous system that will assure me of finding every recipe I clip from newspapers and magazines whenever I need it. And, I will not only save all those recipes, I will use them faithfully, only discarding the ones we don't like. I will keep menu cards, rotating the meals that have worked especially well for us.

All that is the "new me" and since I am still the old me, I am simply enclosing a recipe our family loves. ♥

CAROL KUYKENDALL

Creamy Beef Enchiladas

1 pound ground beef
1 teaspoon salt
8 ounces Cheddar cheese, grated
1 large onion, chopped
2 (10¾ ounce) cans condensed cream of
   chicken soup
¾ cup evaporated milk
1 (8 ounce) package pasteurized processed
   cheese spread (Velveeta), cut in chunks
1 (0.56 ounce) envelope green onion dip mix
1 (4 ounce) can green chili peppers, chopped
1 (4 ounce) can chopped pimentos, drained
12 corn tortillas
oil

Combine beef and salt, brown in skillet. Pour
off drippings and stir in Cheddar cheese and
onion. Remove from heat. Combine soup, milk,
and cheese spread in a medium saucepan. Place
over low heat, stirring constantly, until cheese is
melted. Add onion dip mix, chili peppers, and
pimentos. Remove from heat.

Heat about ½" of oil in a small skillet. Dip
tortillas in hot oil about 3 seconds to soften, drain
well. Spread each tortilla with meat mixture. Roll
tightly and place in a 13"x9"x2" baking dish. Pour
cheese sauce over tortillas. Cover with aluminum
foil, bake at 350 for 30 minutes.

LAREN & JOHN SLOAN

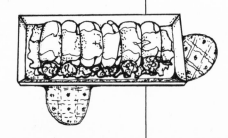

Mysaka

SERVES 4

This Bulgarian casserole is flexible and can be expanded by adding more of the vegetables and milk/egg mixture.

2–3 cups sliced potatoes, eggplant, or summer squash
oil
1 pound ground beef
1 onion, minced
salt
pepper

Milk/egg mixture:

1 cup milk, at room temperature, or slightly warmed*
1 egg, at room temperature, or slightly warmed*
¼ teaspoon salt
dash pepper

In a skillet saute sliced vegetable in a small amount of oil until partially cooked. Remove from skillet and set aside. Brown ground beef and onion in skillet. In a greased ovenproof casserole place alternating layers of meat and sliced vegetable, lightly sprinkling salt and pepper, as desired. Bake at 350F for 45–60 minutes. Turn heat up to 400F. Beat together egg, milk, salt, and pepper and pour slowly over casserole. Bake until set (a knife inserted in the center should come out clean), about 10 minutes.

*To avoid breakage, do not pour cold liquids into a hot breakable container.

RUTH & HARALAN POPOV

Mysaka

I remember well the dear lady in our church in Bourgas by the Black Sea who taught me to cook this dish. She was the last one I saw on the station nearest the border to Yugoslavia. We, I and my children, then 12 and 7 years old, were standing at the window of the train which took us to Sweden, when my husband Haralan Popov was in prison with 15 years hard labor. There we saw her and I called her, she took some steps towards the train, but was stopped by the guard. Nobody was even to get near the train. But I was happy to wave a last good-bye. She is now with the Lord. ♥

RUTH & HARALAN POPOV

Beef Soong

1 pound ground beef
6 tablespoons soy sauce
¼ cup water
¼ teaspoon white pepper
½ teaspoon sugar
2 tablespoons cornstarch
¼ cup chicken broth
⅓ cup corn oil
2 medium onions, diced
½ cup mushrooms, canned or fresh
½ cup water chestnuts
½ cup bamboo shoots
½ cup peas, canned, or cooked fresh or
   frozen

Marinate ground beef for 20 minutes in a mixture of 4 tablespoons of the soy sauce, water, pepper, sugar, and 1 tablespoon cornstarch. Combine chicken broth, remaining soy sauce, and cornstarch and set aside.

Heat 2 tablespoons of corn oil in a wok. Saute onions until translucent. Add mushrooms, water chestnuts, and bamboo shoots. Cook until heated through, approximately 1 minute. Remove to a dish. Wipe the wok clean and add remaining oil. Set wok on high heat. When the oil is hot, add marinated beef. Stir fry until meat is browned. Add chicken broth mixture and cook until the sauce thickens. Add peas and all vegetables, combine well. Heat to simmer.

This dish can be served as is or on a platter lined with lettuce leaves, spooning a small amount onto a piece of lettuce, wrapping it, and eating with fingers. It is also great served with rice or noodles.

Pat McCartney

Teriyaki Meatloaf

SERVES 3–4

1 (8 ounce) can crushed pineapple in syrup
½ pound ground beef
¼ cup soft bread crumbs
2 tablespoons chopped onion
1 clove garlic, minced, or ¼ teaspoon garlic
    powder
2 tablespoons soy sauce
1 tablespoon milk
½ teaspoon salt
¼ teaspoon pepper

Pineapple Glaze:

1 teaspoon cornstarch
¼ teaspoon ginger
1 tablespoon soy sauce
reserved crushed pineapple and syrup

Drain pineapple, reserve syrup and 2 tablespoons pineapple for glaze. Combine remaining pineapple, meat, crumbs, and the rest of the ingredients. Shape and put in a shallow baking pan. Bake at 325F for about 40 minutes or until done.

While loaf bakes prepare glaze. Combine cornstarch and ginger in a small pan. Slowly stir in pineapple syrup, blending until smooth. Add soy sauce and bring to a boil, stirring for 1 minute. Remove from heat and stir in reserved pineapple bits. Pour over cooked meat loaf.

ANNE & R. LAIRD HARRIS

Pizza Meatloaf

1 cup crushed saltine crackers (or Italian
    bread crumbs)
1 cup milk
2 eggs
⅓ cup chopped onion
½ cup Parmesan cheese
1½ teaspoons salt
¼ teaspoon oregano
2 pounds ground beef
1 (8 ounce) can pizza sauce
1–2 cups grated mozzarella cheese

Combine crackers, milk, eggs, onion, Parmesan, salt, and oregano. Mix in ground beef. Pat flat in a loaf pan. Bake at 350F about 60 minutes. Invert into a baking dish. Pour pizza sauce over meatloaf, then top with mozzarella. Bake 10 more minutes.

GRACE & DEAN MERRIL

Barbecue

1½ pounds ground beef
1 cup chopped celery
½ cup chopped onion
2 tablespoons brown sugar
dash salt
2 tablespoons Worcestershire sauce
1 cup or more catsup
1 tablespoon prepared mustard
1 teaspoon vinegar

Brown ground beef, celery, and onions. Add remaining ingredients. Simmer 5 minutes or longer. Serve hot on buns.

MARY JO VRYHOF

My wife and I spent years trying to urge teenagers to eat mushrooms, until it suddenly dawned on us that, far from our being defeated, victory had been handed to us on a china platter. Now, if it looks as if the main dish will be in short supply, my wife regularly includes one or two sliced mushrooms. When I serve it, I announce solemnly: "You children really must have a good helping of this; the mushrooms are marvelous."

True to form, they object. Equally true to form, I become incensed at their gastronomic inflexibility. The beginnings of a scene hover for a moment over the table; but then, with a sigh and a not altogether gracious gesture of resignation, I give in and serve them small portions. My wife and I exchange a knowing glance, and feast quietly in triumph. I commend the strategy to you. It is the only way I know of to serve sweetbreads to a large family and still insure that the people who really care get enough. ♥

ROBERT FARRAR CAPON *(from* The Supper of the Lamb*)*

Barbecued Beef

1 (3–5 pound) roast
salt, to taste
pepper, to taste
1¼ cups water
2 cups diced onion
2 tablespoons oil
1½ cups liquid from roast
14 ounces catsup
¼ cup vinegar
¼ cup brown sugar
2 tablespoons Worcestershire sauce
dash of Tabasco sauce
1 teaspoon prepared mustard

Cook roast, adding salt and pepper to taste and 1¼ cups water. When meat is done, reserve 1½ cups of liquid left in pan (adding water if necessary). Cool meat and cut into small pieces.

Saute onion in oil, add reserved liquid, catsup, vinegar, brown sugar, Worcestershire sauce, Tabasco, and mustard. Cook 55 minutes, stirring frequently. Add beef and simmer 30 minutes. Serve on hamburger buns with chips and pickles.

JUDY BAER

Golden Pot Roast

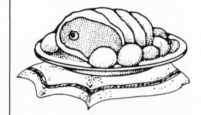

1 (4–5 pound) pot roast
1 package dry onion soup mix
1 can condensed golden mushroom soup

Place roast on a sheet of aluminum foil in a baking pan. Spread undiluted golden mushroom soup over meat. Sprinkle dry onion soup mix on top. Wrap roast in foil and bake at 350F to desire degree of doneness.

MRS. EDWARD GOODRICK

Return Engagement Beef Casserole

"A delicious way to serve leftover beef."

SERVES 4

1 large onion, coarsely chopped
3 stalks celery, coarsely chopped
1 green pepper, coarsely chopped
2 tablespoons margarine
2 cups cooked pot roast, cut in small cubes
1 can condensed cream of mushroom soup
½ cup water
¼ teaspoon salt
dash pepper
1 can chow mein noodles (optional)

Saute onion, celery, and green pepper in margarine until limp. Add beef. Stir in mushroom soup and water. Bake in a greased baking dish at 325F for about 30 minutes. Sprinkle chow mein noodles on top, if desired, and return to oven to bake 5 minutes more.

Variation: 1 pound browned ground beef can be used instead of leftover roast.

ANN & VERNON GROUNDS

Sunday

There's a marvelous line in Hailstones and Halibut Bones by Mary O'Neill, a book about the emotional dimensions of colors. This one is about the color BROWN.

Brown is the color of a country road
Back of a turtle
Back of a toad.
Brown is cinnamon
And morning toast
And the good smell of
The Sunday roast . . .
I say these lines to myself or aloud every time the door is opened upon our arrival home from church on Sunday—and I smell that good smell of the Sunday roast. It may complicate my Sundays, but I cannot give it up. It's such a good time to have people home for dinner, either prearranged or spur of the moment. I prepare the day ahead. It's part of getting ready for the Lord's Day. It's part of our Sunday tradition. It makes what our son used to call "a festive day." ♥

GLADYS HUNT

Beef-Mushroom Stew

1½ pounds lean stewing beef, cut in bite-size
    pieces
oil
salt, to taste
pepper, to taste
water
3 ounces (6 tablespoons) sherry
1 package dry onion soup mix
1 can condensed cream of mushroom soup
1 pound fresh mushrooms, sliced and sauteed
    in butter

Brown meat in a small amount of oil and add
salt and pepper to taste. Add water just to cover
meat. Stir in sherry, onion soup mix, and mushroom soup. Blend mixture and let simmer, covered, for 2 hours, or until meat is tender. Add
mushrooms and cook until heated through. Serve
over rice, or gently mixed together with about 3
cups hot cooked rice.

SHARON & DOUG KUIPERS

*Since I became a steady
cook—by virtue of getting
married—we have lived in seven
different towns and cities, five
in the United States and two in
Ethiopia. In each of these places
our menus have been different,
mostly because of the types of
foods available. My recipes have
also changed.*

*While we were in Ethiopia,
where some products and
ingredients were not available, a
saying among the missionary
ladies was, "If you have the
first three ingredients (in a
recipe) you can make it!" In
other words, improvise,
something which would make
any home economics teacher
shudder, as they always warn
against just that.* ♥

MERILYN & MILTON FISHER

Ethiopian Beef and Vegetable Alecha (Stew)

SERVES 4–6

2 tablespoons oil or shortening
1 pound ground beef (Ethiopians take raw
    beef and chop it finely)
½ cup chopped onion
½ teaspoon salt
1 teaspoon ginger
1 green pepper, cut in chunks, not chopped
8 ounces whole string beans; fresh are best,
    but may use frozen
3 medium carrots cut in 1½" slices
2 medium potatoes cut in pieces
1 cup broken tomatoes (optional)

Brown onion in oil, then add ground beef and brown. Drain off excess fat. Add ginger, salt, raw vegetables, and 1–2 cups water to keep mixture moist while cooking. Cook, covered, in a heavy skillet or Dutch oven, over low heat until vegetables are cooked and flavors blended. May be thickened with flour or cornstarch, if desired. Serve with rice.

Variation: Can also be made with ground beef omitted, for a tasty vegetable dish.

MERILYN & MILTON FISHER

Oxtail Pepper Stew

"This is adapted from an unwritten Ethiopian recipe. Best when made a day ahead and reheated before serving."

½ cup finely chopped onion
¼ cup margarine, butter or shortening
1 pound oxtails, cut into 1½"–3" pieces
1 teaspoon salt
¼ teaspoon ground hot red pepper
¼ teaspoon pepper
⅛ teaspoon cloves
⅛ teaspoon nutmeg
½ teaspoon ginger
¼ teaspoon ground fenugreek
about 3 cups raw or cooked tomatoes, or 1
    (20 ounce) can

Lightly brown onions in melted fat over medium heat in a heavy (preferably iron) skillet. Add oxtails and cook until brown on all sides. Add salt, hot red pepper, pepper, cloves, nutmeg, ginger, and fenugreek. Mix well with onions and oxtail pieces. Add tomatoes. With a spoon break and stir tomatoes into other ingredients. Cover skillet and simmer on low heat for 1 hour or until meat is tender. Serve with spaghetti or spaghetti squash shreds, or Ethiopian injera bread if you can get it.

MERILYN & MILTON FISHER

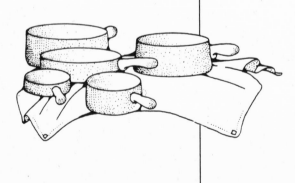

Hungarian Gulyás

1 large onion, chopped
2 tablespoons oil
1 teaspoon caraway seed
1 teaspoon paprika
1 pound stewing beef, cubed
3 carrots, sliced
1 ripe tomato, peeled and sliced
½ green pepper, sliced
1 tablespoon (or more) chopped fresh parsley
4 medium potatoes, cubed
2 teaspoons salt
¼ teaspoon pepper
water, to cover

In a large pot saute onion in oil. When onion is slightly brown add caraway seeds and paprika. Cook 1 minute. Add stewing beef. Stir to coat meat with paprika. Turn heat to low and allow meat to brown, then cover and let simmer in its own juices for 1 hour.

Add carrots, tomato, green pepper, parsley, potatoes, salt, pepper, and enough water to cover meat and vegetables. Simmer, covered, until meat and vegetables are tender.

Julie & Kalman Toth

We hope your Cookbook will not have texts on every page like one of the wedding presents given us which had Steak and Kidney Pudding under "Prepare to meet thy God!" ♥

Donald & Mary Wiseman

Beef Stroganoff

SERVES 3–4

1 pound sirloin or top round steak, cut in
 thin strips across the grain
¼ cup flour
½ teaspoon salt
3 tablespoons butter
1 small onion, chopped
1 cup sliced fresh mushrooms, or 1 (4 ounce)
 can
1 tablespoon tomato paste
1 can beef bouillon
1 clove garlic, crushed, or ¼ teaspoon garlic
 powder
1 cup sour cream
1–2 tablespoons cooking sherry

Dust meat with a mixture of salt and 1 tablespoon of the flour. In a skillet brown meat and
onion in 1 tablespoon butter. Add mushrooms
(saute briefly if using fresh mushrooms). Remove
meat mixture from skillet and set aside. Melt
remaining 2 tablespoons of butter in skillet. Stir in
remaining 3 tablespoons flour and tomato paste.
Gradually add beef bouillon, stirring until thick.
Return meat mixture to skillet and add garlic or
garlic powder. Cover and simmer about 15 minutes, or until meat is of desired doneness. Add
sour cream gradually. Heat through (do not boil).
Stir in sherry. Serve over wild rice or noodles.

SHARON & JAMES ENGEL

Sherried Beef

SERVES 6–8

3 pounds round steak, cut in 1½″ cubes
2 cans condensed cream of mushroom soup
¾ cup cooking sherry
½ package dry onion soup mix

In a saucepan, heat mushroom soup. Gradually stir in sherry. Add onion soup mix and pour over beef in a large casserole. Cover and bake at 325F for 3 hours. Serve over rice or noodles.

LOIS & CARYN DYKSTRA

Pigtails

SERVES 4

2 pounds round steak, sliced ¼″ thick
½ pound pork steak
salt, to taste
pepper, to taste
2 medium onions, chopped
thin slices of dill pickles
2 tablespoons margarine

Remove fat from meat. Cut round steak into pieces 3½″ wide x 5″ long. Cut pork steak into strips 4″ long x ⅓″ wide. Sprinkle salt and pepper on steak. Add a pork strip, 2 thin slices of dill pickle and about 1 teaspoon chopped onion to each piece of round steak. Roll up and close securely with 1–3 toothpicks.

Brown pigtails in margarine. Place in a roaster pan with lid. Add water to cover bottom of pan. Bake at 350F for 2 hours. Use pan juices to make gravy.

LOUISE BAUER

Pigtails

◄ *Also good as snacks when cold, especially good to take along while cross-country skiing, bicycling or on other vigorous outdoor activities.* ♥

LOUISE BAUER

Nystrom's Round Steak

round steak
wine or cooking wine
sliced onions
garlic salt

Pour a little wine in a large skillet, lay the round steak in the wine, pour a little more wine on top. (Slit the surface of the meat to help the wine soak in.) Soak in wine two or three hours. Then turn heat on very low. Lay some sliced onions on top of meat. Shake a little garlic salt on it. Cover and cook for about two hours. (If it starts to curl while cooking, cut the edges so it lies flat.)

CAROLYN NYSTROM

Marinated Flank Steak I

flank steak

Marinade:

1 part unsweetened pineapple juice
1 part soy sauce

Place flank steak in a glass container. Using above proportions mix enough marinade to cover meat. Pour marinade over meat. Cover and refrigerate several hours or overnight, turning meat over several times. Just before serving time remove steak from marinade and broil or grill to medium rare. Thinly slice across the grain and transfer to warm meat platter. Serve immediately.

JOANNE BOER

Nystrom's Round Steak

◄≪ *My husband, a junior high math teacher, works as househusband during the summers. This frees me to write full-time in an office away from home. He does laundry, chauffeuring, cleaning, and yes—even cooking. When I come home from work at 5:00, I experience a pleasure offered few women: dinner is ready and waiting. This is one of his recipes.* ♥

CAROLYN NYSTROM

GARLIC

Marinated Flank Steak II

"Flank steak is a cheaper cut steak and with this marinade it is tender and delicious after just a few minutes on the outdoor barbecue."

flank steak

Marinade:

¼ **cup soy sauce**
3 **tablespoons honey**
2 **tablespoons white vinegar**
1 **teaspoon garlic powder**
¾ **cup oil**
½ **teaspoon onion salt**
1 **teaspoon ginger**

Mix together marinade ingredients (a wire whisk is excellent for this). Pour over flank steak in a shallow glass pan. Refrigerate, covered, four hours or overnight. Cook over glowing coals about 5 minutes on each side for medium steak. To serve, slice in thin strips diagonally across the grain.

Marilyn & William J. McRae

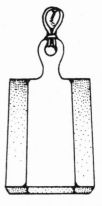

Indonesian Dinner

To be eaten with chopsticks, if possible.

SERVES 4

Oriental Beef:

1 (approximately 2½ pounds) round steak, fat
    removed, cut in small strips
oil
1 can condensed cream of mushroom soup
1 soup can water
¼ cup soy sauce

Chutney:

2 cups finely chopped onions
6 cups chopped peeled tart apples
4 cups brown sugar
2 cups raisins
2 teaspoons cinnamon
1 teaspoon cloves
1 teaspoon ginger
1 teaspoon mace
2 teaspoons salt
3 tablespoons dark molasses
1 (9 ounce) bottle mango chutney

Accompaniments:

3–4 cups hot cooked rice
pineapple tidbits
banana, chopped
cucumber, chopped
green onions, chopped
dry roasted peanuts
raisins
coconut

To prepare Oriental Beef, brown steak strips in
a small amount of oil. Place in a baking dish. Add
mushroom soup, water, and soy sauce. Cover and
bake at 325F for 2–3 hours, or until very tender,
adding water during baking if necessary. ➤➤

To prepare chutney, mix all ingredients together, except bottled mango chutney, and simmer uncovered until thick, about 1 hour. Remove from heat and add mango chutney. (Leftover chutney freezes well.)

To serve:

Serve accompaniments in separate bowls. Serve rice and oriental beef hot. Provide small bowls and chopsticks for each person served.

To eat:

Place a few pieces of Oriental Beef in bottom of bowl. Rice is added next, followed by the other seven ingredients. (Add them all, believe it or not; they really go well together). Chutney is added on top. Mix together with chopsticks, and eat.

MARILYN & WILLIAM J. McRAE

As a family we enjoy MISSIONARY MEALS, as we call those cooked by missionary friends. Or better still, by friends like overseas students to show us what it is like to eat in their country. We persuade them to take over the kitchen and use the ingredients which they have provided (usually at our expense). The whole exercise requires patience and a straight face and often, but not always, leads to a greater understanding of problems in a far country. ♥

DONALD & MARY WISEMAN

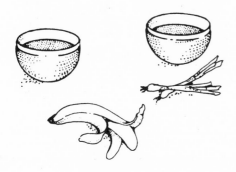

Korean Skewered Beef

"This recipe is great for an outdoor cookout, or you can make it in the oven."

flank, chuck or round steak, cut into chunks
skewers for broiling beef and any or all of
**   the following accompaniments**
cherry tomatoes
small onions
pineapple chunks
green and red pepper chunks
fresh mushroom caps

Marinade:

1 cup oil
¼–½ cup honey
3 tablespoons soy sauce
salt and pepper, as desired
2 cloves garlic
¼ teaspoon ginger
¼ cup sesame seeds

At least 4–6 hours before broiling, or the day before (even better), make marinade: In an electric blender mix together oil, honey, soy sauce, salt and pepper, garlic, ginger, and sesame seeds. Place meat chunks in marinade in a glass container, cover, and refrigerate 4–6 hours or overnight. Stir or turn meat occasionally.

On skewers alternate marinated meat with cherry tomatoes, onions, pineapple, pepper chunks, and mushrooms, as desired. Broil over charcoal, or under an oven broiler until meat is of desired doneness.

JEAN SCHAFER

Any Old Thing—by Candlelight

At least once a week we eat in the dining room by candlelight. Even macaroni and cheese with hot dogs seems fancy when served on good dishes by candlelight. Our prayer takes in more concerns and thank you's, our conversation is more meaningful and substantive, and we all seem to slow down just a little bit when we share our meal in the dining room.

Often after our candlelight dinner we remain at the table when dishes are cleared and all have coffee. The kids have much more milk than coffee in their cups, but the specialness is not in the amount of brown or white liquid. The specialness is

Irish Lamb Stew

"A real Irish Lamb Stew should actually be cooked in an iron kettle hanging from a chain over an open peat fire, but a lamb stew out of the oven tastes just as good."

3 pounds stewing lamb
6 large potatoes
4 yellow onions
2 tablespoons dried parsley flakes
1 teaspoon thyme
1 teaspoon salt
1½ cups chicken broth
1½ tablespoons margarine, softened
1 tablespoon flour
2 tablespoons fresh parsley for garnish
    (optional)

Cut lamb into slices or cubes. Cut peeled potatoes and onions into thin slices or chunks. Mix together parsley and thyme. Butter a large casserole. Arrange ⅓ of potatoes in a layer on bottom of casserole. Cover with a layer of lamb, then a layer of onions. Season with herbs, salt, and pepper. Repeat layers twice, in the above order, seasoning after each addition of onions. Add the broth. Cover and bake at 350F for 1½ hours or until lamb is tender. In a small container mix butter and flour until smooth and add to casserole. Stir and continue cooking 5 minutes, until juices are thickened. Garnish with fresh parsley.

Mary & Ken Regan

in the setting, by candlelight, and sharing a few moments of quiet and very grown-up talk.

Special occasions such as birthdays or Christmas Eve are celebrated by candlelight in the dining room. Perhaps a bit of the magic of those special days is caught up in the flickering of the candles of our dining room dinners. No matter what it is that brings about the atmosphere, it's a part of my week that I cherish and wouldn't give up even for a dinner out. I'll take any old thing, with my family, by candlelight! ♥

Janice Kempe

SEAFOOD

Autumn Fish "Slew" 224
Shrimp Jambalaya 225
Broiled Gulf Scallops 226
Crab Meat Joni 227
Piad Liang Shia 228
Tuna for Two 229
Tuna Lasagna 230

Autumn Fish "Slew"

(Stew)

"Good and filling!"

SERVES 6–8

1 (16 ounce) package frozen fish or shrimp
1 tablespoon oil
1 medium onion, sliced
1 (28 ounce) can tomatoes
2 medium potatoes, peeled and diced
1½ teaspoons salt
½ teaspoon basil
¼ teaspoon pepper
¼ teaspoon sugar (or more, to taste)
1 (10 ounce) package frozen mixed vegetables
½ cup 'whine' (white) wine (optional)

Remove fish from freezer and thaw. In four quart saucepan, over medium heat, saute onion in oil until tender. Add tomatoes, including liquid, potatoes, salt, basil, pepper, and sugar. Bring to a boil, reduce heat to low, cover, and simmer 10 minutes, stirring occasionally. Cut fish into 1" cubes and add fish, mixed vegetables, and wine, if desired. Heat to a boil, then reduce heat and simmer for 5 minutes or until fish is tender. Serve *hot!*

SHIRLEY SCHOLTEN

Shrimp Jambalaya

SERVES 4–6

1 pound fresh shrimp, peeled and deveined
¼ pound fresh mushrooms
4–6 strips bacon
½ cup chopped green pepper
1 clove garlic, chopped
2 tablespoons flour
1 (large) can stewed tomatoes
1 teaspoon curry powder
salt, to taste (about ½ teaspoon)
black pepper, to taste (about ¼ teaspoon)
pinch of red pepper

Fry bacon. Remove bacon and reserve for other uses. In bacon drippings, saute onion, green pepper, and garlic until translucent. Add shrimp. When vegetables are done, stir in flour, mixing well. Add stewed tomatoes, curry powder, salt, and pepper. Heat to boiling. Serve over fluffy rice.

WESLEY MICHAELSON & KARIN GRANBERG-MICHAELSON

Christmas Eve

On Christmas Eve we have a smorgasbord—(not coordinated as a menu)—of all the favorite foods of the family. For example, we end up with: Herring in cream sauce, fried shrimp, deviled eggs, hard salami chunks with cheese, potato chips with special dips, etc. We eat it in the family room, some sitting on the floor, etc. Then we open one special gift, usually a small inexpensive item. After this we attend our church's Christmas Eve service. ♥

TOM & ELEANOR MCCONISKEY

Broiled Gulf Scallops

"Our family has almost as much fun gathering these superb sea creatures, cleaning them and preparing them for the freezer as we do eating them—but not quite!"

scallops
melted butter or margarine
salt
pepper
lemon juice

Preheat broiler. Spread scallops on shallow baking pan. Pour melted butter or margarine over scallops (easy on this, not too much). Season with salt and pepper. Sprinkle with lemon juice. Broil about 10 minutes, shaking pan occasionally to brown evenly. Serve on toast wedges with lemon butter, or plain, with a sprig of fresh parsley. Decorate plate with thin slices of Florida Navel or Temple oranges.

Velma Seawell Daniels

Crab Meat Joni

1 pint half & half
1 pound pimento cheese
½ butter
1 pound broad noodles (I prefer less noodles,
    about ¾ of the package)
½ pound fresh mushrooms (optional)
1 pound crab meat
1 small jar chopped pimento

In a double boiler melt butter and cheese in half & half. Cook noodles according to package instructions. Saute mushrooms, if desired. Drain noodles; when done, arrange in a large dish, or 2 smaller baking dishes. Spread crab meat over noodles. Add pimento and mushrooms to sauce, and pour over noodles and crab. Bake at 350F until bubbly and slightly brown on top (approximately 35 minutes).

JONI EARECKSON TADA

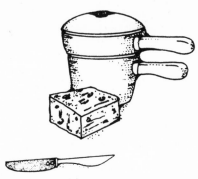

Crab Meat Joni

◄ For me, cooking is a lot of fun—even though my hands can't manage a skillet, spoons or mixing bowls. But the fun doubles when I can use my own recipes while borrowing other people's hands. Then the kitchen becomes more than just a place to work!

Because of my disability, however, everything becomes a bit more streamlined—recipes included. So I offer this simple but delicious seafood dish from Maryland recipe books.

Any native of Maryland loves to eat crab, and this dish is a real East Coast favorite. Oh, as a Marylander, I have one more suggestion—please don't use any old crab meat. West Coast Dungeness crabs taste nothing like the Chesapeake Bay Blue Fin crabs back East. So, when you shop for crab meat, ask for Blue Crab Back Fin meat— that's the best! ♥

JONI EARECKSON TADA

Piad Liang Shia

(Elegant Shrimp)

½ cup sliced almonds
about 1 tablespoon butter
2 pounds small shrimp, shelled and deveined
1 tablespoon minced fresh ginger
2 tablespoons sherry (optional)
1 tablespoon soy sauce
¼ cup peanut oil
2 cups shelled green peas

Lightly brown almond slices in butter. Wash and drain shrimp. Combine cornstarch, ginger, sherry, and soy sauce and marinate shrimp in mixture. Heat oil in wok or heavy skillet. Stir-fry peas briefly, until barely done, and remove to a warm place. Add shrimp to hot oil and stir-fry until they turn pink. Add to peas and serve with rice.

ETHEL RENWICK

Tuna for Two

"A quick, thrifty high protein main dish. Add a fruit salad and bread for a complete meal."

1 (9 ounce) package frozen green beans, cooked
1 (6½ ounce) can tuna, drained
3–4 ounces melting cheese (Cheddar is good)

Optional:

seasoning salt
sesame seeds
buttered bread crumbs
grated Parmesan cheese

Mix cooked green beans, tuna, and cheese together and heat until cheese melts. Season lightly with seasoning salt, if desired. Sprinkle with sesame seeds, buttered bread crumbs, and/or Parmesan cheese, if desired.

SHARON & JAMES ENGEL

King Crab and Artichokes

We often have good family times around meals, but it's difficult to isolate the factors that make the times particularly rewarding. There are two types of foods that come to mind, however, that have offered us good times on many occasions and that are very simple to fix. I usually reserve them for mother-son occasions when Dad is away, since Randy doesn't appreciate these particular delicacies—king crab and artichokes—though not at the same time. The king crab is easy to fix by simply boiling it in water with a little salt and vinegar for 20 minutes or so. After it's cooked we take it piece by piece from a common pile and dig the meat out of the shells and dip it in melted butter. Our mutual excitement

Tuna Lasagna

SERVES 8

½ (16 ounce) package lasagna noodles
2 (10 ounce) packages peas or frozen mixed
    vegetables
2 (10½ ounce) cans condensed cream of
    mushroom soup
½ soup can of milk (about ⅔ cup)
2 (6½ or 7 ounce) cans tuna
1 (16 ounce) package sliced American cheese

Cook lasagna noodles according to package instructions. While noodles cook, in a separate saucepan mix mushroom soup and milk. Heat to bubbling, add peas or frozen vegetables, and reheat to bubbling. Gently fold in tuna.

In a greased 9"x13" baking dish arrange about ⅓ of the noodles lengthwise, spread with ⅓ of tuna-vegetable mixture and ⅓ of the cheese slices. Repeat layers twice. Bake 30 minutes at 350F. Let stand 10–15 minutes before serving.

LOUISE DRUART

about pulling out a big piece of meat intact and the comments about the delicious taste make for a fun meal, and no other side dishes seem necessary.

Artichoke time is usually midafternoon or evening. I try to buy a nice plump artichoke, avoiding the ones that have dry or brown leaves. After cutting off the stem, I place the artichoke in about a half inch of boiling water and simmer it for 20 minutes or so. At the same time I melt butter and add a little lemon juice. It makes for a great social time, just taking turns pulling off the leaves one at a time and dipping them in the butter, and then scraping the pulp from the leaves with our teeth. ♥

RUTH TUCKER

VEGETABLES AND SIDE DISHES

Consommé Rice 233
Rice Pilaf 233
Wild Rice-Broccoli 234
Oven French Fries 234
Restuffed Potatoes 235
Potato Puff 236
Parmesan Potatoes 237
Sour Cream Potatoes I 238
Sour Cream Potatoes II 238
Sour Cream Potatoes III 238
Old-Fashioned Potato Pancakes 240
Squash and Apple Bake 240
Dutch Fried Cabbage 241
Stir-Fry Cabbage and Zucchini 241
Zucchini San Louie 242
Batter for Deep Fried Onion Rings or
    Zucchini 242
Philip Yancey's Summer Squash
    Casserole 243
Donita's Zucchini Casserole 244
Nipponese Eggplant 245
Scalloped Tomatoes and Vegetables
    Italia 246
Stuffed Tomatoes á là Graham 247
Brussels Sprouts with Almonds 248
Debbie's Layered Broccoli Casserole 249
Shelley's Layered Broccoli Casserole 250
Italian Broccoli Casserole 251

Scalloped Spinach 251
Special Spinach 252
Three Bean Bake 252
Wilma's Easy Baked Beans 253
Corn Pudding I 254
Corn Pudding II 254

Consommé Rice

"This simple recipe is one my favorites. It goes especially well with beef or pork."

¼ cup butter
2 onions, thinly sliced
1 cup rice, uncooked
2 cans consommé

Melt butter in a heavy frying pan. Saute onions in butter until translucent. Add rice and stir until rice is coated with butter. Put in a 1½ quart casserole, add undiluted consommé. Cover and bake at 325F for 1½ hours.

CAROL HOLQUIST

Rice Pilaf

"An all-time favorite rice recipe that goes well with chicken or pork."

½ cup thin noodles
¼ cup butter
1 cup long grain rice, uncooked
3 cups boiling water
3–4 tablespoons chicken bouillon crystals

Brown noodles in melted butter until golden. Add rice and heat until rice turns whiter (about 3–4 minutes). Put rice and noodles into boiling water mixed with bouillon. Turn heat to very low, cover, and cook for 35–40 minutes.

D. G. KEHL

Wild Rice-Broccoli

1 (5 ounce or 6¼ ounce) box Uncle Ben's
    Wild Rice, cooked
2 packages frozen chopped broccoli, cooked
    and drained
1 can condensed cream of chicken soup
1 (8 ounce) jar Cheese Whiz or 1 cup grated
    longhorn cheese

Fold rice, broccoli, and soup concentrate together. Spread Cheese Whiz or cheese on top. Place in a greased casserole. Bake at 350F until bubbly.

CHARLIE & MARTHA SHEDD

Oven French Fries

3 scrubbed potatoes
1 tablespoon oil
½ teaspoon salt or Vege-sal

Cut potatoes into strips about ⅓"x3". Toss in a bowl with oil, to coat each strip. Sprinkle evenly with salt. Place on oiled cookie sheet, or line cookie sheet with aluminum foil, then oil. Bake at 375F, turning strips to brown evenly, until done.

PHYLLIS HURLEY

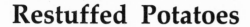

Restuffed Potatoes

8 large baking potatoes
½ cup butter
2–4 cups sour cream
¾ pound bacon, fried and crumbled
¼ pound Cheddar cheese, grated
4 green onions, including tops, chopped
salt, to taste
pepper, to taste
paprika

Scrub potatoes and bake at 375F until done, about 60 minutes. Melt butter in a skillet. Cut potatoes in half lengthwise and spoon pulp into skillet. Mash potatoes and mix with butter, using a fork. Add enough sour cream to make a moist, but not soupy, mixture. Add bacon, cheese, onions, and salt and pepper to taste. Take a heaping tablespoon of mixture and give to daughter or husband to taste. If seasonings are approved, scoop mixture back into potato shells. Sprinkle with paprika. Bake on a cookie sheet at 350F for 45 minutes or until heated through. Can be wrapped securely and frozen before baking. Thaw, then bake.

JOANNE BOER

Mashing Potatoes

It's a shame to throw out the nutritious water from cooked potatoes, only to add milk and mash 'em up. I leave some of the potato water in the bottom of the pan and add nonfat dry milk to it. This way more vitamins and minerals are retained. ♥

JUDY & BILL VRIESEMA

Potato Puff

A good use for leftover or "planned over" mashed potatoes.

2 eggs
2 cups mashed potatoes
¼ cup milk (approximately)

Optional ingredients:

bacon bits or leftover cooked bacon, crumbled
cooked ham, chopped
chives or green onions, chopped
grated cheese
paprika

Beat eggs in a mixing bowl with an electric mixer. Add mashed potatoes and beat thoroughly. Add enough milk to make a light and fluffy, not soupy, mixture. Add any optional ingredients desired. Place in a buttered baking dish and sprinkle top with paprika. Bake at 325F–350F for 30–45 minutes or until lightly browned on top.

Melba Petersen

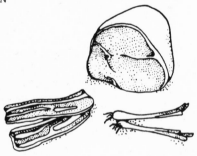

Parmesan Potatoes

SERVES 6

½ cup butter
6 large potatoes
¼ cup grated Parmesan cheese
¼ cup flour
¾ teaspoon salt
⅛ teaspoon pepper

Turn on oven to 375F. Melt butter in a large, shallow baking pan set in the oven while you peel and quarter the potatoes lengthwise. (Check the butter, don't let it burn.) Moisten potato slices with water, and shake a few at a time in a plastic bag with mixture of Parmesan, flour, salt, and pepper. Arrange in baking pan, turning over slices to coat with melted butter. Bake for 30 minutes, turn slices over, bake for 30 minutes more.

NAOMI & JIM RUARK

Mashing Potatoes

When making mashed potatoes, add about 2 tablespoons milk to the water as they boil. This preserves that snowy white color, especially if they have to "sit" in the boiling water while you work on something else. ♥

MARTIN & SHERRY SINGER

Sour Cream Potatoes I

A prepare-ahead recipe. "A favorite when entertaining. Thanks to my sister Sue for this one."

1 (2 pound) bag frozen hash browned
   potatoes
8 ounces grated Cheddar cheese
1 pint sour cream
2 cans condensed cream of potato soup
½ cup chopped onions
salt, to taste (lightly though, there's salt in
   the soup)
pepper, to taste
grated Parmesan cheese
paprika

In a mixing bowl, break up hash browns and mix with Cheddar cheese, sour cream, potato soup, onions, salt, and pepper. Cover and refrigerate overnight. The following day place in a greased 9"x13" baking dish and sprinkle with Parmesan and paprika. Cover and refrigerate until ready to bake. Bake uncovered at 350F for 1½ hours.

Wilma Zondervan Teggelaar

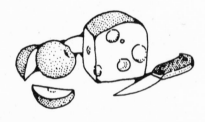

Steamed Potatoes

Are you familiar with the little folding steamer that is found in most hardware stores these days? It's used for steaming vegetables and warming buns. We enjoy potatoes steamed in it, whole. Simply scrub the potato, cut out bad spots, tuck two or even three into the little steamer, set in a pan above an inch or so of water, and turn the fire low when the water is boiling. Check occasionally so that the pan does not run dry. The cover must fit tightly. In about 40 minutes your potatoes are done—not with crusty peeling like baked potatoes, but very easily peeled, and retaining all the good ingredients. ♥

Marion Schoolland

Sour Cream Potatoes II

Can be partially or completely prepared ahead of time.

SERVES 8–10

6 large potatoes
1 large bunch green onions, chopped
1 pint sour cream
1 cup cream, half & half, or milk
salt, to taste
pepper, to taste
poppy seeds, as desired (optional)
¾ pound grated cheese (longhorn or mild
   Cheddar)

The day before, boil potatoes in their skins. When done, cool slightly, remove skins, and refrigerate. The next day, grate potatoes and mix with green onions, sour cream, cream, salt, pepper, poppy seeds, and half the grated cheese. Place in a greased casserole dish, top with remaining cheese, cover, and refrigerate, or bake uncovered at 350F for 60 minutes.

KAY STROM

Sour Cream Potatoes III

"Can be done ahead of time and refrigerated until time to go into the oven. Also great when reheated."

7–8 medium potatoes
½ cup butter or margarine
8 ounces sour cream
2 tablespoons minced green onion
Velveeta cheese, sliced

Peel potatoes, boil until soft. Drain and mash with butter and sour cream. Add onions and beat until fluffy. Put into a casserole dish and add slices of cheese to cover top. Bake at 350F for 20–25 minutes.

DOUG AND SHARON KUIPERS

Old-Fashioned Potato Pancakes

2 cups grated potato
2 eggs
1 tablespoon flour
½ teaspoon salt
a few grains of pepper
butter

If preparing for breakfast, potatoes can be peeled and kept in cold water overnight, drained and grated in the morning. Squeeze excess liquid from grated potatoes, beat eggs and mix all ingredients. Form into thin cakes, brown in skillet in butter.

PAT BERGEN

Squash and Apple Bake

2 pounds butternut or buttercup squash
½ cup brown sugar
¼ cup butter or margarine, melted
1 tablespoon flour
1 teaspoon salt
½ teaspoon mace or cinnamon
2 baking apples, cored and cut into ½" slices

Cut each squash in half. Remove seeds, fibers, and peel. Cut into ½" slices. Arrange squash in ungreased 11½"x7½" baking dish. Arrange apple slices on top of squash. Mix brown sugar, melted butter, salt, and mace or cinnamon and sprinkle over apples and squash. Cover with foil and bake at 350F for 50–60 minutes, or until squash is tender.

SUE MACDONALD

Old-Fashioned Potato Pancakes

◄⋘ *Serve with sausage and homemade applesauce with cinnamon.*

During the Depression my Grandmom invited neighbors on Saturday evenings for the above supper. The pancakes and applesauce were made from potatoes and apples from the garden and eggs from the hen house. She'd make them by huge dishpansful and sometimes spend three or four hours frying as people came in the door. ♥

PAT BERGEN

Dutch Fried Cabbage

3 tablespoons margarine, butter, or lard
medium sized head of cabbage, coarsely
    chopped
1 or 2 cooking apples, cored and chopped
¾ cup raisins, rinsed in hot water and
    drained
2 tablespoons white vinegar
3 tablespoons sugar

In a large frying pan melt margarine, butter, or lard. Fry chopped cabbage in fat over medium heat, stirring frequently. When cabbage is translucent add chopped apples. Continue to fry until cabbage is golden brown. Add raisins, vinegar, and sugar. Cover pan and simmer 5–10 minutes or until raisins are puffed, stirring occasionally.

HELEN ENNS

Stir-Fry Cabbage and Zucchini

Quick & Easy

¼ cup oil
1 large clove garlic, sliced
6 cups (packed) sliced cabbage
2 medium zucchini (about 1 pound), thinly
    sliced
1¼ teaspoons salt
1 teaspoon sugar

In a 5 quart Dutch oven or large skillet, saute garlic in oil until lightly browned. Discard garlic. Add cabbage and zucchini, stir-frying until they are well coated with oil. Add salt and sugar, reduce heat to medium-high. Continue stir-frying 7–8 minutes until vegetables are crisp-tender.

DEBBIE BARR

Zucchini San Louie

1–2 tablespoons olive oil
1 clove garlic, crushed
3–6 small zucchini
salt, to taste (lightly)
½ fresh lemon or lime

In a small or medium sized skillet saute garlic in olive oil for about 2 minutes. Slice zucchini into skillet and saute, uncovered, over medium-high heat for 3–4 minutes, stirring frequently. Salt lightly, reduce heat to low, cover, and steam until zucchini is crisp-tender. Remove garlic. Squeeze several drops of lemon juice over zucchini. Cover for 2 minutes. Serve.

PATRICIA GUNDRY

Batter for Deep-Fried Onion Rings or Zucchini

1 egg, slightly beaten
1 cup milk (may need to add a little more)
3 tablespoons oil
1 cup plus 2 tablespoons flour
½ teaspoon salt
onions, sliced and separated into rings, or
    zucchini cut into strips or rounds for
    frying
additional flour

Mix first 5 ingredients and beat until smooth. Dip onion rings or zucchini pieces in additional flour and then in batter. Fry, a few at a time, in deep hot oil, until lightly browned. Drain on paper towels.

LAURIE GOTT

Zucchini San Louie

◄◄ *On our way back from a visit to relatives in southern Missouri, we stopped for the evening in Saint Louis. We had waited too long to eat our evening meal and everyone was very hungry, but we could not find any place to eat we could all agree on. When we did agree, we discovered the wait would be a long one, too long for us. Back in the car, we decided to go downtown to look for restaurants. None seemed to be open. One son suggested a hotel dining room. So we ended up at the Marriott, where we had just the food we needed to rescue us from progressive indecision and starvation.*

The meal, in peaceful, elegant surroundings, with a gracious and friendly waiter, made a lasting impression. Since I particularly liked the sauteed zucchini, I attempted to duplicate the flavors and technique I guessed were involved. The resulting recipe remains a favorite.

We also formulated a valuable new traveling principle: stop before you're hungry, and if at all possible, plan ahead where you will eat.

PATRICIA GUNDRY

Philip Yancey's Summer Squash Casserole

SERVES 6

2 pounds summer squash, sliced (yellow
   squash, zucchini, etc.)
¼ cup chopped onion
1 can condensed cream of chicken soup
1 cup sour cream
1 cup shredded carrots
1 (8 ounce) package stuffing mix
½ cup melted butter

In saucepan, cook sliced squash and chopped
onion in salted water for 5 minutes, then drain.
Combine soup and sour cream, stir in shredded
carrots. Fold in drained squash and onion. Combine stuffing mix and butter, then spread half of
stuffing mixture in bottom of a 12" baking dish.
Spoon vegetable mixture on top and sprinkle
remaining stuffing over vegetables. Bake at 350F
for 25–30 minutes.

PHILIP YANCEY

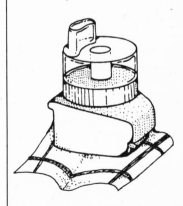

Donita's Zucchini Casserole

4 medium zucchini, sliced ½" thick
½ cup chopped onion
1 (4 ounce) can green chili peppers, diced
1½ cups grated Cheddar cheese
1 cup grated Monterey Jack cheese

Crust:

1 cup biscuit mix
2 eggs, beaten
½ cup milk
½ cup grated Cheddar cheese
sesame seeds

Alternate layers of vegetables and cheese in a buttered casserole dish. Mix together crust ingredients. Either drop by spoonfuls on top of mixture in casserole, or roll out between sheets of plastic wrap or wax paper and place over mixture, making vent holes for steam, or cut into rounds and arrange on top. Sprinkle with sesame seeds and bake at 350F approximately 30 minutes, or until golden brown.

DONITA DYER

Nipponese Eggplant

SERVES 3–4

2 tablespoons margarine or butter
3 medium-size onions, thinly sliced
1 small eggplant
about ¼ cup soy sauce
about ¼ cup water
2–3 tablespoons light brown sugar

In a skillet fry onions in margarine while you peel eggplant and cut it into ½"–¾" cubes. Add to onions. Add soy sauce, water, and brown sugar. (Since the vegetables vary in size and tastes differ, add lesser amounts of soy sauce, water, and brown sugar, stir, and taste the liquid; adjust amounts to your taste.) Cover and simmer 20 minutes or longer.

ANNE & R. LAIRD HARRIS

Nipponese Eggplant

I have for a long time been a collector of recipes and the 14 years I spent in Japan as a missionary with what is now the Mission to the World of the Presbyterian Church in America added a number of goodies to my collection. I am enclosing one that my husband likes, because he likes good things to eat—especially if they are a little sweet. I think he likes it too because of its "origin." It was taught to me by my first Japanese language teacher who is also one of my oldest friends in Tokyo, Miss Shiga (Lydia) Tanabe.

Miss Tanabe, a pharmacist by original profession, graduated from the Tokyo Christian Theological Seminary, where I was teaching, then went to the U.S.A. for further study and received Master's degrees from both Faith Theological Seminary in Philadelphia and Covenant Theological Seminary in St. Louis, where she worked under Laird's direction. While in St.

Scalloped Tomatoes and Vegetables Italia

1 medium onion, chopped
2 or 3 stalks celery, chopped
2 tablespoons olive, or other, oil
1 (16 ounce) can tomatoes
1 (1 pound 4 ounce) bag frozen Italian mixed
　vegetables
1½ teaspoons basil
2 tablespoons sugar
salt to taste
pepper to taste
1 tablespoon cornstarch
about ¼ cup water
½–1 cup bread cut in cubes
garlic salt
Parmesan cheese

Saute onion and celery in oil until onion is translucent. Add tomatoes, vegetables, basil, sugar, and salt and pepper to taste. Simmer 5–10 minutes. Mix cornstarch with water, add to mixture, and stir until thickened. Pour into a buttered 2 quart casserole. top with bread cubes, sprinkle lightly with garlic salt, sprinkle with Parmesan as desired. Bake at 350F until lightly browned on top, about 30 minutes.

ANNE & DONALD GRAY

BASIL

Louis she became seriously ill, and when hope of her recovery was given up, she was sent back to Japan to die among her people. But God had other plans for her. After months of treatment, some surgery and years of special diet, she completely recovered and has for almost 30 years been a valued member of the faculty of T.C.T.S. She has done considerable writing in her own language, and since she is equally at home with Greek and Hebrew, was an important member of the Translation Committee of the modern language edition of the Japanese Bible that was published almost 10 years before the NIV but was worked on in very much the same way by a smaller committee, committed to the truthfulness of the Scripture.

In the summer of 1949 Miss Tanabe and several other friends and I spent several weeks at Gotemba near the foot of Mt. Fuji where she taught us Japanese language and culture

Stuffed Tomatoes á là Graham

"My Dad likes to fix these when our family gets together."

SERVES 6

6 tomatoes, of uniform size
1 cup (rounded) crushed seasoned croutons
2 tablespoons grated Parmesan cheese
2 tablespoons grated American cheese
¼ cup melted butter
salt
pepper
fresh parsley, minced or chopped

Cut out center of tomatoes to provide a place for the stuffing. Lightly sprinkle salt and pepper in the holes. Mix crushed croutons, Parmesan, and American cheese and melted butter. Stuff the tomatoes. Sprinkle parsley on top. Bake in a glass baking dish at 350F for 20 minutes or cook over charcoal until done.

JAMES & MARILYN GRAHAM

and where we shared in Christian fellowship. One night she prepared for us what I call "Nipponese Eggplant." ♥

ANNE & R. LAIRD HARRIS

Brussels Sprouts with Almonds

SERVES 8–10

1 cup water
1 (10¾ ounce) can condensed chicken broth
¼ teaspoon salt
⅛ teaspoon pepper
4 (10 ounce) packages Brussels sprouts
½ cup butter or margarine
½ cup sliced blanched almonds

Combine water, broth, salt, and pepper in a large skillet or Dutch oven. Bring to a boil. Add sprouts, cover, and simmer until just tender. Drain well and keep warm. Melt butter or margarine in a small skillet over medium heat. Add almonds. Cook until golden, stirring constantly. Toss almonds with sprouts and serve immediately.

WILMA ZONDERVAN TEGGELAAR

Debbie's Layered Broccoli Casserole

2 (10 ounce) packages chopped broccoli,
  cooked and drained
1 cup crushed cheese crackers

Sauce:

1 cup salad dressing
1 tablespoon lemon juice
1 tablespoon grated onion
1 can condensed cream of mushroom soup
1 egg, beaten
½ cup grated Cheddar cheese (up to 1 cup is
  okay if you're real cheese fans)
pepper, to taste

Combine sauce ingredients. In a greased baking dish, layer half of each: broccoli, crackers, and sauce, in that order. Repeat layers, in order, with other half. Top with crackers. Bake at 400F for 20 minutes.

Debbie Barr

Freezing Tomatoes the Easy Way

Wash and core fully ripe tomatoes. Place them in plastic freezer bags (quart to gallon size) and store in your freezer.

When you want to use the tomatoes, simply hold them under hot water from the kitchen faucet until you can slip the skins off, then add them to the cooking pot.

Tomatoes frozen in this manner are suitable for any cooked dish in which they do not need to retain their shape. They can't be used for salads because freezing breaks the cell walls so they collapse when thawed. ♥

Patricia Gundry

Shelley's Layered Broccoli Casserole

Layers 1 and 3:

2 (10 ounce) packages frozen broccoli spears, undercooked and drained

Layers 2 and 4:

1 can condensed cream of mushroom soup
½ cup grated sharp Cheddar cheese
2 tablespoons lemon juice

Layer 5:

2 ounces chopped pimento
½ cup crushed Cheese Nip crackers
⅓ cup slivered almonds

In a greased casserole dish layer half of broccoli, half of soup mixed with cheese and lemon juice; repeat with other half. Top with ingredients in layer 5. Bake at 350F for 45–60 minutes.

SHELLEY SMITH

While we were at Gorei all of our children became old enough to learn to pray aloud. We encouraged this by taking turns saying "grace" at meal times. Because of our obvious dependence on our vegetable garden, each of them would thank the Lord for "the vegetables in the garden." One day I playfully asked, "What about the food on the table?" They quickly added this phrase to their prayer, and to this day, though they are grown and married, they always add, "Thank you, Lord, for the food on the table." Thanks for the vegetables in the garden has been long forgotten. ♥

MERILYN & MILTON FISHER

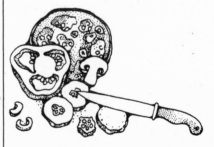

Italian Broccoli Casserole

SERVES 6

2 (10 ounce) packages frozen chopped broccoli
2 eggs, well beaten
1 can Cheddar cheese soup
1 (8 ounce) can stewed tomatoes
3 tablespoons grated Parmesan cheese
½ teaspoon oregano

Cook broccoli according to package directions, drain thoroughly. Turn broccoli into a shallow 2 quart baking dish. Pour eggs over broccoli, spoon soup over eggs. Top with tomatoes; sprinkle cheese and oregano over all. Bake at 350F for 30 minutes.

REA & ALAN JOHNSON

Scalloped Spinach

SERVES 4

1 (10 ounce) package frozen chopped spinach,
    cooked and drained
2 tablespoons finely chopped onion
2 eggs, beaten
½ cup milk
½ cup grated sharp Cheddar cheese
salt, to taste
pepper, to taste
½ cup soft buttered bread crumbs

Combine all ingredients except bread crumbs. Turn into loaf pan or 1½ quart casserole. Top with bread crumbs. Bake at 350F for about 20 minutes or until knife inserted in center comes out clean.

HELEN ENNS

Special Spinach

2 (10 ounce) packages frozen spinach
1 (8 ounce) package cream cheese, softened
3 eggs, well beaten
¼ teaspoon salt
pepper, to taste
¼ cup chopped onion (optional)
1 (4 ounce) package grated Cheddar cheese
crushed croutons

Cook spinach and drain well. Mix cream cheese with beaten eggs, salt, pepper, cheese, and onion. Add spinach and pour into a greased 9"x13" baking pan. Sprinkle with crushed croutons. Bake at 350F for 25–30 minutes.

ARDETH & RON BOSMAN

Three Bean Bake

1 (16 ounce) can pork and beans
1 (15 ounce) can kidney beans
1 (16 ounce) can baby lima beans
1 medium onion, chopped
2 tablespoons bacon drippings or shortening
1 cup brown sugar
1 cup catsup
2 tablespoons prepared mustard
2 tablespoons vinegar

Drain and rinse kidney and lima beans, combine in a baking dish with pork and beans. In a skillet saute onion in bacon drippings until translucent, add brown sugar, catsup, mustard, and vinegar. Bring to a boil and pour over beans. Bake, uncovered, at 350F about 60 minutes.

MRS. DERRALL KINARD

Corn on the Cob

To quickly butter corn on the cob wrap a thickly buttered slice of bread around the cooked ear of corn. Pull the ear of corn through the buttered bread and it is all buttered. ♥

MARY ANN HOWARD

Wilma's Easy Baked Beans

1 large (48 ounce) can Great Northern white
    beans
1 (14 ounce) bottle catsup
1 rounded tablespoon prepared mustard
¾ cup brown sugar
1 medium onion, finely chopped
¼ cup vinegar
¼ teaspoon dill weed
¼ teaspoon basil
2 tablespoons Worcestershire sauce
½ pound bacon, diced and partially fried, or
    1 pound chop suey meat, cut in small
    pieces and partially fried
a few slices of bacon for top (optional)

Mix ingredients and place in a greased 2½ quart casserole. Top with a few slices of bacon, if desired. Bake at 300F for 3–5 hours.

Wilma Zondervan Teggelaar

Corn Pudding I

1 (16 ounce) can whole kernel corn, drained (2 cups)
¼–½ cup sugar
2 tablespoons flour
1 teaspoon salt
1 or 2 eggs
½ cup milk
2 tablespoons butter

Beat together corn, sugar, flour, salt, and egg(s). Stir in milk. Pour into a well-greased baking dish and dot top with butter. Bake at 400F for 30 minutes or at 350F for 50 minutes.

MARILYN & MARVIN MAYERS

Corn Pudding II

SERVES 10–12

1 (16 ounce) can cream style corn
1 (16 ounce) can whole kernel corn, undrained
8 ounces sour cream
⅓ cup sugar
½ cup oil
2 eggs, slightly beaten
1 (8½ ounce) package corn muffin mix

Combine corn, sour cream, sugar, oil, and eggs. Stir in corn muffin mix. Bake in a greased 9"x12" baking dish at 350F for 40–50 minutes.

BETTY & JAMES BUICK

Corn Pudding I

As our own girls got older in junior-high and high school, Marv found it convenient to have business breakfasts—outside the home—and we found that if there were too many of these, that communication between the two of us began to break down. That had become a time for us to "touch base" for the day— and keep communication open and ongoing.

On the other hand, the evening meal was one that we almost always had as a family— and this did the same thing for parents and children—keeping in touch with where they were— and where we were too—a two-way street. ♥

MARILYN A. MAYERS

COOKIES

Best Brownies Ever 257
Gladis's Hong Kong Brownies 258
Berry Favorite Brownies 259
Butterscotch Brownies 260
Jan's Chocolate-Caramel Brownies 261
Oatmeal Caramelites 262
Pear Bars 263
Dream Bars 264
Sunny Lemon Bars 265
Tangy Lemon Bars 266
Chocolate Shortbread 267
Peanut Butter Bars 268
Peanut Butter Rice Krispie Bars 269
Hit of the Party Cookie Bars 270
Seven Layer Bars 271
Patchwork Quilties 272
Gretchen's Oatmeal Molasses Cookies 273
Buttercup Cookies 274
Heath Bar Sugar Cookies 274
Butterscotch Cookies 275
Butter Pecan Cookies 275
Grandma Dee's Imperial Cookies 276
Snowball Cookies 277
Sonja Henie Cookies 278
Rice Krispie Cookies 278
Peanut Butter Chocolate Chip Cookies 279
Easy Koulourakia 280
Hoot Owl Cookies 281
Oatmeal Date Cookies 282
Flemish Almond Cookies 283
Cookie Day Cookies 284
My Grandmother's Tea Cakes 285

Chocolate Heart Cookies 286
Lebkuchen 287
Gingerbread People 288
Non Plus Ultra 289
Great Aunt Margaret's Cereal Cookies 290
Generic Animal Crackers 290
Soft Chocolate Chip Cookies 291
Sour Cream Cocoa Cookies 292
Double Chocolate Cookies 293
Fudge Drop Cookies 294
Pineapple Drop Cookies 294
Julie's Octopus Cookies 295
No-Bake Onos 295
Everybody's No-Bake Cookies 296

Best Brownies Ever

Great frosting for other things, too.

"These are very rich—good served warm with ice cream."

2 cups sugar
½ cup cocoa
1 cup margarine, melted (or half margarine and half shortening)
4 eggs
2 teaspoons vanilla
1½ cups flour
½–1 teaspoon salt (less if all margarine is used)

Frosting:

6 tablespoons margarine, melted
2 tablespoons milk
1 heaping tablespoon cocoa
2 cups confectioner's sugar
½ teaspoon vanilla

Mix together sugar, cocoa, and melted margarine. Add eggs and vanilla and beat well. Sift together flour and salt and stir in. Bake in a well greased 10"x15" pan at 375F for 18–20 minutes. Do not overbake!!! Make frosting while brownies are baking. Mix melted margarine, milk, cocoa, confectioner's sugar, and vanilla, beating until smooth. Let brownies cool about 3 minutes, then spread with frosting.

LAURIE GOTT

Gladis's Hong Kong Brownies

"These deep, dark, and delicious treats have been standard cheer-up, warm-up, and welcome food in our house since 1966, when I discovered them at a Hong Kong coffee break in language school."

½ cup butter or margarine
1 cup sugar
2 eggs, slightly beaten
1½ teaspoons vanilla
½ teaspoon salt
¼ cup cocoa
¾ cup flour
1 cup coarsely broken walnuts

Frosting:

½ box confectioner's sugar
1 tablespoon butter, softened
1½ teaspoons vanilla
dash of salt
2 rounded tablespoons cocoa
undiluted evaporated milk, enough to moisten
    to right consistency
walnuts, shaved or finely chopped, to sprinkle
    on top

Cream butter and sugar, beat in eggs, salt, and vanilla. Mix together dry ingredients and stir into batter until just moistened. Add nuts and bake in a greased 8"x8" pan at 350F for 25 minutes or until just done (when a toothpick inserted in the center comes out clean). While brownies are baking, prepare frosting: Mix butter into confectioner's sugar, add vanilla, salt, and enough evaporated milk to make a *stiff* mixture. Mix thoroughly, beating with a spoon until smooth. Gradually add more evaporated milk, beating well, until frosting

On down the street, past the boat-children's school, a row of stalls stretched long and narrow under a single sun-baked roof. Wong Tai squatted on the pavement in a flowered sam-fu, her round cheery face squinted against the smoke of the wood fire she was poking. Red flames rose lazily in the heat and licked the brown ceramic pot of water. . . .

"Wai, Wong Tai!" I called.
Her face uncrinkled and flashed a smile.
"Ah, Ding Tai, Tisso," she called, . . . "Tell me, where do you like it best, in Mei Gwok, the Beautiful Country or here? Which people are best, Americans or Chinese?"
"Ah, Wong Tai, what can I say? You know not all the good people in the world could possible be Chinese!"
"Ah yah, Ding Tai." She smiled. "Come an have a cup of

➤

is of desired consistency. Spread on hot brownies. Sprinkle with shaved or finely chopped walnuts. Cut in 16 squares. Serve hot. These can be frozen (if there are any left).

GLADIS DEPREE

Berry Favorite Brownies

The small amount of flour is accurate. The recipe works—and it's good.

2 squares unsweetened chocolate
1 cup sugar
½ cup butter or margarine
2 eggs, well beaten
1 teaspoon vanilla
½ cup flour
1 cup black walnuts (optional)
confectioner's sugar, to dust on top

Melt chocolate. Cream sugar and butter well, add eggs and stir well. Blend in chocolate, vanilla, and flour. Add nuts, if desired. Bake in a greased 8"x8"x2" pan at 325F for 35 minutes. Brownies will be moist and chewy. Do not overbake.

When cool, dust lightly with confectioner's sugar and cut into 2" squares.

If you wish to double the recipe, bake in two 8"x8"x2" pans rather than one large one.

JO BERRY

of tea with me."

We squatted on the pavement together, waiting for the water in the pot to boil. . . . The sun beat down mercilessly on the concrete, sending up corrugated heat waves and the fetid odor of the fish market.

"Wah!" I said. "How can you drink hot tea when the sun is already like a ball of fire?"

"Ah, tea is cool," she assured me. "Tea cools the body chemistry. If I drank ice water like you Siyan, I'd die of the heat!"

We looked at each other and laughed, content to be friends and to be different. But in the flash of Wong Tai's laughter something was transmitted, the feeling that on this street, one drank tea and accepted all the way of life that went with it. People drank tea; the rest were nonpeople.

I drank Wong Tai's tea. ♥

GLADIS LENORE DEPREE (from **Festival: An Experiment in Living***)*

Butterscotch Brownies

¼ cup butter
1 cup brown sugar
1 egg
1 teaspoon vanilla
½ cup flour
1 teaspoon baking powder
¼ teaspoon salt
½ cup chopped nuts

In a saucepan over low heat melt butter. Blend in brown sugar and then remove from heat. Cool. Beat in egg and vanilla. Combine flour, baking powder, and salt and stir into mixture. Stir in nuts. Bake in a well greased 8"x8" baking pan at 350F for 25–30 minutes. Do not overbake. Cut into bars while warm.

SHERRY & JERRY PARK

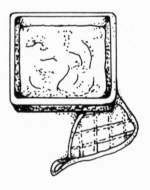

A Picnic Surprise

The day is gloomy. Even the windshield wipers cannot keep up with the rain. The mood inside the car is one of mystery. No one knows for sure where this ride will end—no one except me. The children know only that Daddy has a two o'clock class on the seventh floor of the Loyola Towers. What one does on Chicago's near North Side in the middle of a rainstorm remains part of the mystery. The plot thickens. The rendezvous with Daddy is set for four o'clock, south portico, Fourth Presbyterian Church, Michigan Avenue and Chestnut Street.

All week I'd built the scheme. The last day of summer vacation called for celebration. What better way than a surprise picnic by the lake? We'd have

Jan's Chocolate-Caramel Brownies

14 ounces caramels
¾ cup evaporated milk, or 1 (5 ounce) can
1 chocolate cake mix
⅔ cup margarine, melted
1 (6 ounce) package chocolate chips

In a double boiler, or in a carefully watched saucepan over *low* heat, stirring frequently (it burns very easily), melt the caramels in half of the milk. Keep warm.

Combine the cake mix, remaining milk, and melted margarine. Mix until cake mix is moistened. Spread half of mixture in a greased 9"x13" pan and bake at 350F for 10 minutes. Remove from oven. Pour melted caramel over baked cake mix. (Be careful to keep the caramel away from the sides of the pan. It sticks tenaciously if baked on.) Sprinkle chocolate chips over caramel. Flatten remaining cake mix dough, a spoonful at a time, using your fingers, and cover caramel and chocolate chips. Return to oven and bake twenty minutes longer.

Note: To double recipe use a 12 ounce can of evaporated milk, double other ingredients and bake in a 12"x18" jelly roll pan.

JAN ORTIZ

everybody's favorites: ham and cheese croissants, fresh blueberries with cream, chocolate chip pirouettes, and cider.

The day had begun with the sun but clouds had moved in just about the time I got my big wicker picnic basket down from the top shelf. By the time we were out the door the afternoon had become so gray I went back for candles. The children didn't see the candles. In fact, they didn't even see the basket. I smuggled it all into the trunk of the car while they searched for rain gear and umbrellas.

We create quite a sight as we splash down Michigan Avenue. Nicky holds the umbrella overhead while Jori and I carry the picnic basket, cider, and a bunch of white daisies. Now everyone knows, except Daddy.

We find the spot—my alternative in case of rain—a wide ledge under a Fourth Presbyterian Church gothic arch. We spread the blue-checked tablecloth, arrange the daisies, and light candles. While we

Oatmeal Caramelites

50 candy caramels (2 8½ ounce bags)
½ cup evaporated milk
2 cups flour
1 teaspoon soda
½ teaspoon salt
1½ cups brown sugar
2 cups quick oats
1 cup margarine, melted
1 (6 ounce) package chocolate chips
1 cup chopped nuts

Melt caramels in evaporated milk in a heavy saucepan or double boiler (they burn easily). Set aside to cool slightly. Sift flour, soda, and salt into a mixing bowl. Mix in brown sugar and oats. Add melted margarine and mix until crumbly. Press half of mixture in bottom of a greased 9"x13" baking pan. Bake at 350F for 10 minutes. Remove from oven and sprinkle with chocolate chips and nuts. Spread carefully with caramel mixture. Sprinkle remaining crumb mixture on top. Bake 15–20 minutes more. Chill 1–2 hours before cutting.

Sharon & Doug Kuipers

wait for Daddy we play a guessing game about people under the umbrellas that march down Michigan Avenue. Who is he? Where do you think he is going? What kind of house does she live in? Is she happy or sad? Maybe she's irritated because her feet are wet. But we are warm and dry under our arch.

As the church bells toll four o'clock, the goodies come out of the basket. Yes, Daddy certainly was surprised. We sat secure in our candlelit haven, while fifty feet away people moved along at a hurried pace. Everyone ate as though they had not eaten for days.

That memory will be with us for a long, long time. There is nothing quite like a mysterious surprise picnic. ♥

Ruth Senter

Pear Bars

½ cup margarine, softened
2 cups sugar
2 eggs
2½ cups flour
1½ teaspoons soda
1 teaspoon salt
1 teaspoon cinnamon
½ teaspoon nutmeg
2 cups chopped Bartlett pears
½ cup raisins
½ cup chopped nuts

Frosting:

3 ounces cream or evaporated milk
4 tablespoons margarine, softened
1 teaspoon vanilla
2½ cups confectioner's sugar

Cream margarine and sugar together. Add eggs. Sift together flour, soda, salt, cinnamon, and nutmeg. Add to sugar and egg mixture. Mix well. Add pears, raisins, and nuts. Spread in a greased 9"x13" pan. Bake at 350F for 45 minutes.

Prepare frosting by mixing margarine into confectioner's sugar, gradually add cream or evaporated milk, beating until smooth. Stir in vanilla. Spread over cooled contents of pan and cut into bars.

Judy & Joe Allison

Dream Bars

Part 1:

½ cup butter
½ cup brown sugar
½ teaspoon salt
1 cup flour

Part 2:

¾ cup brown sugar
1 teaspoon vanilla
2 eggs, beaten
2 tablespoons flour
½ teaspoon baking powder
⅛ teaspoon salt
1 cup coconut
½ cup chopped walnuts

Part 1: Mix butter, brown sugar, salt, and flour together until crumbly. Press into a lightly greased 9"x13" baking pan. Bake at 350F for 15–20 minutes.

Part 2: Thoroughly mix together brown sugar, vanilla, and beaten eggs. Stir or sift together flour, baking powder, and salt. Stir into sugar and egg mixture. Stir in coconut and nuts. Spread over baked part 1 ingredients and return to oven to bake 15–20 minutes longer. Cool before cutting into squares.

CLAZIENA & GERARD TERPSTRA

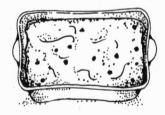

Sunny Lemon Bars

"It takes about 30 minutes, total, to make these."

1 package lemon cake mix
⅓ cup butter, softened
3 eggs
1 cup sugar
½ teaspoon baking powder
¼ teaspoon salt
¼ cup lemon juice
½ teaspoon lemon extract
confectioner's sugar

Mix together lemon cake mix, butter, and one of the eggs. Reserve 1 cup of mixture and set aside. Pat lightly into an ungreased 9"x13" baking pan. Bake at 350F for 10 minutes or until *lightly* browned.

Beat together remaining 2 eggs, sugar, baking powder, salt, lemon juice, and extract until light and foamy. Pour over hot crust. Sprinkle reserved crumb mixture on top and bake an additional 15 minutes, or until light brown. Sprinkle with confectioner's sugar and cut into bars.

Variation: Use orange cake mix, orange juice, and orange extract instead of lemon.

HARRIET & DERRALL KINARD

On the Value of Eating Out

Some of our best "food times" are "eating out" times. The children enjoy eating out so much that we try to go out once a week. (Mother enjoys it, too.) Some fast-food places give you a "dining room" atmosphere (such as Wendy's, Bojangles, Shoney's) and we try to go to those. The children feel grown-up and festive. We have had some very leisurely, philosophical, grown-up talks at those places. We take toys for our preschooler so he will be contented to stay for a while. We cut costs by going to the places that are offering "buy one, get one free," or by sharing drinks, ordering water, whatever! We have found this to be such a worthwhile family experience that we budget it in, and enjoy it! ♥

PHYLLIS & JAMES HURLEY

Tangy Lemon Bars

Very rich, with a strong lemon punch, these bars have a more subdued flavor the second day.

Crust:

1 cup margarine or butter
½ cup confectioner's sugar
2–2½ cups flour

Filling:

2 cups sugar
½ teaspoon baking powder
dash of salt
¼ cup flour
4 eggs
6 tablespoons lemon juice

additional confectioner's sugar to sprinkle on top

To prepare crust, mix margarine, confectioner's sugar, and flour together until crumbly. Press into a 9"x13" baking pan and bake at 350F for 10–15 minutes.

To prepare filling, stir together sugar, baking powder, salt, and flour. In a separate bowl beat together eggs and lemon juice. Stir into sugar mixture. Pour over hot crust and bake an additional 25 minutes. Sprinkle with confectioner's sugar and cut into bars while hot.

Laurie Gott
Latayne Scott

Chocolate Shortbread

British shortbread enhanced with chocolate and coconut.

½ **cup margarine or butter**
⅔ **cup sugar**
½ **teaspoon vanilla**
2 **heaping teaspoons cocoa**
1 **cup self-rising flour**
1 **cup coconut**
½ **cup chocolate chips**

Cream margarine and sugar together. Stir in vanilla and cocoa. Using your fingertips, work the flour in lightly. Gently mix in coconut. Pat into an 8"x8" baking pan and bake at 350F for about 25 minutes. Remove from oven and sprinkle chocolate chips over the top of shortbread. Return to oven for 2 minutes, until chocolate chips are spreadable. Spread melted chips over shortbread. Cut into squares while still warm. Cool thoroughly before removing from pan.

Mary & Donald Wiseman

Kay Kuzma, Ed.D., mother of three and associate professor of Loma Linda University School of Health in California, where she conducts parenting classes, encourages families to stimulate interesting conversations around the dinner table by using a talk-about-it bowl. In her book Working Mothers, *Kuzma advises, "During the day, the children can put objects, notes, newspaper clippings or articles into the bowl that they would like to talk about during dinner."*

She then encourages parents to be good listeners by looking at the child who is speaking and not correcting, contradicting, or interrupting. Each child should have a chance to participate in mealtime conversation—which means parents should avoid the temptation to engage in adult-only conversation. ♥

Carol Kuykendall
(Excerpted from an article that appeared in the February, 1983 issue of Parents Magazine, *p. 62.)*

Peanut Butter Bars

Makes 1½ to 2 dozen bars

1½ cups brown sugar
⅔ cup chunky peanut butter
½ cup shortening
2 eggs
1 teaspoon vanilla
1½ cups flour
1½ teaspoons baking powder
½ teaspoon salt
¼ cup milk

Frosting (optional):

⅓ cup chunky peanut butter
2 tablespoons butter or margarine, softened
2 cups sifted confectioner's sugar
light cream or half & half

Cream together brown sugar, peanut butter, and shortening. Add eggs and vanilla; beat well. Stir together flour, baking powder, and salt. Add to the creamed mixture alternately with milk, beating well. Spread in a greased 9"x13" baking pan. Bake at 350F for about 30 minutes. (Center should still be slightly soft when done.) Cool.

To prepare frosting, cream together peanut butter and margarine. Slowly beat in confectioner's sugar and enough cream or milk to make of spreading consistency. Spread frosting over cooled cookie mixture. Cut into diamond-shaped bars.

JEAN SHAFER

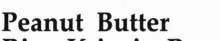

Peanut Butter Rice Krispie Bars

6 cups Rice Krispies
1 cup peanut butter
1 cup light corn syrup
⅔ cup sugar
1 (6 ounce) package butterscotch chips
1 (6 ounce) package chocolate chips

In a large saucepan bring peanut butter, corn syrup, and granulated sugar to a boil. Remove from heat and add Rice Krispies, mixing well. Spread in a buttered 9"x13" baking pan.

Melt butterscotch chips and chocolate chips together. Spread on top of peanut butter-Rice Krispies mixture. Refrigerate until the topping sets. Cut into bars.

MARK COSGROVE

Cookie Parties

A food tradition has developed in our family that sprang from my attempt to make up for being cross with my sons. Several years ago, after losing my temper with my two preschool boys, I took cookies and milk to their bedroom and awoke them. We sat in the dark room, eating cookies and talking about fun things. We enjoyed the time so much that from then on, several times a month, my wife and I would wake them up for a cookie party. Now we have three preschool boys and still sit with cookies and flashlights and talk about dreams, God, angels, stars, cowboys, school, bugs, etc. Cookie parties have helped this father slow down in his world of work and take time to enter a child's world of cookies and milk. ♥

MARK COSGROVE

Hit of the Party
Cookie Bars

1 (12 ounce) package butterscotch chips
1 (6 ounce) package chocolate chips
1 cup sugar
1 cup light corn syrup
1 cup chunky peanut butter (½ of an 18
   ounce jar)
5 cups cereal flakes (Kirkie uses Special K)

In a small saucepan over low heat melt butterscotch and chocolate chips. In a large saucepan bring sugar and corn syrup to a boil, add peanut butter, and mix well. Stir in 2 cups of the cereal flakes, then 2 more cups, and finally the last cup.

Spread cereal mixture in a buttered 10″x15″x1″ baking pan, pressing with a buttered spoon. Pour melted chips over mixture and spread evenly.

Refrigerate for no more than 30 minutes. Cut into bars. Refrigerate 1 hour longer. Then they're ready to eat.

KIRKIE MORISSEY

Seven Layer Bars

Rich and chewy.

½ cup margarine
1 cup graham cracker crumbs, finely crushed
1 (6 ounce) package chocolate chips
1 (6 ounce) package butterscotch chips
1 cup chopped nuts
1 cup coconut (optional)
1 can sweetened condensed milk

Melt margarine in a 9"x13" baking pan. Tilt pan so sides are coated about 1" up. Sprinkle crumbs, chocolate chips, coconut, butterscotch chips, and nuts in layers. Dribble sweetened condensed milk over the top. Microwave on high for 8–9 minutes, or bake at 350F for 30 minutes. Let stand for 10 minutes on a rack to cool. Cut while warm.

Hint:

I like to put the graham crackers in a large Zip-Loc bag before I crush them with a rolling pin. Much less mess!

DEBBIE ROBERTS

Working Together

Unless you must have total peace and quiet to produce a meal, get the family to participate. This can be as simple as putting the napkins on the table for a three-year-old. The point is, family participation develops a greater appreciation and anticipation of the final result.

A divorced working mother finds that preparing food with her five- and seven-year-old daughters "is important to our sense of being a family." They spend many Saturdays together making cookies and preparing meals for the upcoming week. ♥

CAROL KUYKENDALL
(Excerpted from an article that appeared in the February, 1983 issue of Parents Magazine, p. 62.)

Patchwork Quilties

1 cup butter or margarine
1 cup brown sugar
1 egg
1½ teaspoons vanilla
2 cups flour
1 (12 ounce) package chocolate chips

Cream together butter and sugar. Beat in egg and vanilla. Add flour ½ cup at a time, mixing well after each addition. Spread in a greased 15"x10"x1" baking pan. Bake at 350F for 15 minutes. Remove from oven and immediately sprinkle chocolate chips over cookie base. Return to oven for 2 minutes, then remove from oven and spread melted chocolate chips. Mark off into squares, but do not cut while hot. Decorate squares individually with coconut, candies, nuts, icing, or whatever your imagination can dream up. Chill in refrigerator about 1 hour and then cut into squares.

SHIRLEY BLEDSOE

Gretchen's Oatmeal Molasses Cookies

"One day Gretchen, age 5, was making a 'mixture' and we turned them into these cookies."

½ cup brown sugar
½ cup shortening
1 egg
¼ cup molasses
1 teaspoon vanilla
1 teaspoon cinnamon
¼ teaspoon ginger
½ teaspoon baking soda
1 teaspoon baking powder
¼ teaspoon salt
1 cup whole wheat pastry flour
1½ cups rolled oats

Mix sugar and shortening, add egg, molasses, and vanilla. Add dry ingredients in order given. May form into balls and roll in sugar, if desired, or drop by teaspoon on a greased cookie sheet. Bake at 350F for 10 minutes.

KAREN VANDER WEELE

Cooking is a family affair; as soon as the mixer starts there are children on chairs waiting to help. We use wooden spoons because they are light-weight. The children do a lot of fetching and carrying. Heidi, age 2, can even crack eggs. Becky, age 8, is learning how to measure, and Gretchen, age 6, loves to make "mixtures," not too often, though.

At the stove they stand with the chair back against the stove and hold the pan handles as they stir under adult supervision.

I call it organized mayhem. ♥

KAREN VANDER WEELE

Buttercup Cookies

1½ cups butter or Imperial margarine,
    softened
1 cup sugar
2 egg yolks
1 teaspoon vanilla
3½ cups flour

Cream together butter and sugar, mix in egg yolks and vanilla. Stir in flour and knead a bit until smooth. Roll into balls (about 1 rounded teaspoon of dough each). Press each down on a cookie sheet and bake at 350F for 10 minutes.

DIANE BRUMMEL BLOEM

Heath Bar Sugar Cookies

1½ cups sugar
1½ cups margarine
2 teaspoons vanilla
3 cups flour
1 teaspoon soda
½–1 teaspoon salt
5 Heath Bar candy bars, broken in pieces (Put
    in freezer, then pound them with a
    rolling pin while still in their wrappers.)

Cream together margarine and sugar, blend in vanilla. Sift together flour, soda, and salt and stir into creamed mixture. Add broken Heath Bars. Roll in balls and place on a greased cookie sheet. Flatten with the bottom of a glass, greased and dipped in sugar. Bake at 325F–350F for 12–15 minutes.

JOANNE BOER

Buttercup Cookies

◄≪*We had a mystery here the first time I made these cookies. I looked around the kitchen for something which would make a pattern when I flattened the cookies. As I opened a drawer I felt the drawer knob. Aha! It was round and had grooves in it. I unscrewed it, washed it, and dipped it in sugar before using it to flatten each cookie. It made a pretty flower impression. I made the whole family search the kitchen until they found what made the pattern. My kitchen has been remodeled but I have kept a knob for making buttercup cookies.* ♥

DIANE BRUMMEL BLOEM

Butterscotch Cookies

1 cup butter
1½ cups brown sugar
1 egg
1 cup All Bran cereal
1 teaspoon vanilla
2 cups sifted flour
1¾ teaspoons baking powder
1 cup chopped walnuts or pecans (optional)

Cream together butter and sugar. Beat in eggs and vanilla. Stir in All Bran. Sift together flour and baking powder and stir into dough. Add nuts, if desired. Form into walnut-sized balls and place on a lightly greased cookie sheet. Flatten with a fork. Bake at 350F for 10–12 minutes or until lightly browned.

Rozella Rinzema

Butter Pecan Cookies

"Delicious with tea or ice cream."

1 cup Imperial margarine, softened
½ cup sugar
2 cups flour
1 cup finely broken pecan pieces
additional sugar

Cream together margarine and sugar, mix in flour and pecans. Roll teaspoonfuls into balls, place on an ungreased cookie sheet, and flatten with a fork. Bake at 350F for about 20 minutes, or until lightly browned. Cool 2–3 minutes, then roll in granulated sugar.

Diane Brummel Bloem

Grandma Dee's Imperial Cookies

"Makes about 2 dozen, which will not be nearly enough."

1 cup Imperial margarine, softened (no substitution)
¾ cup sugar
½ teaspoon vinegar
½ teaspoon soda
1½ cups unsifted flour

Cream margarine and sugar together, by hand, until fluffy. (Do not use a mixer.) Add vinegar, soda, and flour, mixing well. Drop by teaspoonfuls, about the size of a walnut, on an ungreased cookie sheet. (Grandma Dee flattens them with a wet paper towel folded in fourths and placed over the end of a glass. We tested them both flattened and not, and they were about the same.) Bake at 310F for 15 to 20 minutes, until very lightly brown.

ARLENE & PETER KLADDER

Grandma Dee's
Imperial Cookies

◄ *My mother, Harriet De Borest, who is 86 years old now, bakes these cookies every Saturday. All the grandchildren come by after church for Sunday Coffee. Mother's coffee, lemonade, and cookies keep the cousins and extended family together.* ♥

ARLENE & PETER KLADDER

Snowball Cookies

This popular cookie has many names, including Polvorones and Wedding Cakes. Many varieties add ½ to 1 cup of chopped nuts.

MAKES 4–5 dozen

1 cup butter or margarine
½ cup confectioner's sugar
2¼ cups flour
½ teaspoon salt (optional)
1 teaspoon vanilla
additional confectioner's sugar

In a mixing bowl cream together butter and sugar, add salt, if desired, and vanilla. Add flour gradually. Or use hands to mix all ingredients thoroughly. Form into balls 1" in diameter and bake on an ungreased cookie sheet at 350F–375F for 16–20 minutes or until very lightly browned. Remove from pan immediately and roll in more confectioner's sugar.

PATRICIA GUNDRY
RONNIE CARDER
WILMA ZONDERVAN TEGGELAAR
MELODIE DAVIS

Variation:

Irish Crescents: Reduce flour to 2 cups, omit salt, and add 1 cup chopped nuts. Shape into crescents instead of balls. Sprinkle with confectioner's sugar when cool.

MARY & KEN REGAN

Sonja Henie Cookies

½ cup butter
½ cup brown sugar
1 egg yolk
1 cup flour
½ cup chopped nuts
1 egg white, beaten lightly with a fork

Filling:

jelly of your choice
chopped nuts

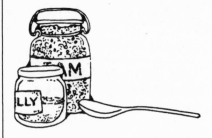

Cream together butter and brown sugar. Mix in egg yolk, flour, and chopped nuts. Dip teaspoonfuls of dough in egg white, then place on a lightly greased cookie sheet. Press with finger to form indentation in the center of each cookie, fill with jelly and nuts. Bake at 325F for 10–15 minutes, until very lightly browned.

ISABELLE & KENNETH BARKER

Rice Krispie Cookies

1 cup butter
1 cup sugar
1 teaspoon vanilla
2 cups flour
½ teaspoon soda
½ teaspoon baking powder
½ cup Rice Krispies
½ cup chopped nuts

With an electric mixer cream together butter, sugar, and vanilla. Sift flour, soda, and baking powder together and add to creamed mixture. Add Rice Krispies and beat with mixer to break up Krispies. Stir in nuts. Form into walnut-sized balls. Bake on an ungreased cookie sheet at 350F for 8–12 minutes (they won't be browned).

SUE MacDONALD

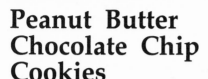

Peanut Butter Chocolate Chip Cookies

Delicate and crumbly texture, like a sand tart, breaks easily when taken off the cookie sheet, so let it cool on the sheet a couple of minutes before carefully removing. For people who love chocolate and peanut butter together this cookie is wonderful.

1 cup margarine
1 cup brown sugar
2 eggs
1 teaspoon vanilla
1 cup peanut butter
2 cups flour
2 teaspoons soda
½ teaspoon salt
1 (12 ounce) package chocolate chips

Cream together margarine and sugar. Add eggs and vanilla, beating until fluffy. Add peanut butter. Sift together flour, soda, and salt. Add to batter. Stir in chocolate chips. Drop by teaspoon on lightly greased cookie sheet. Flatten with a glass dipped in sugar. Bake at 350F for about 10–12 minutes.

LOIS & CARYN DYKSTRA

House of _An_
A Christmas Eve Tradition

The first Christmas Eve in our own home in Shanghai, China, in 1919, we began this tradition of reading the Christmas Story, Luke 2:1-20, in as many different languages as could be read by our guests, each taking a turn in reading successive verses. At the end we went around once more for each one to read verse 14 in his or her language. Then we sang hymns, had a prayer, and a Swedish Smorgasbord, keeping the family tradition of my husband Elam's Swedish family, and adding some Chinese dishes.

After Elam's death in 1944, I continued this tradition, and now when one or more of our three children are not here, they continue the reading in their own homes. ♥

COLENA M. ANDERSON

House of _An_
_An_ 安 Peace

Easy Koulourakia

(Greek Sesame Cookies)

1 cup butter
½ cup sugar
2 eggs (reserve 1 yolk for glaze)
1 tablespoon lemon juice or orange juice
3 cups flour
1 teaspoon baking powder
2 tablespoons water
sesame seeds for topping

Soften butter, gradually add sugar, and cream together thoroughly. Add eggs and beat well. Stir in lemon or orange juice. Sift flour and baking powder together and stir into creamed mixture. Turn out on a lightly floured surface and knead until dough is smooth. Pinch off walnut-sized pieces, roll lightly by hand to desired length, and shape into twists. Place on a greased cookie sheet. Mix reserved egg yolk with water and brush on cookies. Sprinkle with sesame seeds and bake at 350F for about 15 minutes, or until lightly browned.

OLIVIA & PAUL HILLMAN

Hoot Owl Cookies

"This recipe is fun to make with pre-school children at Halloween."

¾ cup butter or margarine
1 cup brown sugar
1 egg
1 teaspoon vanilla
2½ cups unbleached flour
2 teaspoons baking powder
½ teaspoon salt (optional)
2 squares unsweetened chocolate, melted and
   cooled
¼ teaspoon baking soda
chocolate chips and cashews for decoration

Cream together butter and brown sugar. Beat in egg and vanilla. Add flour, baking powder, and salt. Combine cooled chocolate and baking soda. Remove ⅔ of the dough and blend with chocolate mixture. Roll out the chocolate dough into a 10"x4" strip. Shape the light dough into a 10" long roll. Place the roll on the dark strip and mold the chocolate dough around the light dough, sealing in the edges. Wrap and chill the roll. Cut dough into ⅛" slices. Pinch the upper part of the circle to form two ears. Add chocolate chips for eyes and a cashew for the beak. Bake on a lightly greased cookie sheet at 350F for 8–12 minutes.

JULIE L. & S. RICKLY CHRISTIAN

Entertaining

I was born of missionary parents in India. Entertaining there was very simple, that is, of high-caste friends. The menu was always nuts in their shells. That way food could not be defiled by our touch. On one occasion we had as our guest the rani (queen) of our district. She stayed and stayed. Finally one of the servants called Mother out of the room and told her she was being very rude to her distinguished guest. The rani had to stay until she was told to leave. That was the custom of the land. Whereupon Mother thanked the queen for her visit and bid her farewell. With great relief the rani and her retinue said their salaams and left.

I have often thought how wise that etiquette is. It is always difficult, as a guest, to judge a gracious terminal point of a visit. ♥

EDNA & JOHN GERSTNER

Oatmeal Date Cookies

MAKES about 4 dozen

1 cup butter
½ cup sugar
½ cup brown sugar
1 egg
1 teaspoon vanilla
1 cup flour
1 teaspoon soda
1½ cups corn flakes
2½ cups oats
1 cup chopped dates
1 cup chopped nuts

Cream together butter and sugars, beat in egg and vanilla. Stir or sift together flour and soda and stir into creamed mixture. Stir in corn flakes, oats, dates, and nuts. Form into 1 or more long rolls about 2″ in diameter, wrap in plastic wrap, and chill in refrigerator or freeze until ready to bake. Slice and bake on a greased cookie sheet at 350F about 10 minutes. Can also be baked, without chilling, as a drop cookie.

MARTHA AND CHARLIE SHEDD

Flemish Almond Cookies

These cookies are very crisp and sweet, almost like candy.

1 cup butter, softened
3 cups brown sugar
3 cups flour
1½ teaspoons soda
1½ teaspoons cinnamon
¼ cup boiling water
½ cup slivered almonds

Cream together butter and brown sugar. Sift flour, soda, and cinnamon together, and mix with creamed mixture until combined and crumbly. Stir in boiling water, then slivered almonds. Form into long rolls about 2½" in diameter and wrap in plastic wrap. Freeze until ready to bake:

Slice *thin* and bake on a greased baking sheet at 350F for about 11–12 minutes, until golden brown. Watch very carefully during final minutes as they burn easily.

ELEANOR & TOM MCCONISKEY

Flemish Almond Cookies

◄─ *This recipe for cookies was given to me by a Flemish lady who was our landlady. Every Christmas she gave us some as a gift, but would not give us the recipe until we moved away. We continue to make them because they are so special.* ♥

ELEANOR & TOM MCCONISKEY

Cookie Day Cookies

Makes:

6 doz.	12 doz.	18 doz.	24 doz.	
1	2	3	4	cup(s) margarine
¾	1½	2¼	3	cup(s) sugar
1	2	3	4	egg(s), slightly beaten
2	4	6	8	tablespoons evaporated milk
1½	3	4½	6	teaspoons vanilla
3	6	9	12	cups flour
1	2	3	4	teaspoon(s) baking powder
½	1	1½	2	teaspoon(s) salt

Cream margarine and sugar together until smooth. Stir in eggs, milk, and vanilla. Add flour, baking powder, and salt and stir well. Refrigerate overnight. Roll dough on well-floured surface, or between waxed paper, or plastic wrap to ⅛" thickness. Cut out with cookie cutters and bake at 400F for 5–8 minutes. Decorate to your taste and personality.

JO BERRY

Cookie Day Cookies

◄⏜ "Cookie Day" is a pre-Christmas tradition in our family. My daughters and their friends, as well as my friends and their children and surrogate family all gather early on a Saturday morning to make holiday cookies. The recipe we use has been handed down through my family for generations, but the secret of the "yumminess" of the cookies isn't so much in the taste as in their appearance. Decorating the cookies is an art. We use a regular buttercream frosting recipe and color the frosting to get the various shades we need. We serve the cookies during the holidays, as well as giving them for gifts. Some recipients even use them as decorations on their Christmas trees. ♥

JO BERRY

My Grandmother's Tea Cakes

An old fashioned "hands-in" recipe. A fun job for children with very clean hands.

2¼ cups flour
2 teaspoons baking powder
pinch of allspice (scant ⅛ teaspoon)
1 egg
1 cup sugar
⅓ cup melted butter or margarine
¼ cup milk
1 teaspoon (or less) vanilla

Into a large bowl sift together flour, baking powder, and allspice. Push a hole in flour mixture with fist. Into the hole dump egg, sugar, melted butter, milk, and vanilla. Work slowly *with hand*, pulling flour into mixture until all flour is used up. (Pulling flour into mixture makes a better cookie.) Roll out dough on a floured surface. Cut and bake on a lightly greased cookie sheet at 350F until lightly browned.

VERDELL & CREATH DAVIS

Among my fondest memories of growing up in a small central Texas farming and ranching community in the 40s and 50s were sharing a dishpan full of popcorn with my mother and daddy and brothers and listening to "Gunsmoke" on the radio, spending lazy summer days on the farm—and my grandmother, Pearl Watson, baking tea cakes in her wood cookstove. (How she knew how many sticks of wood to put in that stove to get 350 degrees I'll never know!) My grandmother always made them by the sacks full and we could eat to our heart's, or stomach's, content. Even today my 88-year-old grandmother still bakes up dozens of her tea cakes, though not in a wood stove, and they are everybody's favorite! But somehow it's not just the tea cake itself, but the warmth their very mention creates, even among the third and fourth generation. ♥

VERDELL DAVIS

Chocolate Heart Cookies

MAKES 4½ dozen

½ cup soft margarine
1¼ cups sugar
2 eggs
1 teaspoon vanilla
2 cups flour
2 teaspoons baking powder
½ teaspoon salt
½ cup cocoa
sugar to sprinkle on top of cookies

Mix together margarine and sugar until fluffy. Beat in eggs, stir in vanilla. Sift together flour, baking powder, salt, and cocoa and add to mixture. Chill dough. Roll out on a floured surface and cut with a heart-shaped cookie cutter. Sprinkle with sugar and bake on a greased cookie sheet at 325F for 8–10 minutes.

LAURIE GOTT

Lebkuchen

(German Honey Cake)

Make these 4–6 weeks ahead.

1 cup honey
3 tablespoons sugar
3 tablespoons butter
2 eggs
4 drops lemon extract
⅓ cup candied citron
3½ cups flour
2 tablespoons cocoa
1 tablespoon baking powder
¼ teaspoon cloves
¼ teaspoon allspice
1 teaspoon cinnamon
½ cup pecan halves

Glaze:

½ box confectioner's sugar
milk
¼ teaspoon vanilla

In a small saucepan over low heat, warm honey, sugar, and butter slowly. Pour into a mixing bowl and allow to cool. When mixture is cool stir in eggs, one at a time. Add citron and lemon extract. Sift together flour, cocoa, baking powder, cloves, allspice, and cinnamon and add to mixture. Spread on a 10"x15"x1" greased baking pan. (A spatula dipped in cold water helps spread dough evenly.) Bake at 350F for 25 minutes. Cool, then cut into 2½"x2½" squares.

Mix glaze ingredients, adding milk until of spreading consistency. Spread on top of Lebkuchen and place a pecan half on each square. Store in an airtight container for 4–6 weeks. Lebkuchen will be hard when baked but become soft after being stored in a container for 4–6 weeks.

BEA FOSMIRE

My mother came to the United States in 1922 as a German war bride leaving her mother, brothers, and sister. And so it was with some excitement that we found ourselves stationed in that country for six and a half years. Visiting relatives and meeting the German people was particularly delightful and we soon found ourselves adopting some of the German holiday customs. Especially joyful for our children was St. Nicholas Day on December 6.

On that day the children put their shoes outside the front door of the apartment hoping that St. Nicholas would fill them with cookies, candy, and fruit. This was a sign that they were extremely good children during the year. If they had not been good, they would find switches and coals in their shoes. My husband and I would place cookies, candy, and fruit in the shoes but place some switches and coals beside each to insure continued good behavior.

Gingerbread People

"A Christmas Tradition."
MAKES 2½ dozen.

⅓ cup shortening, softened
1 cup brown sugar
1½ cups dark molasses
⅔ cup water
6½ cups flour
2 teaspoons soda
1 teaspoon salt
1 teaspoon allspice
1 teaspoon ginger
1 teaspoon cloves
1 teaspoon cinnamon
raisins, nuts, chocolate chips, candied fruits,
    M&M candies (optional), confectioner's
    sugar, icing (optional)

Mix together shortening, brown sugar, and molasses. Stir in water. Blend together flour, soda, salt, allspice, ginger, cloves, and cinnamon and mix in. On a floured surface roll out dough to ¼" thickness and cut out with a large gingerbread man cookie cutter. Place cookies on lightly greased cookie sheet.

To decorate before baking, use a toothpick to make a face, buttons, clothing designs, etc. Using scraps of dough, add pieces to the sides of cookies to make hats, skirts, fluffy hair, puffed sleeves, or shoes. Chocolate chips, nuts, candied fruits, and candy can be pressed into the unbaked cookie to make noses, buttons, clothing outlines, and designs. When ready, bake at 350F for about 10 minutes. Allow to cool briefly before removing from pan to cool on racks.

To decorate after baking, frost with a mixture of confectioner's sugar, vanilla, and enough milk to make frosting of spreading consistency. While frosting is still wet, add decorative elements as above. ➥

We could never understand why, when the children went outside to see what was in their shoes, there were never any switches or coals (only goodies). One St. Nicholas Day we learned the secret of the missing switches and coals. The children would wake very early to check out their shoes and finding the switches and coals they would throw them away, hoping that we would not discover that St. Nicholas had left something other than the cookies, candies, and fruit.♥

BEA FOSMIRE

Notes: For small children, you may want to reduce the amount of salt and spices to ¾ teaspoon or less of each.

For added nutrition reduce flour to 6 cups and add 2 tablespoons wheat germ and ½ cup instant nonfat dry milk.

DOROTHY YOUNG

Non Plus Ultra

The Latin name of this Hungarian cookie means literally "no more beyond." In other words, "none better."

1½ cups butter
1½ cups flour
½ cup confectioner's sugar
½ teaspoon vanilla
3 egg yolks
about ¼ cup jam
1 egg white
3 tablespoons confectioner's sugar
¼ teaspoon vinegar

With a pastry blender, fork, or fingertips, mix butter, ½ cup confectioner's sugar, and flour together to a crumb-like consistency. Stir in vanilla and egg yolks. Turn out on a floured surface and knead briefly, about 1 minute. Roll out to about ⅛" thickness and cut into circles with a 2" cutter. Using the center of a doughnut cutter or a bottle cap, form rings by cutting out the center of half of the circles. Cover solid circles with a thin layer of jam. Top each with a ring. Lightly beat together egg white, 3 tablespoons confectioner's sugar, and vinegar. Brush or spread on tops of assembled cookies. Transfer to an ungreased cookie sheet and bake at 325F for 25 minutes, or until lightly browned.

JULIE & KALMAN TOTH

Non Plus Ultra

◄ *The Latin name of this rich Hungarian cookie means, literally, "no more beyond." It is a variant of the phrase "ne plus ultra," which marked the Strait of Gibraltar on Roman maps as a warning to sailors not to enter the Atlantic Ocean.* ♥

JULIE & KALMAN TOTH

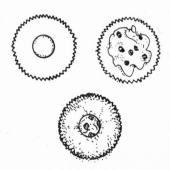

Great Aunt Margaret's Cereal Cookies

½ cup shortening
½ cup sugar
½ cup brown sugar
1 egg
2 teaspoons milk
1 teaspoon vanilla
1 cup flour
½ teaspoon salt
½ teaspoon soda
¼ teaspoon baking powder
1 cup rolled oats (not instant)
1 cup corn flakes

Beat together shortening, sugar, and brown sugar. Add egg, milk, and vanilla. Beat until creamy. Blend in flour, salt, soda, and baking powder. Stir in cereals. Drop by teaspoon on an ungreased cookie sheet and bake at 350F for 10–15 minutes.

Doris Rikkers

*Great Aunt Margaret's
Cereal Cookies*

◄ *This has been a family favorite for three generations. It's a great way to use up the last crumbs in the cereal boxes. Any kind of flake cereal can be used instead of corn flakes. I usually double the recipe.* ♥

Doris Rikkers

Generic Animal Crackers

1 cup shortening
1½ cups sugar
2 eggs
2¾ cups flour
2 teaspoons cream of tartar
1 teaspoon soda
¼ teaspoon salt

Mix shortening, sugar, and eggs thoroughly. Mix the flour, cream of tartar, soda, and salt separately and then blend them in the goo you mixed previously. Drop spoon-sized blobs of dough onto a lightly greased cookie sheet. (Do not

➥

drop from a height exceeding 14 feet.)

Bake at 400F for 8–10 minutes. When you rescue these succulent critters from the oven you will find that they have formed, as if by magic, into the shape of our no-frills animal, the amoeba.

Variation: If you like your amoebas more flavorful, substitute butter or margarine for shortening and/or add 1 teaspoon vanilla or almond extract.

RICHARD P. WALTERS

Soft Chocolate Chip Cookies

Ann's grandmother's recipe.

½ **cup shortening, margarine or butter**
1 **cup brown sugar**
2 **eggs**
1 **cup evaporated milk**
1 **teaspoon vanilla**
2¾ **cups flour**
½ **teaspoon soda**
1 **teaspoon salt**
1 **(12 ounce) package chocolate chips**
1 **cup chopped walnuts (optional)**

Mix shortening, sugar, and eggs thoroughly. Stir in milk and vanilla. Sift together and add flour, soda, and salt. Stir in chocolate chips and nuts, if desired. Drop by teaspoon on a greased cookie sheet. Bake at 350F–375F for about 10 minutes.

ANN KIEMEL ANDERSON

Nutrition Booster

I fortify white flour for homemade baked goods by putting 1 teaspoon of wheat germ and 1 tablespoon of nonfat dry milk in the bottom of each cup of flour measured. A small amount can be added to mixes also. ♥

DOROTHY & DAVIS A. YOUNG

Sour Cream Cocoa Cookies

Soft and cake-like.

½ cup butter or margarine
1 cup sugar
1 egg
1 cup sour cream
1 teaspoon vanilla
2 cups flour
½ cup cocoa
½ teaspoon soda
½ teaspoon salt
1 (12 ounce) package chocolate chips
    (optional)

Cream butter and sugar together, beat in egg, sour cream, and vanilla. Sift together flour, cocoa, soda, and salt. Stir into creamed mixture, add chocolate chips, if desired. Drop by teaspoon onto a greased cookie sheet. Bake at 350F–375F for 8–10 minutes.

ANN KIEMEL ANDERSON

Special places in the dining room have been arranged to meet the needs of children. Many a restless tyke has been transformed into a content and courageous cowboy by the wicker rocking horse grazing in the archway between the living room and dining room. A reading chair has been placed near the shelves which house their most treasured books. Each child has been assigned space in the wall cupboards: storage for games, puzzles, workbooks, and other equipment. Art supplies— fingerpaints, watercolors, construction paper, scissors, glue, colored pencils—are kept in the cupboard nearest the kitchen.

The kitchen, too, needs activity centers for little people. Magnetic letters of the alphabet cling to the refrigerator for little fingers to arrange by color or words. On the top of the

Double Chocolate Cookies

Crisp and delicious, a great combination of tastes and textures.

1 cup shortening or margarine
¾ cup sugar
¾ cup brown sugar
2 eggs
1 teaspoon vanilla
1½ cups flour
3 tablespoons cocoa
1 teaspoon salt
1 teaspoon soda
1 teaspoon hot water
2 cups quick oats (not instant)
1 cup chopped nuts
1 (12 ounce) package chocolate chips

Cream together shortening and sugars. Add eggs, one at a time, blending well after each addition. Add vanilla. Sift flour, cocoa, and salt together and stir into creamed mixture. Dissolve soda in hot water and stir into mixture. Stir in oats, nuts, and chocolate chips. Drop by teaspoon onto an ungreased cookie sheet.

Bake at 350F for 10–12 minutes.

KAY & DON GLENN

refrigerator is a large reed clothes basket of games containing many little pieces. This basket is available on request upon condition that all pieces be returned to their proper coffee can. The stoneware crock next to the stove is filled with miniature vehicles and pull toys that glide smoothly across kitchen tile surfaces. ♥

MIRIAM HUFFMAN ROCKNESS (from A Time to Play)

Fudge Drop Cookies

1 (6 ounce) package chocolate chips
1 (6 ounce) package butterscotch chips
1¼ cups Quaker 100% Natural Cereal
1 cup cocktail peanuts

In a double boiler melt chocolate and butterscotch chips. Stir in cereal and peanuts. Leave
over hot water while dropping by teaspoon on
wax paper or greased surface. Refrigerate until
firm. Store in a cool place to prevent chocolate
from melting.

HARRIET & DERRALL KINARD

Fudge Drop Cookies

◄◄ *Favorite cookie recipe of our
children, also voted favorite
recipe in my son's 2nd grade
class at school when the children
made up a recipe booklet.* ♥

HARRIET & DERRALL KINARD

Pineapple Drop Cookies

MAKES about 60 cookies

1 cup sugar
1 cup brown sugar
1 cup shortening
1 cup crushed pineapple, undrained
2 teaspoons vanilla
4 cups flour
1 teaspoon soda
2 teaspoons baking powder
1 teaspoon salt
1 cup chopped nuts

Cream together sugars and shortening, add
crushed pineapple. Sift together flour, soda, baking powder, and salt; add and mix well. Stir in
nuts. Drop by teaspoon on a greased cookie sheet
and bake at 350F for 10–15 minutes.

RUTH THOMAS

Julie's Octopus Cookies

1 large can Chinese (chow mein) noodles
2 (6 ounce) packages butterscotch morsels
1 (12 ounce) can cocktail peanuts

Melt butterscotch morsels in a double boiler. Immediately stir in noodles and peanuts, stirring until all are coated. Drop by teaspoon onto waxed paper or greased surface. Refrigerate until firm.

BRENDA KNIGHT GRAHAM

No-Bake Onos (Ono is Hawaiian for "tasty" or "delicious")

MAKES about 4 dozen

2 cups rolled oats
1 cup seedless raisins
½ cup peanut butter
¼ cup carob powder
¾ cup honey
¼ cup butter or margarine
1 teaspoon vanilla
a few drops of peppermint extract

In a large bowl combine oats, raisins, peanut butter, and carob powder. In a saucepan boil honey and butter for 1 minute. Remove from heat and stir in vanilla and peppermint extract. Add to oats mixture and stir until blended. Drop by teaspoon onto tray or baking sheet greased or lined with wax paper. Chill until firm.

JOYCE LEENSVAART

Everybody's No-Bake Cookies

2 cups sugar
2 tablespoons–½ cup cocoa
½ cup milk
½ cup butter or margarine
½ cup peanut butter (optional)
1–1½ teaspoons vanilla
3–3½ cups quick oats
1 cup coconut (optional)
1 cup pecans or other nuts (optional)

In a large saucepan combine sugar, cocoa, and milk. Add butter and heat mixture to boiling. Boil 1 minute, stirring constantly. Remove from heat and stir in peanut butter, if desired, vanilla, oats, coconut, and nuts, if desired. Drop by teaspoon onto wax paper or greased surface. Cool.

ANN & RICHARD PATTERSON
ISABEL & KENNETH BARKER
LATAYNE SCOTT
MARY & KEN REGAN

DESSERTS

Peach, Blueberry, or Cherry Cobbler 299
J. D. Douglas's Apricot Dessert 300
Mrs. Truman's Ozark Pudding 302
Willie-Mae 303
Fruit Crumble 304
Noodle Kugel 305
Christmas Porridge 306
Fructsoppa (Swedish Fruit Soup) 307
Old-Fashioned Creamy Rice Pudding 308
Mother's Old-Fashioned Bread
     Pudding 309
Fudge Pudding with Ice Cream Sauce 310
Baklava 311
Banket 312
Almond Tassies 313
Dutch Krinkle 314
Funny Cake 315
Dream Cake 316
Easy Pineapple-Cherry Dessert 317
Melba's Torte 317
Poppy Seed Torte 318
Helen's Fancy Pancake 319
The "Bs'" Cheese Crepes 320
Strawberry Crepes 322
Cherry Cool Comfort 323
Blueberry or Cherry Cream Cheese
     Dessert 323
Uldine's Cheesecake 324
Slim Lemon Cheesecake 325
Quick and Easy English Trifle 326
Angel Bavarian Cake 327
Pavlova 328

Chocolate Slice 329
Chocolate Eclair Dessert 330
Toffee Squares 331
*Family Favorite Low-Calorie Ice
    Cream* 332
Ice Cream Grasshoppers 333
Frozen Cheese Cream 333
Sherbet Cream Cake 334
Crunchy Ice Cream 335
Turtle Sundae Dessert 336
Oreo Pie 336
Danny Penwell's Pumpkin Pie Cake 337
Melba's Dessert Topping 337

Peach, Blueberry, or Cherry Cobbler

SERVES 5–8

4 cups sliced fresh peaches, or blueberries*
(fresh or frozen), or cherries* (fresh,
frozen or canned)
¾–1 cup sugar
½ cup butter or margarine

Batter:

1 cup sugar
¼ teaspoon salt
1 teaspoon baking powder
¾ cup flour
1½ teaspoons cinnamon
¾ cup milk

Mix together fruit and sugar. Set aside. Melt butter in a large (2 quart) casserole. Prepare batter by mixing together dry ingredients, then add milk and beat until smooth. Pour batter into melted butter in casserole. *Do not stir.* Spoon fruit over top of batter. *Do not stir.* Bake at 350F for 45 minutes or until top is browned. Serve with fresh or sour cream. May be reheated.

*Optional: If using blueberries, add 1 or 2 teaspoons of lemon juice. If using cherries, add ½–1 teaspoon almond extract.

CAROL HOLQUIST

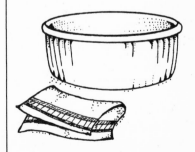

J. D. Douglas's Apricot Dessert

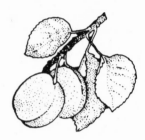

Producing the Zondervan Family Cookbook has been a long and sometimes maddening project. But it has also been satisfying, challenging, vastly educational, enjoyable and at times downright delightful. One of the pleasures in the job came from reading the authors' comments accompanying the recipes and their imaginative apologies for late submissions. I'm including the following letter just as I received it (my only additions are measurement equivalents in parentheses) to share with you one of those pleasant experiences. It's from J. D. Douglas, general editor of several reference books, whose Scottish wit seems to be flavored with just a bit of Irish blarney.

The S. N. Gundry he refers to is my husband Stan who, as Zondervan Academic Publisher, was working with him on a book project, and mentioned that I would love to receive a recipe Douglas had suggested sending.

Dear Lady:

S. N. Gundry, whose qualifications to be my friend are of the sketchiest, has the disagreeable habit (you will recognize it at once) of picking up on throwaway lines and Making A Meal of them. Some idle words of mine in a recent letter, thrown in just to keep the correspondence going, have given him just such a cue. In menace-fraught phrases he gets it across that your wrath is the sort of thing I would want less of. He did not spell it out in so many words (he's not a Zondervanian for nothing), but there was the distinct implication that non-compliance would lead to my being creamed in my own end zone. So . . .

2 ounces (¼ cup) soft butter
4 ounces (½ cup) brown sugar
3 ounces (½ cup) self-raising flour

➥

2 egg yolks
2 egg whites
½ pint (1¼ cups) milk
1 medium or small tin apricots

heat oven to 350
mix butter and sugar
mix (separately) egg yolks and milk with mixer at
medium speed
add yolk/milk mixture to butter/sugar, and add
flour simultaneously
mix well
add 2 tablespoons apricot juice
mix
beat well the egg whites and fold them into above
mixture
lightly grease a medium-sized oven dish
drain juice from apricots and place them at bottom
of dish
pour in mixture
bake for 45 minutes
eat with cream (Scotsmen prefer milk; not just
because it's cheaper). I call it Doocot Delight
(doocot is a Scots word for dovecote; there is a
15th-century one I can see from my window as I
type).

I wish you well in your great endeavor. Be
assured that I will be the first to scrutinize the
complete book for the slightest whiff of Eutychian-
ism. I would not be upset, indeed I would be
relieved since I have a reputation for eccentricity
to keep up, if you did not use the above offering.

Jim Douglas

*I love a beautiful table. . . . I
don't put away my good things
for Sundays, but use them every
day. I like fresh flowers on the
table and throughout my house.
Things I don't like are milk
cartons or salt boxes on the
table. I think a meal should be
served with a little dignity, even
in the poorest and simplest of
circumstances. Order and
neatness aid in good digestion
and good health.* ♥

June Carter Cash (from Among
My Klediments)

Mrs. Truman's Ozark Pudding

SERVES 6–8

2 eggs
1 cup sugar
1 teaspoon vanilla
⅓ cup flour
1 tablespoon baking powder
⅛ teaspoon salt
2 cups chopped peeled apples
½ cup chopped walnuts
unsweetened whipped cream
poached apple slices (optional)

In a large mixing bowl beat together eggs, sugar, and vanilla until light and fluffy. Sift together flour, baking powder, and salt. Blend into creamed mixture. Fold in apples and walnuts. Pour into a greased and floured 9"x9"x2" baking pan. Bake at 325F for 30–35 minutes. Spoon into dessert dishes. Serve warm with whipped cream and apple slices, if desired.

CAROLYN & ROBERT DE VRIES

Willie-Mae

1½ cups flour
1½ cups sugar
2 teaspoons soda
½ teaspoon salt
½ teaspoon cinnamon
½ cup oil
4 eggs
1 teaspoon vanilla
5 cups finely chopped tart apples
2 cups finely chopped walnuts

Combine flour, sugar, soda, cinnamon, oil, eggs, and vanilla. Beat with an electric mixer on medium speed until well blended. Stir in apples and nuts. Bake in a greased tube pan at 350F for about 60 minutes. When done it will be soft and gooey. Spoon into dessert dishes while still warm and serve with whipped cream or, better still, ice cream.

JANE PEART

Willie-Mae

◄ *When we were children our family had a cook named Willie-Mae. A great cook! And as cooks go, she went, taking most of her recipes with her. My sisters and I have tried to reconstruct one of our favorites of hers. This is our best try.* ♥

JANE PEART

Fruit Crumble

"Since we raised our 4 sons in the context of a Torchbearer International Youth Center in England, our situation was rather one of an 'extended family' living with some 200 young people most of the time, and often cooking for, and eating with them. My recipes are sufficient for 200, so need to be adapted for a 'normal' family!

"There is one dessert which has always proved a 'winner,' particularly amongst our North American visitors, and it is as simple as the proverbial ABC. We call it 'Fruit Crumble.' For the 200 hungry youth, it would call for about 12 English pounds of plain flour, but for a family of 4, here in the United States, you would take **2 cups of flour** in a basin, and with the fingers, crumble into that **1 cup of margarine,** and **1 cup of granulated sugar.** The result should resemble fine breadcrumbs. Next, take a medium sized baking tray, or Pyrex dish, of about 3 or 4 inches in depth, place some **fruit** about half way up from the base. Fresh cooking **apples** are good, skinned and sliced, but **rhubarb, apricots,** etc. are fine, though the raw fruit is usually better than canned. Sprinkle **sugar** over the fruit if it is sour. Cover with the crumbled mixture, cook in moderate oven for about half to three quarters of an hour, until brown on top. In England we serve with 'custard,' which is an egg based sauce made with hot milk, but ice cream (vanilla) is very acceptable, or whipped fresh cream. There are many possibilities for variations of fruit crumble, such as adding some canned blackberries to the apples, or some cinnamon, or adding a touch of ginger to rhubarb, etc."

E. JOAN & MAJOR THOMAS

Noodle Kugel

"I have many recipes for kugel, but this one has always made a hit with those who eat it. In particular, I have used this recipe for *Chanukkah* parties for students and they just love it."

SERVES 10–12

1 pound medium size noodles
1 cup dairy sour cream
4 eggs, beaten
½ cup sugar
pinch of salt
1 cup creamed cottage cheese
¼ teaspoon cinnamon
1 teaspoon vanilla
⅓ cup golden raisins
2 tablespoons butter
¼ cup brown sugar
1 (8 ounce) package whole pecans

Cook noodles until tender, rinse and drain, and then fold in the sour cream, eggs, sugar, salt, cottage cheese, cinnamon, vanilla, and raisins. Melt butter in a 9"x13" baking pan and sprinkle brown sugar evenly over butter, then press nuts into the pan. Pour noodle mixture into pan. Bake at 350F for 60 minutes. Cool 10 minutes. Loosen the kugel and invert on a serving plate.

MRS. LOUIS GOLDBERG

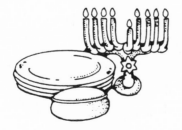

Eating is important at our house, not just because it's a physical necessity but also because of its spiritual significance, its role as a key metaphor in Scripture for spiritual fellowship. Jesus promises that if we hear His voice and open the door, He will come in and eat with us— and we with Him (Revelation 3:20). And we are exhorted whether we eat or drink or whatever we do, to do it all for the glory of God (I Corinthians 10:31). It's interesting to contemplate how we can bring glory to God by the way we eat and drink.

This metaphoric significance of eating is a part of our language. For example, the word companion *comes from two Latin words,* com, *"together," plus* panis, *"bread." A "companion" is one who eats bread with another, a "bread-fellow." These times of "companionship" are very special at our house.* ♥

D. G. KEHL

Christmas Porridge

SERVES 6–8

1 cup white rice, uncooked
1 teaspoon salt
1 tablespoon butter
4 cups whole milk
1 stick cinnamon
1 tablespoon sugar
1 teaspoon vanilla

Cover the rice with water, add salt and butter, and cook at a rapid boil for ten minutes. Add milk and cinnamon stick and simmer for 30 minutes to an hour, until milk is absorbed. Near the end of cooking time add sugar and vanilla. Serve in dessert bowls while hot. Top with butter, sugar, and cinnamon.

KARIN GRANBERG-MICHAELSON

Christmas Porridge

◄≋ *This one comes from my Scandinavian family roots. You can serve it on Christmas Eve and hide an almond in the bowl of one of your guests. The person receiving the almond must compose a song or a poem to share with the gathered friends.* ♥

KARIN GRANBERG-MICHAELSON

Fructsoppa

(Swedish Fruit Soup)

SERVES 4–6

1 cup dried apricots
¾ cup dried apples
½ cup pitted dried prunes
½ cup seedless raisins
2 quarts water
¼ cup sugar
3 tablespoons quick tapioca
1 cinnamon stick
6 whole cloves
1 tablespoon grated orange peel
1 cup raspberry or strawberry juice
whipped cream
slivered blanched almonds

Soak apricots, apples, prunes, and raisins in water for 2 hours. Without draining, add sugar, tapioca, cinnamon stick, cloves, and orange peel. Bring to a boil. Simmer, covered, until fruits are very tender. Remove from heat and add raspberry or strawberry juice. (You may want to remove cinnamon stick and cloves at this point.) Chill. To serve, top with whipped cream sprinkled with slivered blanched almonds.

KAY STROM

Fructsoppa

◄≪ *Fructsoppa is our traditional Christmas breakfast—along with Swedish Christmas bread. This fits into our generally Swedish Christmas celebration, traditional from my Swedish husband's childhood.* ♥

KAY STROM

Old-Fashioned Creamy Rice Pudding

SERVES 4–6 (depending on whether they are *true* pudding lovers)

¼ cup short-grain rice
¼ teaspoon salt
3 tablespoons honey or ¼ cup sugar
4 cups milk
1 teaspoon vanilla
⅓ cup raisins
cinnamon, to taste

Combine rice, salt, honey, and milk in baking dish. Bake at 325F for 2½ hours. Stir often during the first hour, three times the second hour. After pudding has baked for 2 hours add vanilla and raisins, sprinkle with cinnamon, and bake the last half hour without stirring. Good hot or cold.

JUDITH MARKHAM

Old-Fashioned Creamy Rice Pudding

◄ *My Grandmother Weimer made the best rice pudding in the whole world. Unfortunately, like the rest of her recipes, it was in her head, not in a recipe book. Thus I spent years combing the world for the perfect rice pudding like Grandmother made. A few years ago I found this recipe, which delivers what it promises. But don't try to cheat on the stirring or the time.* ♥

JUDITH MARKHAM

Mother's Old-Fashioned Bread Pudding

⅓ cup raisins
½ cup sherry
6 slices bread
1 (15 ounce) can peaches
3 eggs, beaten
2 cups milk

Soak raisins in sherry for 15 minutes. Butter 3 slices of bread and arrange in the bottom of a greased 2 quart baking dish. Drain juice from fruit and pour half of juice over bread in dish. Arrange peaches on top. Drain raisins and reserve sherry. Sprinkle raisins over peaches. Cut remaining bread into small triangles and arrange on top of fruit. Beat eggs, add milk and sherry. Pour over pudding and allow to stand for 30 minutes. Set baking dish in a larger pan containing hot water about 1" deep. Bake at 375F for about 60 minutes or until set and a golden brown.

ISA & J. SIDLOW BAXTER

Fudge Pudding with Ice Cream Sauce

SERVES 6

½ cup boiling water
⅓ cup soft butter
¼ cup cocoa
1 cup sugar
1 egg, beaten
1 cup flour
½ teaspoon salt
1 teaspoon baking powder
¼ cup milk
1 teaspoon vanilla
½ cup chopped nuts

Pour boiling water over butter and cocoa; stir until blended. Add sugar and egg, mix until smooth. Sift together flour, salt, and baking powder. Add alternately with milk. Blend in vanilla and nuts. Pour into a greased 1½ quart casserole. Cover and bake at 350F for 60 minutes. Serve with ice cream sauce.

Ice Cream Sauce

MAKES 3 cups

1 cup whipping cream
1 egg
1 teaspoon vanilla
¼ teaspoon salt
¼ cup sugar
⅓ cup butter, melted

Whip cream until stiff, set aside. Beat egg until thick and foamy. Gradually add vanilla, salt, sugar, and butter, beat well. Fold in whipped cream. Chill and serve with warm fudge pudding or gingerbread.

MRS. WALTER HENRICHSEN

Using Raw Eggs

Editorial Note: *When preparing recipes that contain raw or partially cooked eggs, it is important to remember to: (1) Use only eggs that are free of cracks, (2) Refrigerate promptly and keep cold, and (3) Use up the food soon.* ♥

Baklava

1 pound pecans, finely chopped
1 pound walnuts, finely chopped
½ teaspoon cinnamon
1½ pounds phyllo dough leaves (buy it by
    the box, pre-made; just unfold it)
1½ cups butter

Syrup:

8 cups sugar
2 cups honey
4 cups water
1 small cinnamon stick
¼ cup lemon juice

Combine nuts and cinnamon in a bowl. Grease a 10"x15" baking pan or rectangular casserole dish. You can use any size, really, just cut the dough to fit. Line the bottom of the baking pan with 5 layers of phyllo dough. Sprinkle with an extra-thin layer of nut mixture. Cover nut mixture with one layer of phyllo dough. Sprinkle with nut mixture and again cover with 1 layer phyllo. Repeat until nut mixture is gone or the pan is full. Top with 5 layers of phyllo dough. Melt butter and pour over phyllo, covering all the dough. Cut into traditional (about 1½"–2" per side) diamond shaped pieces. Bake at 250F for 2 hours.

To prepare syrup boil together sugar, honey, water, and cinnamon stick for 10 minutes. Remove from heat and add lemon juice. Remove cinnamon stick. When baklava is done remove from oven and immediately cover with hot syrup. Let sit for 15–30 minutes before serving.

Jo E. Hentz

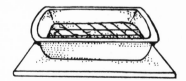

Banket (BON-kett)

Pastry:

2 cups flour
½ teaspoon soda
2 cups butter or margarine (or half of each)
1 scant cup *cold* **water**

Paste Filling:

2 eggs, beaten
1 cup sugar
1 pound almond paste, crumbled

Glaze:

1 egg beaten with 1 teaspoon water
sugar

To prepare pastry sift together flour and soda. Cut in butter until crumbly. Stir in water. Chill thoroughly. Prepare paste filling by mixing together eggs and sugar. Add almond paste. Mix well and chill thoroughly.

When ready to use, cut pastry into 8 equal pieces. Roll each piece into an oblong 5"x15" strip. Divide paste into 8 portions and arrange one portion along the center of the length of each pastry strip. Bring pastry edges together to form rolls and seal edges and ends well.

Place the rolls on cookie sheets, 4 to a sheet, with space between them so sides will brown. Brush each roll with egg and water mixture and sprinkle with a little sugar.*

Rolls should be frozen before baking to get a flaky pastry. Bake at 425F for 15 minutes, then at 350F until nicely browned, about 30 minutes. The baked rolls can be frozen after they have cooled. Wrap well in plastic or aluminum foil.

WILMA ZONDERVAN TEGGELAAR

Banket

A traditional Dutch holiday favorite. This may seem complicated but it really isn't— it's worth the effort.

After the strips are ready, they can be formed into letters, numbers, etc., before being put in the freezer. For many years I made the first initial of each of my grandchildren's names and also my nephews' and nieces', at Christmas time. The family became so large that some time ago I gave up the practice. ♥

WILMA ZONDERVAN TEGGELAAR

Almond Tassies

MAKES 24

Crust:

½ cup margarine, softened
1 (6 ounce) package cream cheese, softened
1 cup flour
pinch of salt

Filling:

¾ cup almond paste
½ cup plus 1 tablespoon sugar
2 eggs
½ teaspoon almond extract
confectioner's sugar
water
maraschino cherries

Mix together margarine and cream cheese. Add flour and salt, blending well. Form into a ball and divide into 24 pieces. Roll the pieces into balls. Refrigerate for 2 hours so dough is more firm. Then press into bottoms and sides of miniature muffin tins.

To prepare filling, beat together all ingredients with an electric mixer. Spoon into pastry-lined tins. Bake at 350F for 20–25 minutes, or until golden brown. Cool on rack. Make a glaze of confectioner's sugar and water. Top each tassie with glaze and ¼ maraschino cherry.

LOIS & CARYN DYKSTRA

Dutch Krinkle

Pastry:

1 cup flour
¼ teaspoon salt
½ cup butter or margarine
2 tablespoons water

Filling:

½ cup butter or margarine
1 cup water
1½ teaspoons almond extract
1 cup flour
¼ teaspoon salt
3 eggs

Glaze:

1 cup confectioner's sugar
2½ tablespoons (⅓ stick) butter or margarine
1 tablespoon milk
1½ teaspoons almond extract

To prepare pastry mix flour and salt, cut in butter with pastry blender, fork, or fingers, until crumbly. Sprinkle water over mixture. Divide in two portions. On a cookie sheet pat each portion into a 4"x10" strip.

To prepare filling bring butter and water to a rolling boil in saucepan. Add almond extract. Remove from heat. Stir in flour and salt. Stir until mixture is smooth and forms a ball. Add eggs, one at a time, beating after each addition until smooth. Spread half of mixture on each pastry strip. Bake at 375F for 45 minutes. When cool, frost with glaze.

To prepare glaze mix powdered sugar and butter until smooth. Mix in milk and almond extract.

KATHY THOMPSON

Funny Cake

"This recipe is a tradition from my childhood. When the pie is cut the inside reveals a chocolate sauce on the bottom and a white cake on top."

Pastry:

10″ unbaked pie shell

Cake:

1¼ cups flour
1 teaspoon baking powder
½ teaspoon salt
¾ cup sugar
¼ cup shortening
½ cup milk
1 teaspoon vanilla
1 egg
3 tablespoons chopped nuts

Topping:

1 square unsweetened baking chocolate
½ cup water
⅔ cup sugar
¼ cup butter
1 teaspoon vanilla

With an electric mixer mix flour, baking powder, salt, shortening, milk, and vanilla on low speed for 2 minutes. Add egg and mix for 1 more minute. Stir in nuts. Pour mixture into unbaked pie shell.

To prepare topping combine chocolate and water in a medium saucepan over low heat. When chocolate is melted add sugar and bring to a boil while stirring. Remove from heat and add butter and vanilla. Stir until butter melts. Pour over batter in pie shell. Bake at 350F for 50–55 minutes.

ANNE WILCOX

How long is long enough at the table? Again, flexibility seems to be the key. Usually, children under six cannot be expected to last more that 20 minutes. And remember, 15 minutes of gratifying time together is worth more than a rigid 30-minute stint marked by uncomfortable silence or forced conversation.

In our family, when the meal is over, the children ask to be excused and clear their plates as they go. Sometimes one child lingers, indicating a need for more attention or private conversation. The setting is perfect to fulfill this need. ♥

CAROL KUYKENDALL

(Excerpted from an article that appeared in the February, 1983 issue of Parents Magazine, *p. 62.)*

Dream Cake

"Almost every holiday found this cake gracing the table as I grew up. It was a favorite of my father and grandmother."

Crust:

½ cup brown sugar
1 cup butter or margarine
2 cups flour
1 teaspoon vanilla

Topping:

4 eggs
2 teaspoons vanilla
3 cups brown sugar
¼ cup flour
2 teaspoons baking powder
1½ cups coconut
2 cups walnuts or pecans

Use a pastry blender to combine crust ingredients. Press into a greased 13"x9" baking pan. Bake at 350F for 10 minutes. To prepare topping beat eggs well and add remaining ingredients. Stir until blended. Spread topping over baked crust and return to oven for 45 minutes.

ANNE WILCOX

When the three older children left home, my parents had only two rather quiet boys left at home. To get them to talk at supper, a fund was set up, in which each person who didn't tell at least one thing that had happened to them during the day had to put a quarter. The plan was to go out to a restaurant when enough money was saved, but they never got enough. Everyone began getting to know each other better, and saving their money at the same time. ♥

SANDRA DRESCHER LEHMAN

Easy Pineapple-Cherry Dessert

"Really great topped with ice cream."

1 (20 ounce) can crushed pineapple, undrained
1 (20 ounce) can cherry pie filling
1 large package cake mix
½ cup margarine, melted
¾ cup chopped nuts

Dump undrained pineapple in a lightly greased 9"x13" baking pan. Swirl it around to fill all corners. Cover pineapple with cherry pie filling. Sprinkle dry cake mix over pie filling. Pour melted margarine over cake mix. Sprinkle nuts on top, if desired. Bake at 350F for 50–55 minutes, or until lightly browned.

MARY & KEN REGAN

Melba's Torte

pound cake, purchased, or made from a mix*
cream cheese
apricot preserves
buttercream frosting, canned or prepared from scratch

Slice pound cake horizontally into 3 or more layers. Whip cream cheese, beat in apricot preserves until of desired consistency. Fill between pound cake layers. Cover assembled torte with buttercream frosting. Refrigerate.

*If making pound cake from a mix, bake in four round cake pans to make layers.

MELBA PETERSEN

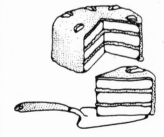

Poppy Seed Torte

⅓ cup poppy seeds
¾ cup milk
¾ cup butter or margarine
1½ cups sugar
1½ teaspoons vanilla
2 cups flour
2½ teaspoons baking powder
¼ teaspoon salt
4 egg whites, stiffly beaten
confectioner's sugar for top

Filling:

½ cup sugar
1 tablespoon cornstarch
1½ cups milk
4 egg yolks, slightly beaten
1 teaspoon vanilla
¼ cup coarsely chopped walnuts

Soak poppy seeds in milk for one hour. Cream together butter and sugar. Stir in vanilla, milk, and poppy seeds. Mix flour, baking powder, and salt. Add to creamed mixture. Fold in egg whites. Pour into 2 greased 8" or 9" round baking pans. Bake at 375F for 20–25 minutes. Cool 10 minutes and remove from pans.

To prepare filling, in a saucepan mix together sugar and cornstarch. Add milk and egg yolks. Cook and stir until thickened. Cool and add walnuts and vanilla. Split baked layers horizontally. Stack the 4 layers on a serving plate spreading filling between layers. Sift confectioner's sugar on top. Chill 2–3 hours before serving.

CAROL HOLQUIST

Helen's Fancy Pancake

This Hungarian dessert consists of stacked crepes with flavorful filling between each layer. It is served warm, cut in wedges like a torte.

Batter:

⅓ cup plus 2 tablespoons milk
3 eggs, separated
⅛ teaspoon salt
¾ cup flour
5 tablespoons butter, melted

Filling choices:

grated chocolate
jam
vanilla sugar

Remove milk and eggs from refrigerator. Separate eggs. Set aside egg whites to allow to come to room temperature. Beat together egg yolks, milk, salt, and flour until smooth. Set aside to rest for 1 hour. Beat egg whites until they form stiff peaks. Add melted butter and beaten egg whites to milk mixture.

Fry crepes on a hot (400F) pan greased with a few drops of oil. Cook on one side only (except the last one), tipping pan to produce thin crepes. Place crepes on serving plate, cooked side down. Sprinkle grated chocolate, or vanilla sugar, or spread a thin layer of jam on each crepe, stacking them on serving plate. Top with final crepe, cooked on both sides. Place in a 350F oven for 15–20 minutes. Cut in wedges. Serve hot.

Julie & Kalman Toth

"Animal Farm"

A typical problem with kids is that they like to lean back on two chair legs—which is good for neither the furniture nor the person. (One of our kids went through the window once, but fortunately suffered no physical injury.)

When any of the kids forgets the rules and leans back, I send a signal that avoids reprimand in front of company and enables him or her to save face. I simply say, "Animal farm." The kids all know that, based on George Orwell's book of that name, it means "four legs good, two legs bad." ♥

Jim Ruark

The "Bs'" Cheese Crepes

Crepe batter:

1½ cups milk
2 tablespoons oil
3 eggs
1½ cups flour
⅛ teaspoon salt

Filling:

2 (8 ounce) packages cream cheese
1 cup sugar
1 teaspoon vanilla

Milk Sauce:

2 cups milk
2 tablespoons butter
3 tablespoons sugar
1 teaspoon vanilla

To prepare batter put all batter ingredients into a blender and process at "blend" setting (medium-high) until smooth. To prepare with an electric mixer beat eggs thoroughly in a large mixing bowl at medium speed. Gradually add dry ingredients alternately with liquid ingredients. Beat until smooth.

Batter may be cooked immediately or stored, covered, in the refrigerator until ready to use, up to 3 days. Stir before using. To cook crepes you may use a crepe maker or a 10″ skillet. Oil skillet with 1 teaspoon oil. When hot pour about ¼ cup batter into skillet and rotate, making a thin round crepe. Cook until dry on top and then turn over and cook until steaming stops. Repeat until all batter is used.

To prepare filling soften cream cheese, add sugar and vanilla, mixing until smooth. Fill each crepe with 1 tablespoon of filling, roll, and place

The "Bs'" Cheese Crepes

◄≪ *These crepes along with baked ham are the Bustanoby family traditional Christmas Eve dinner. We started this tradition when our four sons were still all living at home and have continued it even though three sons now are married and have families of their own. When any of our sons and their families are able to be in our home for Christmas we all enjoy sitting around the table on Christmas Eve with our traditional dinner and reminisce about fun times as a family.*

After dinner we all adjourn to the living room in front of a blazing fire and each member of the family relates what significant things have happened in their life over the past year, and we all rejoice in the Lord together." ♥

Fay & André Bustanoby

in a buttered glass 13″x9″x2″ baking dish. Cover with milk sauce.

To prepare milk sauce mix all ingredients in a saucepan and heat on low until butter melts. Pour over crepes. Bake crepes at 350F for 15 minutes or until puffy.

"Our family likes a warm fruit sauce served over the crepes (any favorite sauce with do)."

Suggested blueberry sauce:

1 large can blueberries in heavy syrup
2 teaspoons corn starch
sugar, to taste (optional)

Drain blueberries, reserving juice. Place juice in small pan and mix with corn starch and sugar (if desired) and cook over medium heat until thickened. Add berries and serve.

FAY & ANDRÉ BUSTANOBY

Strawberry Crepes

4 eggs
½ cup milk
½ cup water
1 cup flour
½ teaspoon salt
2 tablespoons melted butter
2 teaspoons sugar
1 teaspoon vanilla
4 cups fresh strawberries, sliced and sugared
whipping cream

In a large bowl with an electric mixer beat eggs, milk, water, salt, melted butter, sugar, and vanilla at medium speed. Gradually add flour. If small lumps are present pour batter through strainer.

To cook crepes, pour a small amount of batter (about ¼ cup) into a lightly oiled skillet or crepe maker. Tip skillet to spread batter into a thin round pancake. Cook until dry on top. Turn crepe over and cook until steaming stops. Repeat until all batter is used.

Fill each crepe with ¼ cup sweetened strawberries, rolling crepe up with strawberries inside. Top with whipped cream.

DIANE HEAD

The Emergency Cupboard

I find it useful to keep frozen bread dough on hand to thaw for pizza or breadsticks. It will thaw quickly in a plastic bag placed in a large bowl of hot water if the water is changed as it cools and the dough flattened with a few squeezes as it thaws.

Cooking double portions, one to eat and one for the freezer, is another easy way to stockpile ready food for late arrivals, tight schedules, and those times you just don't care to cook. Before the birth of my fourth child, I prepared and froze my own TV dinners by doubling recipes I routinely cooked and freezing the excess. Those TV dinners were some of the most welcome meals I ever ate or served.

I also like having cookie dough in the freezer ready to slice and bake. Hot cookies from the oven have a way of

Cherry Cool Comfort

SERVES 12

½ cup butter
1½ cups confectioner's sugar
2 eggs
1 package vanilla wafers, finely crushed
1 (1 pound 6 ounce) can cherry pie filling
1 cup cream, whipped

Cream butter and sugar until light and fluffy. Beat in eggs, one at a time. Place half the vanilla wafer crumbs in a 13"x9"x2" pan. Spread butter mixture over crumbs. Top with cherry pie filling. Cover with whipped cream and sprinkle remaining crumbs on top. Chill for several hours or overnight. Keep refrigerated.

ANNE & DONALD GRAY

Blueberry or Cherry Cream Cheese Dessert

1½ cups crushed graham crackers
1 cup sugar
¾ cup butter, melted
1 (8 ounce) package cream cheese, softened
2 eggs
1 can blueberry or cherry pie filling

Mix together crushed graham crackers, ½ cup of the sugar and melted butter. Place in the bottom of a 9"x13" baking pan. With an electric mixer beat eggs, add remaining ½ cup of sugar and the cream cheese. Beat well. Pour over graham cracker mixture and bake at 350F for 15 minutes. Top with pie filling. Serve warm with whipped cream.

KATHY LYNN

satisfying guests, weary students home from a hard day at school, and family members who say, "I'm hungry, but I don't know what I want to eat."

And the ultimate in preparedness is the Emergency Shelf, a corner of the kitchen cupboard reserved for a whole meal's worth of ingredients that can be prepared quickly and easily. Knowing that the food is there, and having a specific plan for using it, enlisting all hands available, makes apprehensive hostesses feel confident again. It also helps to have a family plan of action for those situations when the house is a mess, no food is prepared, but a phone call reveals fast approaching guests, or they arrive unannounced. It's amazing what can be accomplished in ten minutes by several fast working people (of all ages) who know exactly what they are to do. ♥

PATRICIA GUNDRY

Uldine's Cheesecake

Crust:

½ cup butter
1 cup whole wheat flour
1 cup chopped pecans
2 tablespoons wheat germ

Filling:

2 eggs
½ cup honey
2 teaspoons vanilla
¾ teaspoon almond extract
2 cups cottage cheese
¼ cup nonfat dry milk

Topping:

1 pint kefir cheese (buy at health food store)
¼ cup honey
juice of one lemon
coconut, strawberries or blueberries

With fingers mix together butter, flour, pecans, and wheat germ until crumbly. Pat into the bottom of an 8″ or 9″ square baking pan. Bake at 350F for 10 minutes. In a blender whirl together eggs, honey, vanilla, almond extract, cottage cheese, and nonfat dry milk until smooth. Pour filling onto crust. Set pan on a rack or jar lids in a pan of hot water. Bake at 350F for 45 minutes. Remove from oven and cool 20 minutes. Mix together kefir cheese, honey, and lemon juice. Spread over cheesecake. Return to oven and bake 10 minutes longer. Chill. Top with coconut, strawberries or blueberries.

ULDINE BISAGNO

Natural Foods

We eat natural foods at our house! What is the big difference between our natural food diet and the average American diet? Simple—"If man made it, don't eat it!" We eat the food God made.

If you've been telling yourself it's time to do something about your nutrition, you're right. Good nutrition is the way God planned it! Wheat germ, bran, sprouts sandwiches, steamed vegetables, yogurt, whole grains, nuts and seeds, fresh fruit, plus moderate amounts of fish, fowl, and lean meats and eggs for protein. More and more people every day are getting excited about eating natural foods. It's a good thing to do.

The rewards are great too— more pep and energy, nice skin, shining hair, trim bodies. But even better—fewer colds, calmer children, less depression and heart attacks.

Try it. Soon it will become your way of life. It will be so easy and the food will be so good that you'll wish you had switched over sooner. ♥

ULDINE BISAGNO

Slim Lemon Cheesecake

1 package lemon-flavored gelatin
1 cup boiling water
1 large carton lowfat or regular cottage cheese
3 packets Equal sweetener or 3 tablespoons
  sugar
2 packets (20 crackers) graham crackers,
  crushed
¾ cup margarine
¼ cup brown sugar

Dissolve gelatin in boiling water. In electric blender, blend cottage cheese, sweetener, and dissolved gelatin until smooth. Using hands, mix crushed graham crackers, margarine, and brown sugar together. Reserve ½ cup for topping. Press remainder into two 9" pie pans or one 9"x13" baking pan and bake at 400F for 5 minutes or until just browned at edges. Pour filling over crust (no need to cool first). Sprinkle reserved crumb mixture on top. Refrigerate until firm.

Variation: Fruity Lemon Cheesecake. Before pouring in filling put drained canned mixed fruit in crust.

AUDREY HINTEN

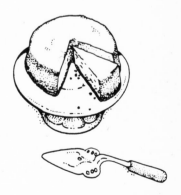

Quick & Easy English Trifle

"Very attractive, best if made shortly before serving."

SERVES 12–15

1 yellow cake mix
2 quarts sweetened fresh or frozen
   strawberries
2 packages French vanilla pudding mix
1 package non-dairy whipped topping
a few strawberries for garnish

Prepare cake mix and bake in 2 layers. Cool. Prepare pudding mix according to package instructions. In a large clear glass flat-bottomed bowl, place 1 layer of the cake. Top with half of strawberries, then half of pudding. Repeat with second cake layer, remaining strawberries, and pudding. Top with non-dairy whipped topping. To decorate pipe topping around edge and garnish with fresh strawberries. Refrigerate until served.

DEBORAH SNYDER

Christmas Eve

About three years ago we began a very special family tradition on Christmas Eve. Our immediate family enjoys a candlelight formal dinner. The children (Kevin, 8; Carol, 5; Beth and Carl, 2½) and I spend the day baking and cleaning. We set the table with the lace tablecloth and china. This is such a contrast from our normal informal meals that the children realize a special event is taking place and it is just for them. The boys dress up in their suits and we girls put on our long special dresses. Just before Wayne arrives home we light every candle in the house and put on our best manners. It has proved to be a real special celebration of the end of a hectic time for our family because of the intense Christmas rush at the bookstore. Following dinner, we gather by the fireplace to read the Christmas Story. Sure, it is extra work on Mom, the cook, but it is worth it. ♥

BRENDA & WAYNE SPRUILL

Angel Bavarian Cake

SERVES 12–15

2 cups milk
4 eggs, separated
1 cup sugar
2 tablespoons flour
¼ teaspoon salt
2 envelopes unflavored gelatin
½ cup cold water
1½ pints whipping cream
1 large angel food cake
2 tablespoons confectioner's sugar
1 teaspoon vanilla
grated coconut for garnish

In a double boiler make a custard of milk, egg yolks, sugar, flour, and salt by cooking until mixture is thickened, stirring occasionally. Soak gelatin in cold water. While custard is hot, add gelatin mixture, and stir until gelatin dissolves. Cool in refrigerator until mixture is thick and mounds slightly. Whip 1 pint of cream and beat egg whites until they form stiff peaks. Fold whipped cream and egg whites into custard. Tear cake into bite-sized pieces and, beginning with cake, alternate with custard in angel food cake pan. Chill overnight. Whip remaining half pint of cream with confectioner's sugar, add vanilla. Remove cake from pan and frost with whipped cream. Sprinkle cake lightly with coconut. Keep refrigerated.

CAROL HOLQUIST

Pavlova

An airy Australian dessert named in honor of the great Russian ballerina Anna Pavlova, representing her role as the ethereal bird in Swan Lake.

4 egg whites, at room temperature
¼ teaspoon salt
1–1½ cups sugar
1 teaspoon vanilla
1 teaspoon vinegar
2 teaspoons cornstarch

Filling:

whipped cream
strawberries
kiwi fruit

Add salt to egg whites and beat until stiff. Gradually beat in sugar one tablespoon at a time. Beat until stiff and glossy. Combine vanilla, vinegar, and cornstarch. Using a metal spoon fold into egg white until thoroughly blended. Grease and flour, or line with greased cooking parchment, a cookie sheet or 9" pie pan. Spoon mixture into a round mound about 7"–9" in diameter. Make a wide well in the center about 1" deep so it can be filled later. Bake at 250F–300F about an hour and a half in center or lower half of oven. Remove from oven and allow to cool on rack 15 minutes before removing from pan, or if using cooking parchment allow to cool completely, then carefully peel off parchment. Frost with whipped cream, fill, and decorate with fruit just before serving.

LEON MORRIS
SHARON & JAMES ENGEL

Chocolate Slice

Layer 1:

½ cup butter
5 tablespoons sugar
5 tablespoons cocoa
1 teaspoon vanilla
1 egg
2 cups graham cracker crumbs
1 cup coconut
½ cup nuts, chopped

Layer 2:

¼ cup butter, softened
3 tablespoons milk
1 package instant vanilla pudding mix
1½ cups confectioner's sugar

Layer 3:

4 squares semi-sweet baking chocolate
1 tablespoon butter

Evening meals throughout the week offer the opportunity for our family to share the day's activities. Often we take turns sharing the best thing that happened to us during the day. ♥

D. G. KEHL

To prepare layer 1: Cook butter, sugar, cocoa, vanilla, and egg in double boiler until thickened, stirring frequently. Mix crumbs, coconut, and nuts together, add thickened mixture, and spread in a greased 7"x11" pan.

To prepare layer 2: Cream butter, combine milk and pudding mix, and add to butter. Mix in confectioner's sugar. Spread over layer 1 in pan. Allow to stiffen slightly.

To prepare layer 3: Melt and mix together chocolate and butter. Spread over layer 2 in pan. When cool cut into about 20 bars. Refrigerate. Freezes well.

HELEN ENNS

Chocolate Eclair Dessert

graham crackers
2 packages French vanilla instant pudding
3 cups milk
1 (8 ounce) container non-dairy whipped
   topping
2 squares unsweetened baking chocolate*
3 tablespoons margarine or butter, softened
2 tablespoons light corn syrup
1½ cups confectioner's sugar
3 tablespoons milk
1 teaspoon vanilla

Place a layer of graham crackers in the bottom of a greased 9"x13" baking pan or glass dish. Combine pudding with milk and beat according to package directions. Fold in non-dairy whipped topping. Spread half of mixture over the graham crackers. Add another layer of graham crackers and spread with the rest of the pudding mixture. Refrigerate until pudding is set.

Melt chocolate and butter or margarine. With an electric mixer combine melted chocolate and butter with corn syrup, confectioner's sugar, milk, and vanilla. Beat until smooth. Spread over chilled pudding mixture and refrigerate overnight or longer.

*You can also use 2 squares semi-sweet baking chocolate or 1 (6 ounce) package semi-sweet chocolate chips, reducing confectioner's sugar to ½ cup.

RONNIE CARDER
DENA KORFKER
DELORIS VANDER SCHUUR

Toffee Squares

SERVES 9

1 cup crushed vanilla wafers
1 cup chopped pecans
½ cup butter, softened
1 cup confectioner's sugar
3 eggs, separated
1½ squares unsweetened baking chocolate,
   melted
½ teaspoon vanilla
whipped cream

Mix vanilla wafer crumbs and pecans together. Using half the mixture cover the bottom of a buttered 9"x9" pan. Cream butter and sugar. Beat egg yolks. Add egg yolks, melted chocolate, and vanilla to sugar-butter mixture, beat well. Beat egg whites until they form stiff peaks, then fold into mixture. Pour over wafers and spread remaining crumbs on top. Refrigerate overnight. Cut in squares and serve with whipped cream. Keep refrigerated. May be prepared ahead and frozen.

HELEN ENNS

We had our five children in ten years and this sometimes created bedlam at the table. At one point in our family life together we determined that something had to be done to make eating a happy experience for all of us. This was our plan. Each person should come to the evening meal prepared to share the best thing that happened to them all day or pay a penny penalty. This began a happy ending to our dinner time dilemma. ♥

BETTY DRESCHER

Family Favorite Low-Calorie Ice Cream

MAKES 1 gallon

3½ quarts *skim* milk
8 junket rennet tablets
2 tablespoons water
2 cups sugar
2 tablespoons vanilla

Pour milk into a one gallon sized ice cream freezer container. Set container in a pan or sink of hot, *not* boiling, water. Do not heat on stove. Rennet will cause milk to curdle if overheated. Allow milk to heat to room temperature. Dissolve rennet tablets in water. Quickly stir in dissolved rennet, sugar, and vanilla. Then *do not touch* for about 5 minutes. If not disturbed, junket will turn mixture into a custard. When it has reached custard consistency freeze according to freezer instructions.

BONNIE & HADDON ROBINSON

Family Favorite Low-Calorie Ice Cream

◄ *When Haddon is home on those rare Sunday evenings we make this low calorie (1 cup serving only 120 calories) ice cream our Sunday meal, winter and summer. It was a favorite of my parents. I grew up on this recipe.* ♥

BONNIE ROBINSON

Ice Cream Grasshoppers

SERVES 4

8 chocolate wafers
1 pint vanilla ice cream, slightly softened
1 tablespoon green creme de menthe

About 40 minutes before serving: Pulverize chocolate wafers to fine crumbs at medium speed in a blender or in a food processor with knife blade attached. In a small bowl, with electric mixer at low speed, beat together ice cream and creme de menthe. Layer ice cream mixture and chocolate wafer crumbs in freezer-safe parfait or dessert glasses. Freeze until ready to serve. Makes 4 servings.

JOIE & MIKE VANDER WALL

Frozen Cheese Cream

"Prepare early in the day or up to 2 weeks ahead."

1½ cups creamed cottage cheese
½ cup sugar
1 egg
¾ teaspoon almond extract
2 pints vanilla ice cream, softened
grated lemon peel for garnish

Line a 9"x5" loaf pan with plastic wrap. In a blender or food processor with knife blade attached, blend cottage cheese, sugar, egg, and almond extract until smooth. In a large bowl with electric mixer at low speed beat ice cream with cheese mixture until well blended. Pour into loaf pan, cover with plastic wrap, and freeze until firm, about 6 hours.

JOIE & MIKE VANDER WALL

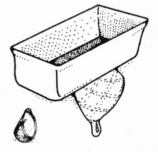

Sherbet Cream Cake

SERVES 10–12

1½ pints raspberry sherbet
1½ pints orange sherbet
1½ pints pistachio ice cream
3 quarts vanilla ice cream
2 cups chopped pecans
2 cups shaved sweet chocolate
1 pint heavy cream
green food coloring
fresh berries for garnish

Make 8 balls of each kind of sherbet and of the pistachio ice cream (24 balls in all). Place them in a chilled flat pan and freeze. Chill a 10″ tube pan. Slightly soften vanilla ice cream* and beat in a large bowl with electric mixer until smooth. Stir in 1 cup chopped pecans and 1 cup shaved chocolate. Spoon enough ice cream mixture into chilled tube pan to make a 1″ layer. Quickly arrange 3 balls of each color sherbet and pistachio on top, against center tube and along sides of pan. Spoon rest of soft ice cream over balls. Return to freezer.

Slightly soften remaining half of vanilla ice cream,* beat as above, and add remaining chopped pecans and chocolate. Alternate colored balls as before and cover with soft ice cream to fill pan. Cover with foil. Return to freezer until firm or until day to serve.

Early in the day of serving cover a 10″ circle of cardboard with foil. Remove frozen cake from freezer, run a knife around edges of pan and tube. Quickly dip cake pan in and out of lukewarm water. Lay foil-covered cardboard circle on top of pan, invert, and unmold. Return to freezer.

Two hours before serving, whip cream and tint it a delicate green. Remove the cake from freezer. Quickly frost it and return to freezer until serving time. Garnish with fresh strawberries or other berries and small leaves if desired.   ➥

*Do not oversoften; keep ice cream frozen to avoid bacterial contamination.

Variation: Can be made with any compatible combination of ice creams or sherbets.

JOANNE BOER

Crunchy Ice Cream

SERVES 12–15

½ gallon ice cream
16 graham crackers, finely crushed
6 Heath bars, finely crushed
½ cup chopped maraschino cherries
2 tablespoons crunchy peanut butter

Mix together all ingredients except ice cream. With a sharp knife cut sides of ice cream carton and open flat. Cut ice cream into 12–15 pieces. Roll each piece in mixture. Place on cookie sheet or individual serving dishes and return to freezer until serving time.

MRS. WALTER HENRICHSEN

Turtle Sundae Dessert

 Quick & Easy

26 oreo cookies, crushed
⅓ cup butter or margarine, melted
½ gallon vanilla ice cream
1 small jar caramel ice cream topping
1 small jar chocolate ice cream topping
pecans

Mix cookies and margarine and press into a 9"x13" pan. Refrigerate. Soften ice cream and spread over crushed cookies. Return to freezer to harden. Drizzle caramel topping, then chocolate topping over ice cream. Top with pecans. Cover and store in freezer.

SUE MacDONALD

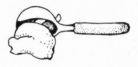

Oreo Pie

  Quick & Easy

30–35 Oreo cookies
½ gallon vanilla ice cream, softened
½ teaspoon vanilla
1 (12 ounce) container frozen non-dairy
    whipped topping
chocolate syrup (about ¼ of a 16 ounce can)
⅔ cup chopped pecans or other nuts

Crush Oreo cookies. Reserve about ¾ cup for topping and use the rest to line the bottom of a 9"x13" pan. Mix together ice cream, vanilla, and frozen non-dairy whipped topping. Drop by spoon over crushed cookies. Smooth ice cream mixture carefully to avoid mixing with cookies. Drizzle chocolate syrup in a zig-zag pattern over top. Sprinkle with pecans and reserved crushed cookies. Freeze until firm. Cut in squares to serve. Keep frozen.

HARRIET & DERRALL KINARD

Sharing

For most of the 12 years Dick and I have been married we have both worked full time. Therefore, meal planning and preparation must be streamlined. My husband, a mathematics professor, does the grocery shopping and dishwashing. I am the cook and dish drier. I also do the meal planning. I plan menus two weeks ahead and Dick does the major food shopping approximately every two weeks. In between we make quick stops at the market for perishables. ♥

MARTHA STOUT

Danny Penwell's Pumpkin Pie Cake

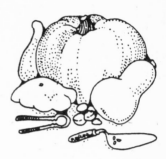

1 yellow cake mix
½ cup margarine, melted
3 eggs
1 (30 ounce) can pumpkin pie mix
½ cup milk
¼ cup sugar
¼ cup margarine, unmelted
½ cup chopped nuts
whipped topping

Reserve and set aside ¾ cup of dry cake mix. Combine remaining cake mix with melted margarine and one of the eggs, reserving the other two eggs. Press mixture into the bottom of a greased 9"x13" baking pan.

Combine pumpkin pie mix, remaining two eggs, and milk. Pour over mixture pressed in pan.

Combine reserved cake mix, sugar, and unmelted margarine by cutting margarine into dry ingredients. Sprinkle over filling. Sprinkle nuts over all. Bake at 350F for about 50 minutes. Serve with whipped topping.

DANNY PENWELL

Melba's Dessert Topping

cream cheese, softened
maraschino cherry juice, orange juice, or juice drained from canned fruit

Whip together cream cheese and a small amount of the juice of your choice, gradually adding juice until of desired consistency.

MELBA PETERSEN

CAKES

Pumpkin Cake 341
Cream Cheese Frosting 341
Carrot Cake I 342
Carrot Cake II 342
Carrot Bundt Cake 343
Rhubarb Coffee Cake 344
Rhubarb Upsidedown Cake 345
Grandma's Fresh Fruit Cake 346
Cranberry Coffee Cake 347
Mother's Shortcake 347
Quick Pineapple Cake 348
Apple Pound Cake 349
Apple Cake 350
Applesauce Cake 351
Orange Cake 352
Chocolate Cream Cupcakes 353
Chocolate Sheet Cake 354
Turtle Cake 355
Milky Way Cake 356
Chocolate Zucchini Cake 357
Zucchini Chocolate Bundt Cake 358
Surprise Chocolate Cake 359
Milk Chocolate Cake 360
Mashed Potato Cake 361
Sour Cream Coffee Cake 362
Easy Coffee Cake 363
Super Quick Coffee Cake 364
Butter Farm Coffee Cake 365
Spicy Oatmeal Cake 366

Praline Pound Cake 367
Dutch Nutmeg Cake 367
Twyla's Christmas Fruit Cake 368
Light Fruit Cake 369
Halley's Kentucky Fruitcake 370

Pumpkin Cake

4 eggs
2 cups sugar
1 cup corn oil
2 cups flour
2 teaspoons soda
2 teaspoons cinnamon
½ teaspoon salt
2 cups pumpkin

With an electric mixer, beat together eggs, sugar, and oil. Sift together and add flour, soda, cinnamon, and salt. Stir in pumpkin. Pour into a greased and floured 9"x13" baking pan or a tube cake pan. For flat cake bake at 350F for about 45 minutes. For tube cake bake at 325F for about 1 hour, then at 350F for 15–20 minutes. When cool frost with Cream Cheese Frosting.

Variation for Pumpkin Bread: bake in 2 loaf pans at 350F for 45–55 minutes.

JOY MACKENZIE

Cream Cheese Frosting

8 ounces cream cheese, softened
½ cup margarine, softened
1 (1 pound) box confectioner's sugar
1 teaspoon vanilla

Cream together cream cheese and margarine, mix in confectioner's sugar, then vanilla. Spread on cooled cake.

BETTY DRESCHER
RONNIE CARDER

Carrot Cake I

"My husband's favorite."

1½ cups oil (may use only 1 cup for a lighter cake)
2 cups sugar
3 eggs
2 cups flour
2 teaspoons baking powder
1½ teaspoons soda
2 teaspoons cinnamon
1 teaspoon salt
2 cups grated carrots
1 (8 ounce) can crushed pineapple, undrained
½ cup chopped pecans

Mix oil and sugar together well. Beat in eggs, one at a time. Sift together and add flour, baking powder, cinnamon, soda, and salt. Mix well. Stir in carrots, pineapple, and nuts. Bake in a greased 9"x13" baking pan at 350F for about 45 minutes. Cool and frost with Cream Cheese Frosting.

RONNIE CARDER

Carrot Cake II

1 cup oil
2 cups sugar
2 teaspoons soda
1 teaspoon salt
2 teaspoons cinnamon
3 cups grated carrots
1½ cups chopped nuts
4 eggs, beaten
2 cups flour
dash cloves

Dump together ingredients and stir well. Bake in a greased and floured 9"x13" baking pan at 300F for 50–60 minutes.

JUDY VRIESEMA

Carrot Bundt Cake

1½ cups oil
1¾ cups brown sugar
4 eggs, separated
5 tablespoons hot water
2½ cups flour
1½ teaspoons baking powder
½ teaspoon soda
½ teaspoon salt
1 teaspoon nutmeg
1 teaspoon cloves
2 teaspoons cinnamon
1¾ cups grated carrots
1 cup chopped pecans

Cream Cheese Glaze:

2 tablespoons cream cheese
¼ teaspoon vanilla or almond extract
1 cup confectioner's sugar
milk, as needed for proper consistency

Mix together oil and sugar. Beat in egg yolks, one at a time. Add hot water. Sift together and add flour, baking powder, soda, salt, nutmeg, cloves, and cinnamon. Stir in carrots and pecans. Beat egg whites to soft peaks and fold into batter. Bake in a well greased bundt pan at 350F for 60–70 minutes. Cool and glaze if desired.

To prepare glaze, combine cream cheese, vanilla, and confectioner's sugar. Gradually add milk until of desired consistency. Drizzle over cake.

Julie L. & S. Rickly Christian

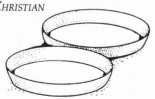

Baking Pan Substitutes ♥

I just came across an article on baking pan substitutes and found it very useful. Remember that when you alter the size of a dish or substitute glass for metal, cooking time and temperature must be adjusted accordingly. Reduce oven temperatures by 25 degrees when using glass pans. The substitutions were as follows:

For 8x1½ inch round pan use:
   10x6x2 inch dish
   9x1½ inch round pan
   8x4x2 inch loaf pan
   9 inch pie plate
   Approximate volume: 1½ quarts

For 8x8x2 inch pan use:
   11x7x1½ inch pan
   12x7½x2 inch pan
   9x5x3 inch loaf pan
   two 8x1½ inch round pans
   Approximate volume: 2 quarts

For 13x9x2 inch pan use:
   14x11x2 inch baking dish
   two 9x1½ inch round pans
   three 8x1½ inch round pans
   Approximate volume: 3 quarts

Barbara & Stephen G. Cobb

Rhubarb Coffee Cake

½ cup shortening
1½ cups sugar
1 egg, beaten
2 cups flour
1 teaspoon soda
pinch of salt
1 cup sour milk
1½ cups cut up rhubarb

Topping:

½ cup sugar
1 teaspoon cinnamon
1 cup chopped pecans

Cream together shortening and sugar. Add beaten egg. Sift together flour, soda, and salt. Add to creamed mixture alternately with sour milk. Fold in rhubarb. Spread in a greased and floured 9"x13" baking pan. Mix together topping ingredients and sprinkle on top of cake. Bake at 350F for 35 minutes.

Isabelle & Kenneth Barker

Rhubarb Upsidedown Cake

5 cups rhubarb cut up in ½" pieces
1 cup sugar
2 (3 ounce) packages red fruit-flavored gelatin
2 cups miniature marshmallows
1 package yellow cake mix

Grease a 9"x13"x2" glass baking pan. Spread rhubarb evenly in pan. Sprinkle sugar over rhubarb. Sprinkle dry fruit-flavored gelatin over sugar. Scatter marshmallows over gelatin.

Prepare cake mix according to package instructions. Pour over other ingredients. Bake at 350F for 55 minutes. Turn out on a serving platter or tray. Cool. Serve with whipped cream.

RUTH THOMAS

Rhubarb Upsidedown Cake

◄ *This recipe was given to me by Rita Bentley of Bentley's Restaurant, St. Ignace, Michigan. Rita likes to cut the cake, freeze it, and take a couple of pieces out at a time for her and her husband, Ralph. It freezes beautifully, and is a very colorful dessert.* ♥

RUTH THOMAS

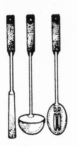

Grandma's Fresh Fruit Cake

½ cup butter or margarine
½ cup sugar
3 eggs
¼ teaspoon lemon juice
3 cups flour
1 tablespoon baking powder
½ teaspoon salt
1 cup minus 2 tablespoons milk
about 2 pounds sliced fresh fruit (cooking
    apples, peaches, plums, pitted cherries)

Topping:

¼–½ cup sugar (depending on tartness of
    fruit)
1 egg, slightly beaten
¼ cup milk

Divide butter into two ¼ cup portions. Melt one portion and set aside. Cream other portion with sugar. Beat in eggs, one at a time. Add lemon juice. Sift together flour, baking powder and salt. Beat in alternately with milk. Spread batter in a lightly greased 10½"x15½"x1" baking pan. Spread reserved melted butter over batter. Arrange fruit over batter. To prepare topping, sprinkle sugar over fruit. Mix egg and milk together and pour over all. Bake at 425F for 15 minutes, reduce heat to 350F and bake 15 minutes longer, or until golden brown.

ELAINE L. SCHULTE

Grandma's Fresh Fruit Cake

◄≡ *Delicious plain, or topped with whipped cream or ice cream.*

When my mother baked her mother's fresh fruit cake—often using apples, peaches, plums, or cherries from our trees or from a friend's bumper crop—it was always far more than just a special treat. My grandmother brought the recipe to America from Austria on an immigrant ship at the turn of the century.

Every time I bake this unusual cake, I remember my lovely grandmother Matthew and marvel at the faith and courage it must have taken when she emigrated alone at the age of sixteen. I'm overwhelmed too by the wondrous love of her poverty-stricken parents, depriving themselves even more so that their daughter might

Cranberry Coffee Cake

½ cup margarine
1 cup sugar
2 eggs, beaten
1 teaspoon vanilla
1 cup sour cream
2 cups flour
1 teaspoon baking powder
½ teaspoon soda
¼ teaspoon salt
1 cup whole cranberry sauce

Combine margarine and sugar, mix in eggs, vanilla, and sour cream. Sift together flour, baking powder, soda, and salt. Lightly stir into batter. Spoon half of batter into a greased 7"x11" baking pan. Spread with cranberry sauce. Spoon remaining batter over top. Bake at 350F for about 35–45 minutes.

JEAN SHAW

have an opportunity for a better life in a new land. Surely they suspected that they would never see her on earth again. And they never did.

This recipe not only carries on a family tradition, but it links me and my children and their future children to our forebears in a tangible way, reminding us of one of our trails through the family of mankind. ♥

ELAINE L. SHULTE

Mother's Shortcake

2 cups flour
3 tablespoons sugar
½ teaspoon salt
4 teaspoons baking powder
3 tablespoons margarine
1 egg, beaten
1 cup milk
crushed sweetened strawberries
whipped cream

Into a mixing bowl sift together flour, sugar, salt, and baking powder. With fingers, work in margarine until crumbly. Stir in egg and milk. Bake in a greased 9" round or 9" square baking pan at 425F for 15 minutes.

While still warm cut into portions and serve with crushed sweetened strawberries and whipped cream.

DIANE BRUMMEL BLOEM

Quick Pineapple Cake

This unusual cake contains no shortening. It
tastes particularly good warm.

2 cups sugar
2 teaspoons soda
1 (20 ounce) can crushed pineapple, undrained
2 cups flour
2 eggs
1 teaspoon vanilla
½ cup chopped nuts

Frosting:

¼ cup margarine or butter
1 (8 ounce) package cream cheese
¾ of a (1 pound) box confectioner's sugar
1 teaspoon vanilla or almond extract
½ cup chopped nuts (optional)

Do not use electric mixer. In a mixing bowl, stir
together sugar and soda. Add crushed pineapple
with its juice. Stir in flour. Beat in eggs and
vanilla. Stir in nuts. Bake in a greased and floured
9"x13" baking pan at 325F for about 35–45 minutes. To make frosting mix first 4 ingredients
together until smooth. Stir in nuts, if desired.
Frost while hot.

David M. Martin

Apple Pound Cake

2 cups sugar
1½ cups vegetable oil
3 eggs
3 cups flour
1 teaspoon soda
1 teaspoon salt
2 tablespoons cinnamon (optional)
1½ teaspoons vanilla
3 cups peeled diced apples
1 cup chopped nuts

In a mixing bowl mix together sugar and oil. Beat in eggs. Sift together and add flour, soda, salt, and cinnamon, if desired. Mix well. Stir in vanilla. Mix in diced apples and nuts. Bake in a well greased tube cake pan at 300F for about 1 hour and 20 minutes.

BLANCHE E. RYDEL

Christmas

Our family, in an attempt to emphasize Christmas as Jesus' birthday, features a birthday cake with one large white candle. Singing "Happy Birthday to Jesus" while the youngest child blows out the candle helps us remember. ♥

LORETTA R. WILSON

Apple Cake

Rich and chewy-gooey, crunchy and chocolate all in one. "The favorite of Bernard D. Zondervan, Jr."

2 cups sugar
½ cup margarine
2 eggs
½ teaspoon salt
2 teaspoons cinnamon
½ teaspoon nutmeg
2 teaspoons soda
5 teaspoons warm water
5 cups unpeeled diced apples
2 cups coarsely chopped nuts
2 cups flour
1 (6 ounce) package chocolate chips

Cream together sugar and margarine, beat in eggs. Stir in salt, cinnamon, and nutmeg. Dissolve soda in warm water and add, mixing well. Combine chopped apples, half of the nuts, and flour. Add to batter, mixing together thoroughly. Pour into a greased and floured 9"x13" baking pan. Sprinkle chocolate chips and remaining nuts over the top. Bake at 350F for 45–60 minutes. Delicious as is. Can also be served with ice cream or whipped cream.

WILMA ZONDERVAN TEGGELAAR

Applesauce Cake

1 yellow cake mix
1 (16 ounce) can applesauce
⅓ cup oil
2 eggs

Crumb mixture:

½ cup flour
½ cup brown sugar
2 teaspoons cinnamon
⅓ cup butter

With an electric mixer beat together cake mix, applesauce, oil, and eggs for 2 minutes at medium speed. Spread in a greased and floured 9"x13" baking pan. Mix together flour, brown sugar, cinnamon, and butter with fingers or a fork, until crumbly, and spread on top of cake mixture. Bake at 350F for 30 minutes.

ISABELLE & KENNETH BARKER

Orange Cake

1 (7¼ ounce) package dates
1 cup chopped pecans
1 cup oil or margarine
2 cups sugar
4 eggs, separated
1 teaspoon soda
1⅓ cups buttermilk
2 teaspoons baking powder
4 cups flour
½ teaspoon salt

Topping:

candied cherries (optional)
pecan halves (optional)
2 cups brown sugar
1 cup *fresh* orange juice

Dredge dates in a small amount of the flour and cut in small bits. Mix with chopped nuts. Cream together shortening and sugar. Beat egg yolks thoroughly and add to butter and sugar. Dissolve soda in buttermilk and add to mixture. Stir in flour sifted with baking powder and salt. Add dates and nuts. Beat egg whites until they form stiff peaks, fold into batter. Blend well. Bake in a large, well greased and floured tube pan at 350F for 1½ hours. Or bake in 3–4 loaf pans for 30–40 minutes. Cake is done when knife inserted in the middle comes out clean.

To prepare topping, while cake is baking, squeeze orange juice and combine with brown sugar, stirring to dissolve sugar. (These make great jobs for little hands.) After cake is removed from the oven and still warm, punch holes all over cake top (an ice pick is good for this) and spoon on mixture, allowing it to seep into the holes in the cake. Repeat process until all mixture is used. Remove from pans to a sheet of foil, wrap, and store in refrigerator or freeze. (This cake freezes

Orange Cake

My childhood was essentially a rural one, filled with sips of cold well water from long-handled dippers, frosty morning trips to the outhouse, and Mason jars filled with fireflies. Christmas seemed the highlight of every year. For weeks preceding that special day, our kitchen was as fragrant with the smells of Christmas goodies as our living room was pungent with the smell of fresh-cut pine.

But one scent will forever mean Christmas for me—fresh oranges. My mother would begin baking and freezing her Orange Cakes before we had even finished Thanksgiving leftovers. An old family recipe, these cakes were given as presents to teachers, neighbors, friends. When I was old enough, I took orders for Mother's specialty. Many times, it was the money made from baking these Orange Cakes that paid for our Christmas presents.

Now I have my own daughter, as well as my own

➤➤

very well.) For a festive look, cherries and pecan halves may be arranged on top of the cake and topping spooned over these, also.

MARY LOU CARNEY

Chocolate Cream Cupcakes

Batter:

1½ cups flour
½ teaspoon salt
¼ cup cocoa
⅓ cup oil
1 tablespoon vinegar
1 teaspoon soda
1 cup sugar
1 teaspoon vanilla
1 cup water

Cream Cheese Center:

1 (8 ounce) package cream cheese
⅓ cup sugar
1 egg
⅛ teaspoon salt
1 (6 ounce) package chocolate chips

To prepare batter mix all ingredients together thoroughly, using an electric mixer. Fill cupcake paper cups ½ full. Prepare cream cheese center by creaming together cream cheese and sugar. Add egg and salt and mix well. Stir in chocolate chips. Place 1 generous tablespoon of cream cheese mixture on top of each cupcake before baking. Bake at 350F for about 30 minutes. Cool and freeze, if desired.

SANDRA ZUIDERSMA

son. *Together we bake Orange Cakes each holiday. My mother has graciously consented to let me share her/my/my daughter's recipe with you. I hope it will give to many people the pleasure it has given to me and mine.* ♥

MARY LOU CARNEY

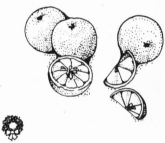

A Kansas Christmas

Christmas, 1971. My husband had been drafted in 1970, and now, 18 months and four states later, was assigned to Fort Riley, Kansas. Until then, my only connection with Kansas had been Dorothy and Toto. Now I was to have a Kansas Christmas and a Kansas baby.

I pulled the collar of my worn wool coat tightly around

Chocolate Sheet Cake

A super-favorite among cakes because it's easy to make, easy to frost, easy to transport, and tastes fudgy-good.

1 cup margarine or ½ cup margarine and ½
    cup oil
4 tablespoons cocoa
1 cup milk or water
2 cups flour
2 cups sugar
pinch of cinnamon (optional)
2 eggs, beaten
½ cup buttermilk or milk soured with 1½
    teaspoons vinegar
1 teaspoon soda
1 teaspoon vanilla

Frosting:

⅓–½ cup margarine
4 tablespoons cocoa
6 tablespoons milk or evaporated milk
1 (1 pound) box confectioner's sugar (a little
    less if using ⅓ cup margarine)
1 teaspoon vanilla
½–1 cup chopped pecans or walnuts
    (optional)

In a saucepan bring to a rapid boil margarine, cocoa, and milk or water. While mixture is heating combine flour, sugar, and cinnamon, if desired, in a mixing bowl. Pour boiling mixture over flour and sugar mixture. Mix well. Add eggs, buttermilk, soda, and vanilla. Mix well. Bake in a greased and floured 10"x15"x1" baking pan at 350F–400F for about 20 minutes. ➥

my neck. The tattered vinyl belt barely reached around my bulging middle. Half-frozen droplets stung my cheeks and clung to my eyelashes as I hurried down the slushy Junction City sidewalk, splashing through murky puddles and floating chunks of gray snow. It was the bleakness of the scene before me, as much as the sleeting weather, that made me look for a place out of the storm.

The USO sign swayed in the December wind. Red, white, and blue stars had been painted on the front of the building and the entrance wore a faded plastic wreath. Inside, the room smelled of space heaters and cigars. Two soldiers were playing checkers on a card table nearby. A warped ping pong table stood near the back wall. Rows of battered paperbacks—their corners mended with masking tape— were shelved along one side.

A weathered-faced soldier leaned lazily against the bookshelves, peeling an orange.

While cake bakes prepare frosting. In a sauce-pan heat together margarine, cocoa, and milk until hot. Remove from heat and add confectioner's sugar, beating until smooth. Stir in vanilla and nuts, if desired. Pour over hot cake.

RONNIE CARDER
CHERYL ROSE
PATRICIA GUNDRY
DIANE HEAD
CAROL KUYKENDALL

Turtle Cake

1 German Chocolate cake mix
1 (14 ounce) package caramels
½ cup evaporated milk
¾ cup margarine, melted
2 cups chopped nuts
1 (6 ounce) package chocolate chips

Prepare cake mix according to package instructions. Pour half the batter into a greased and floured 9"x13" baking pan and bake at 350F for 15 minutes. While cake is baking melt together caramels, evaporated milk and margarine in a double boiler or in a saucepan over low heat, stirring constantly. (Watch carefully, it burns easily.)

Pour caramel mixture over baked batter. Sprinkle half the nuts and half the chocolate chips on top. Pour remaining cake batter on top. Sprinkle with remaining nuts and chocolate chips. Bake 20 minutes longer.

DELORIS VANDER SCHUUR

The pungent citrus smell filled the dingy room and unexpectedly carried me back in time, as the tornado had transported Dorothy.

I was suddenly back home in Indiana, and Mother was baking her famous orange cakes for the Christmas festivities. I, a child again, was pushing orange halves against the juicer, watching the golden liquid spill into the bowl. Outside, fresh snow whirled playfully, caressing fenceposts and silos. Birch trees, like virgin brides, boasted white on white. Pine trees posed for Christmas cards. Children's voices could be heard as young carolers made their way to our inviting front porch . . .

"Merry Christmas!" a voice rang out. Startled, I watched the room do a scene change. My daydream faded and I was abruptly back in the present. A small but very brisk woman was peering intently into my face. "Say," she wanted to know, "are you okay?"

Standing erect, I managed a

Milky Way Cake

"Delicious even without the rich frosting. This is definitely *not* a cake for calorie-counters!"

8 (1 ounce) snack-size, or 5 (2.24 ounce) regular Milky Way candy bars
1 cup margarine or butter
2 cups sugar
4 eggs
2½ cups flour
½ teaspoon soda
1¼ cups buttermilk
1 cup chopped pecans (optional)

Frosting:

2½ cups sugar
1 cup evaporated milk
1 (6 ounce) package chocolate chips
1 cup marshmallow creme
½ cup margarine

Melt together candy and ½ cup of the margarine. Set aside. Cream sugar and remaining margarine. Add eggs. Sift together flour and soda and add alternately with buttermilk. Then add pecans. Bake in a greased and floured tube pan at 325F for about 1½ hours. Frost when cool, if desired.

To prepare frosting, cook sugar, and milk together to soft ball stage. Add chocolate chips, marshmallow creme, and margarine. Stir until all are melted. Cool, stirring occasionally, until of spreading consistency.

OLIVIA & PAUL HILLMAN

weak smile. "Guess I'm a little tired," I murmured self-consciously.

The woman's name was Molly. "Here, let me take your coat," she said, as she hustled me toward a well-used, overstuffed chair. "How about a cup of peppermint tea? When is your baby due?" Somehow the concern in her voice made the worn upholstery of the chair feel friendly and more familiar.

I found myself not only answering her businesslike questions, but soon I was stringing popcorn, testing lights and searching through stacks of ancient record albums for Christmas music. When I next noticed the clock on the wall, a pleasant hour had slipped by. First impressions aside, the room seemed to have gained a warm, homey personality.

I mumbled something about getting home to start dinner, but as I was about to leave, Molly took my face between her gnarled hands. "You and your husband will eat Christmas

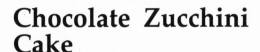

Chocolate Zucchini Cake

½ cup margarine
½ cup oil
1¾ cups sugar
2 eggs
1 teaspoon vanilla
½ cup sour milk
2½ cups flour
4 tablespoons cocoa
1 teaspoon soda
½ teaspoon cinnamon
½ teaspoon cloves
½ teaspoon salt
2 cups grated zucchini
½ cup chopped nuts
½ cup chocolate chips

Mix together margarine, oil, and sugar. Add eggs, vanilla, and sour milk. Sift together and add flour, cocoa, soda, cinnamon, cloves, and salt. Stir in grated zucchini. Pour into a greased 9"x13" baking pan. Sprinkle nuts and chocolate chips on top. Bake at 325F for 45–55 minutes.

LAURIE GOTT

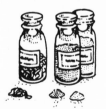

dinner here with us," she said. "We have turkey and all the trimmings." For an instant the idea repulsed me—a charity meal served on plastic trays. "We're family," Molly added, as though she sensed my feelings, "and it's Christmas." Then, quickly and with surprising strength, she hugged me.

Warmed both in body and soul, I began to walk toward the base and our quarters. Then I noticed the sleet had turned to snow and huge, airy flakes floated around me. Already a sparkly film covered the ground. Christmas lights winked through wisps of white.

I stopped at the commissary. Gingerly, I handled the oranges—searching out the juiciest for the orange cakes I would make for the USO Christmas dinner.

"You certainly are particular," a friendly stranger smiled at me. "I bet you're baking a little something for your family."

I held the oranges in my

Zucchini Chocolate Bundt Cake

¾ cup butter or margarine
2 cups sugar
2 ounces unsweetened baking chocolate, melted
3 eggs
2 teaspoons vanilla
2 teaspoons grated orange peel
2½ cups flour
2½ teaspoons baking powder
1½ teaspoons soda
1 teaspoon salt
1 teaspoon cinnamon
½ cup milk
2 cups coarsely grated zucchini
1 cup chopped pecans
1 cup mini-chocolate chips
confectioner's sugar

Cream together butter and sugar. Add chocolate. Beat in eggs, one at a time. Add vanilla and orange peel. Sift together flour, baking powder, soda, salt, and cinnamon. Add alternately with milk, beating until blended. Stir in zucchini, pecans, and chocolate chips. Bake in a buttered and floured bundt pan at 350F for about 60 minutes. When cool remove from pan and dust with sifted confectioner's sugar.

Donita Dyer

arms. *"You're absolutely right,"* I beamed.
Suddenly I was very glad— for oranges and Christmas and Kansas. ♥

Mary Lou Carney (article first appeared in Off Duty. *Reprinted by author's permission.)*

Surprise Chocolate Cake

Mixed right in the pan.

1 cup sugar
1½ cups flour
3 tablespoons cocoa
1 teaspoon soda
½ teaspoon salt
6 tablespoons oil
1 cup cold water
1 tablespoon vinegar
1 teaspoon vanilla

Frosting:

3 tablespoons brown sugar
3 tablespoons margarine
3 tablespoons milk
1 heaping tablespoon cocoa
¼ teaspoon vanilla
confectioner's sugar, sifted

Into an 8"x8" baking pan sift together sugar, flour, cocoa, soda, and salt. Make a well in the middle and pour in oil, water, vinegar, and vanilla. Beat with a fork until well mixed. Bake at 350F for about 35 minutes. Cool and frost.

To prepare frosting, in a saucepan bring to a boil brown sugar, margarine, and milk. Remove from heat and add cocoa and vanilla, then enough confectioner's sugar to make of spreading consistency.

DOROTHY HALVERSON

Milk Chocolate Cake

MAKES 3 layers

**2 squares unsweetened baking chocolate,
    melted
2¼ cups sugar
3 tablespoons water
¾ cup butter
1 teaspoon vanilla
4 eggs, separated
2¼ cups sifted cake flour
1 teaspoon cream of tartar
½ teaspoon soda
½ teaspoon salt
1 cup milk**

In a saucepan over low heat melt chocolate with ¼ cup of the sugar and water. Set aside. In a mixing bowl cream butter well. Gradually add remaining 2 cups sugar, beating until light and fluffy. Add vanilla, then egg yolks, one at a time, beating well after each addition. Add chocolate mixture and blend thoroughly. Sift together flour, cream of tartar, soda, and salt. Add alternately with milk, beating until smooth. Beat egg whites until stiff, but not dry. Fold into batter. Pour into 3 round 9″ cake pans, lined with wax paper or greased cooking parchment. Bake at 350F for about 30 minutes. Cool, fill, and frost as desired.

LOUISE DRUART

Birthdays

The honored person has the privilege of choosing his favorite menu. Another birthday tradition for our boys has been a cake in the form of a cutout figure: train, Snoopy, space ship, football field, racing car, basketball, etc. Part of the "birthright" is the choice of the figure. ♥

D. G. KEHL

Mashed Potato Cake

2 cups sugar
½ cup shortening
1 cup mashed potatoes
2 eggs
2 cups flour
1 teaspoon baking soda
pinch of salt
1 teaspoon cinnamon
1 teaspoon cloves
6 tablespoons cocoa
1 cup buttermilk, or milk soured with 1
    tablespoon of vinegar

Cream together sugar and shortening. Add mashed potatoes, mixing well. Beat in eggs, one at a time. Sift together flour, soda, salt, cinnamon, cloves, and cocoa. Add alternately with buttermilk, beating well after each addition. Bake in 3 greased and floured 8" or 9" round baking pans at 350F for about 30 minutes, or until a toothpick comes out clean. Cool, and frost as desired.

JOYCE LEENSVAART

Sour Cream Coffee Cake

1 cup sour cream
1 teaspoon soda
½ cup margarine
1 cup sugar
2 eggs
1 teaspoon vanilla
2 cups flour
1¾ teaspoons baking powder
½ teaspoon salt

Filling mixture:

¼ cup sugar
1 teaspoon cinnamon
¾ cup chopped nuts

One half hour before starting, dissolve soda in sour cream.

Beat margarine, sugar, eggs, and vanilla together. Combine and add flour, baking powder, and salt. Beat together. Add sour cream, a little at a time. Beat until light and fluffy.

Pour half of the batter into a greased 10″ tube pan or bundt pan. Combine and sprinkle half the filling mixture on top of batter. Add rest of batter. Sprinkle with remainder of filling mixture. Bake at 350F for 40–45 minutes.

DORIS RIKKERS

How to Feed Your Picky Eater

I was a picky eater. My mother was a picky eater; so was my brother, my husband, and his father.

I always thought there would have been a reasonable solution to that. I figured I was picky— and probably the others too— because our mothers hadn't known how to feed us what we needed, or too much candy was available, or some simple cause-effect situation existed, like not enough siblings to eat the food up if we didn't dig in and get ours.

My Epps cousins ate all the food they could get their hands on. My aunt Ida cooked just the right amount of food for any one meal. No one was thin or ever went hungry—unless they dawdled. Which, if any of them ever did, was only once or twice at the most and before I happened to be eating with them.

Easy Coffee Cake

1 egg, beaten
½ cup sugar
½ cup milk
¼ cup oil
1 cup flour
2 teaspoons baking powder
¼ teaspoon salt

Topping:

¼ cup brown sugar
1 teaspoon cinnamon
1 tablespoon flour
1 tablespoon oil

Mix together beaten egg, sugar, milk, and oil. Combine flour and baking powder and add to mixture. Pour into a greased 8"x8" baking pan. Blend topping ingredients with a fork until crumbly and sprinkle over batter. Bake at 350F–375F for about 20 minutes.

SUE MACDONALD

At our house my mother liked to cook extra so she wouldn't have to cook so often. She would say with a certain relief, "Oh, we have plenty left, we won't need to cook supper." My brother and I knew we wouldn't run out; in fact, we often dreaded those pronouncements because one reason there was so much left over was because we hadn't touched whatever it was. Mama worried about our health and our skinny frames, and would try to get us to eat it. She'd say with surprise, "Why I thought you liked potato soup, boiled turnips," etc. "You should try it. It's good." Her sisters and their plump daughters would echo the philosophy with, "You don't know what's good!"

When I grew up and was about to become a parent myself, I determined to avoid the whole picky scene. Fortified with Gessell and Spock, I would approach this logically. Children given a choice among a variety

Super Quick Coffee Cake

"I keep two cans of biscuits on hand most of the time so I can quickly make this coffee cake. The aroma itself is friendly and inviting."

2 cans refrigerated biscuits
¼ cup melted margarine
½ cup sugar
2 teaspoons cinnamon

Frosting:

1–1½ cups confectioner's sugar
1 teaspoon vanilla
milk

Dip each biscuit in melted margarine, then in mixture of sugar and cinnamon. Stand biscuits on end in an aluminum ring mold. Bake at 350F for about 30 minutes. Remove from oven and invert on serving plate. Mix together confectioner's sugar, vanilla, and enough milk to make a spreading consistency. Drizzle over slightly cooled coffee cake. Serve warm.

Variation: See Easy Cinnamon Rolls in Bread section.

DIANE BRUMMEL BLOEM

of nutritious *foods would choose a balanced diet. Not balanced daily—maybe they'd eat only eggs for a day or two or three. But it would even out over time.*

So I presented only nutritious foods. My first three children ate few sweets and almost no junk food or fast food at all. And yet, they were in varying degrees picky, one and all. One avoided all cooked vegetables except corn; one could not eat sack lunches—she would starve first; one was a gourmet, disdaining things not up to his own standards.

I compromised; everyone had to have a small helping of everything served. That didn't work either. The pea hater literally swallowed his unchewed, like medicine, or made trips to the bathroom to spit them out in the toilet. And I discovered my daughter got headaches from lima beans, the gourmet from watermelon. And since we didn't eat candy, soda pop, or go to fast-food places, those foods

Butter Farm Coffee Cake

An attractive cake with a rich buttery flavor accented by lemon.

1 cup butter, softened
1½ cups sugar
3 eggs
grated rind of 1 lemon
1 tablespoon lemon juice
3 cups flour
1 tablespoon baking powder
1 teaspoon salt
1 cup milk
¾ cup raisins (tossed in a little bit of flour)
½ cup chopped nuts
confectioner's sugar

Cream together butter and sugar. Beat in eggs. Add lemon rind and juice. Sift together flour, baking powder, and salt and add alternately with milk, beating well after each addition. Stir in raisins. Sprinkle nuts in the bottom of a well greased tube pan. Pour in batter and bake at 350F for 60 minutes. When cool, remove from pan, position upside down, and sprinkle sides of cake with confectioner's sugar.

DORIS RIKKERS

assumed an unnatural glamour. Okay, so I would give them some things occasionally for their mental health, if not for their optimal physical benefit.

Enter child number four. Mother has been defeated in her quest for nonpickiness, but she's still trying. This child was so discriminating, he wrinkled his nose at the taste of his pacifier, refusing it for a more acceptable-tasting finger. He had tummy aches from things with tomato, Italian seasoning, and citrus juices. He became the most particular of all.

My conclusions, from twenty-nine years of picky-eater children and more than I will say of personal experience, is: it's hereditary. Don't fight it. Pickies become great cooks and chefs. They notice that the food is spoiled or substandard and save everyone from eating stuff that would make them sick. The only thing I've found that helps is to teach them to cook. If they cook it, they'll eat it. ♥

PATRICIA GUNDRY

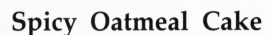

Spicy Oatmeal Cake

1¼ cups boiling water
1 cup rolled oats
½ cup butter or margarine, softened
1½ cups brown sugar
1 teaspoon vanilla
2 eggs
1½ cups flour
1 teaspoon soda
1 teaspoon cinnamon
½ teaspoon salt
½ teaspoon nutmeg (optional)

Lazy Daisy Frosting:

¼ cup butter or margarine, softened
½ cup brown sugar
¼ cup evaporated milk
1 teaspoon vanilla
1 cup coconut
½ cup chopped pecans or walnuts (optional)

In a small mixing bowl pour boiling water over oats, cover with a saucer, and set aside. In another mixing bowl cream together butter and brown sugar. Beat in vanilla and eggs. Add oats mixture. Stir well. Sift together and add flour, soda, cinnamon, salt, and nutmeg, if desired. Stir until well blended. Bake in a greased 9"x13" baking pan at 350F for 25–30 minutes or until cake tests done.

While cake is baking make Lazy Daisy Frosting. Mix butter and brown sugar, stir in evaporated milk and vanilla. Add coconut and chopped nuts, if desired. Spread on baked cake and place under broiler until bubbly and lightly browned.

PATRICIA GUNDRY
MARILYN & WILLIAM J. McRAE

Birthdays

The birthday person is honored and talked about during the whole meal time—things we remember about them, words to describe his character—in other words, ALL attention is centered on the birthday person.

Larry and the boys have had a tradition since their fifth birthdays. Larry takes the birthday boy out for a meal to the place of the boy's choosing and asks the same questions every year. Some of them are:

What do you like best about yourself?

What do you like best about our family?

Who do you admire, and

Praline Pound Cake

SERVES 12–16

1½ cups butter
1 cup sugar
1 pound light brown sugar
5 large eggs
1 teaspoon vanilla
3 cups flour
½ teaspoon baking powder
1 cup milk
1 cup chopped pecans

Beat butter, sugars, eggs, and vanilla until creamy. Sift together flour and baking powder. Add alternately with milk to creamed mixture. Stir in nuts. Bake in a greased and floured 10" tube pan at 325F for 1 hour and 15 minutes–1 hour and 30 minutes. If desired, sprinkle with confectioner's sugar just before serving.

JUDITH MARKHAM

Dutch Nutmeg Cake

6 eggs
1½ cups sugar
2 cups flour
1 teaspoon soda
1 teaspoon nutmeg
1 cup butter, melted

With an electric mixer beat eggs. Gradually add sugar, beating until mixture is light and fluffy. Sift together and add at low speed flour, soda, and nutmeg. Add melted butter, mix in thoroughly. Bake in a greased and floured tube pan at 350F for about 45 minutes.

MRS. DAVID KOK

why?
  What is God like?
  In what do you see the greatest beauty?
  What gives you the most joy?
  What do you want to be when you are an adult?

The answers have been saved, and we plan to present them to the boys at their 21st birthday. ♥

RACHEL & LARRY CRABB

Twyla's Christmas Fruit Cake

2 cups butter
3 cups brown sugar
6 eggs, whites and yolks beaten separately
½ cup molasses
½ cup brandy
4 cups flour
1 teaspoon nutmeg
1 tablespoon cinnamon
1 teaspoon cloves
1 teaspoon mace
1 teaspoon soda
2 teaspoons warm water
1 cup cooked or canned prunes, pitted and
    drained
1 cup spiced gum drops, cut up with scissors
1 pound raisins
1 pound dried currants
1 or 2 cups walnut pieces

Cream together butter and sugar. Mix in beaten egg yolks, molasses, and brandy. Sift together and add flour, nutmeg, cinnamon, cloves, and mace. Mix well. Mix soda with warm water and stir in. Add prunes, gum drops, raisins, currants, and walnuts. Fold in stiffly beaten egg whites.

Line various greased baking tins or coffee cans with wax paper. Fill ⅔ full and bake at 325F until a toothpick inserted in the center comes out clean. Remove from cans, peel off paper. Cool and store wrapped in foil or in tightly covered cans.

TWYLA M. LUBBEN

Twyla's Christmas Fruit Cake

◄ ⚞ Yes, having had 70 children (*never less than 6 around our tree*) *at Christmas we have built some lovely traditions.*

The nativity is always the first thing we put up in our house. I've had the joy of "showing" a blind child the nativity for the first time, letting her run her sensitive fingers over each figure, and seeing the thrill this brought to her.

Always there are little cakes to decorate and of course cookies, but the traditional centerpiece of the cakes is the dark fruit cake whose recipe came down through generations of my family. ♥

TWYLA M. LUBBEN

Light Fruit Cake

MAKES 3 regular loaves and one small loaf.

2 cups margarine, or shortening, softened
2 cups sugar
10 eggs
4 cups flour
½ teaspoon salt (may omit if using margarine)
8 ounces candied pineapple, cut up
8 ounces candied cherries, cut up
2 cups chopped walnuts or pecans
2 (15 ounce) packages golden raisins

Cream together margarine and sugar. Add eggs one at a time, beating well after each addition. Stir in 2 cups of the flour. Combine candied pineapple, cherries, nuts, and raisins and mix with remaining 2 cups of flour. Add to batter. Mix and pour into 3 greased and floured 9"x5" and one 8"x4" loaf pans. Bake at 300F for 2 hours or until light brown and a toothpick inserted in the center comes out clean. Store wrapped in foil or plastic.

Note: Recipe contains no baking powder or soda.

MARY ELLEN & ROBERT FISCHER

Christmas Kaleidoscope

I had thought it would be a simple thing to resurrect the recipe for my grandmother's delectable Christmas fruitcake, but the journey, the pacing off of memories has been kaleidoscopic in its dimensions and its colors. The first memory of our adored grandparents frames them in an exotic Christmas setting of roses tumbling in a fall of colors from the very peaks of our California bungalow. There was no snow for Santa's reindeer, only falling petals. The snow came later, when we all climbed nearby Mt. Wilson following a path that started with lush ferns and ended at the snow-covered observatory at its summit. The occasion was a weekend honoring Father and Grandfather as kin of

Halley's Kentucky Fruitcake

"There is a Noel lilt to our name, for in England and Virginia and Kentucky where our history unfolded, it is still pronounced 'holly.'

"Grandmother Halley was fortunate that two of her sons settled in California—one on a ranch as a grower of apricots and other delectables. Sam's freshly dried apricots and fat raisins in great natural clusters, plus walnuts from his own trees, were jewels as from heaven for her fruitcakes, as were figs, dates, and almonds. Grandmother was ahead of her time and had her own ideas about chopping and mincing—she wanted her fruits to be enjoyed individually and instructed that they be cut accordingly, that is, in identifiable bites. Her cakes were lovely mosaics of color and from such a start, I began to see the possibilities in limited combinations, as well as the grand jubilee. For one: dates, pecans, cherries, sultanas, and apricots, with candied orange peel or ginger; another with candied pineapple, apricots, coconut, and almonds.

"But for those who followed in her steps and for us who follow in theirs, there is only one Christmas fruitcake, and the recipe follows.

"In days gone by, currants and raisins were at least half of the cake. Grandmother shared her traditions with change."

Fruit/nut assembly:

1 pound seedless raisins
1 pound seedless sultana raisins
1 pound candied apricots (or dried, simmered in orange juice till puffed, cut into fourths)
1 pound dates, stoned and halved
1 pound (at least) candied red cherries

➤➤

Edmund Halley, the "Comet's astronomer."

It was perhaps the following Christmas that I had my first feel of a holly-berried, snowy celebration that tingled the toes and warmed the heart and crowded my small head with memories. This was also my first Kentucky Christmas.

In Lexington, Christmas began in an awesomely beautiful, candlelit service of hymns and carol singing. I know now how intensely happy my Father felt to be home. After the last note of "Silent Night" had been sung, there were delighted greeting and renewals. Half the church it seemed to this youngster were cousins, second cousins and kissin' cousins to Hen's family (from up noath, as in Noah); "Hen" was family for Henry, and Henry Halley is my father—at home now with an eternity of angels and his beloved Lord.

Christmas celebrations were divided between Father's sisters. This year at Fan and Graham

1½ pounds candied pineapple, cut into bite-
    size wedges
¼ pound candied orange peel
¼ pound candied ginger
1½ pounds pecans (or include nuts of your
    choice)

(For *light fruitcake,* use only 1 pound sultanas
and 1 pound each of pecans and blanched almonds.)

Separate each item into equal parts and assemble in two *large* bowls for easier handling. Macer-
ate with ½ to 1 cup sherry or peach or apple
brandy per bowl, for a 24 hour period, turning the
mixtures over from time to time. Mix well.

The "paste" (batter) must not be mixed until all
the fruits are prepared and assembled.

Batter:

3½–3¾ cups flour
2 teaspoons allspice
1 teaspoon cloves
1 teaspoon nutmeg
1 teaspoon cinnamon
1 teaspoon ginger
2 teaspoons baking powder (if molasses is
    used instead of honey or maple syrup,
    substitute soda)
1 teaspoon salt
½–1 pound butter
1 cup honey or maple syrup or light molasses
    (For light fruit cake substitute 1 [14
    ounce] can sweetened condensed milk)
1 cup brown sugar (For light fruit cake
    substitute white sugar)
6 extra large eggs, separated

Cream butter and sugar until fluffy; add syrup,
or sweetened condensed milk. Beat egg yolks into
butter/sugar mixture. Beat egg whites until stiff
and fold in.

*Kerr's gracious house and
garden in town, the next
reunion to be at Julia and
Charlie Marvin's "Audobon" a
few miles out of town in
bluegrass country. For each, a
different turn of the kaleidoscope.*

*For the children, nothing
could match the drama of those
first Christmas tree viewings at
either home. No child ever
witnessed the production taking
place behind locked doors,
climaxed at last when all were
assembled, each spiral candle
lighted and the doors opened
wide. In later years, spaced
apart more widely for this
viewer, it lost none of its
magic. Like the Nutcracker's
tree, as ever I watched, it grew
taller and larger and more
shimmering. All the love that
went into the collection of its
ornaments and the filling of its
cornucopias, poured forth to its
viewers. I wonder whether any
of that spun glass fairyland has
survived the years—the birds
with their long arching tails, the
angels and cherubs and fruits*

Drain soaked fruits thoroughly, adding fluid to butter/sugar mixture; there should be at least ½ cup for batter. Dredge fruit lightly with ¾ cup of the flour and mix in. Sift together and add remaining flour, spices, baking powder or soda, and salt.

Grease and line with wax paper, also greased, cake pans or loaf pans of your choice. Fill ⅔ full and bake at 275F, about 4 hours for large tube pans down to two hours for small loaves.

Bake at mid-oven with pans of water on the bottom shelf. An inch of water will do, replenish as needed. Watch the smaller cakes and take them out when firm to the touch, *before* the surface fruit gets dry and crusty. (Even 250F is better than a scorched cake.) Watch it with love. When done, cool and wrap in liquor moistened muslin and store in airtight containers. Cool-to-cold storage is best, and an occasional wine or brandy moistening will keep nuts and fruit at their peak for at least a year.

JOLLY HALLEY BERRY, *author's daughter, and reviser of Halley's Bible Handbook*

galore; cornucopias, radiant with marzipan fancies, pastel bonbons and other delights.

Candles were snuffed almost immediately; logs lighted in the hearth, a winter necessity (but foregone this once for old Santa). What an imprint it made, just to close my eyes now and to see it, hear it all over again, and ponder too the less spectacular but equally love-enveloping Christmases that my own mother and father never failed to create. While Grandfather and Grandmother Halley were strong enough, their Christmas express crates provided all the makings of a Christmas feast and for many a day afterward, when our own visits south were not possible. All the signatures of Kentucky were in those boxes: Kentucky ham and sausage, a gross or more of beaten biscuits, a plum pudding and the heartbeat of Grandmother's offering, her luscious fruitcake. ♥

JOLLY HALLEY BERRY

PIES

French Cherry Pie 374
Strawberry Yogurt Pie 375
Fresh Strawberry Pie 376
Raspberry Rapture Pie 377
Fresh Peach Pie 378
Summer Pie 378
Toffee Ice Cream Pie and Sauce 379
Peanutty-Crunch Pie 380
Sugarless Banana Cream Pie 381
Impossible French Apple Pie 382
Macaroon Apple Pie 383
Elegant French Chocolate Pie 384
French Silk Chocolate Pie 384
Chocolate Cheese Pie 385
Money in the Bank Pie 386
One-Bowl Brownie Pie 387
Pecan Pie 388
Southern Chess Pie 388
Pumpkin Chiffon Pie 389
Stir and Roll Pastry 390
Old-Fashioned Pumpkin Pie 391
Raisin Tarts 392

French Cherry Pie

"Our children have requested this in place of a birthday cake."

Crust:

3 egg whites
1 cup sugar
1 teaspoon vanilla
1 teaspoon baking powder
1 teaspoon vinegar
12 saltine crackers, finely crushed (rounded ⅓ cup)
½ cup chopped nuts

Filling:

1 cup whipping cream (or 1 package nondairy topping)
1 (3 ounce) package cream cheese, softened
½ cup confectioner's sugar
1 can cherry pie filling

Whip egg whites until stiff, gradually fold in sugar. Add vanilla, baking powder, vinegar, crushed saltines, and nuts. Stir gently until mixed. Bake in a greased 8" pie plate or 7"x11" pan at 350F for 30 minutes. Cool.

Whip cream, add softened cream cheese and confectioner's sugar, and continue beating until very fluffy. Spread over cooled crust. Refrigerate until set. Cover with cherry pie filling and continue to chill until served.

KAY & DON GLENN

Variation for Pantry Pie: Omit cherry pie filling and cream cheese. Top whipped cream with fresh strawberries or grated German sweet chocolate and/or more nuts.

HELEN ENNS   ➤➤

Variation for Divinity Pie: Use pecans in crust and increase to 1 cup. Use nondairy whipped topping instead of whipped cream and confectioner's sugar. Omit cherry pie filling.

AILEEN HANEY

Strawberry Yogurt Pie

Crust:

1 cup graham cracker crumbs
1 cup wheat germ
1 tablespoon cinnamon
4 tablespoons oil
1 tablespoon honey

Filling:

2 cups strawberry yogurt
medium (8 ounce) container frozen nondairy
    whipped topping, softened
fresh or frozen strawberries (optional)

In a bowl blend cracker crumbs, wheat germ, and cinnamon. Blend oil and honey and combine with cracker-wheat germ mixture. Form into a crust in a greased pie pan and bake at 300F for 10 to 15 minutes. Cool.

Mix yogurt and nondairy whipped topping. Add strawberries, if desired. Pour filling into pie shell and decorate top with more strawberries. Freeze. Thaw at least one hour before serving.

PHYLLIS & JAMES HURLEY

Recently a university student commented to me as we sat down to dinner at Cedar Campus, our InterVarsity training center, "I really enjoy the meals here!" He said it with enthusiasm, but I interpreted it as the comment of a hungry man. So I said, "The food is good, isn't it?" But, no, it wasn't just the food. It was the sitting down together and talking. It was sharing ideas and having someone listen—that was what made our meals so important to him. At home in his family he said, every one eats when they want to from food the mother leaves on the stove! Every time I hear such an accounting of family life—now all too common—I feel the same sense of surprise that people value meal times so little. When do all the family members get caught up on what is happening in each other's lives? How do they cope with all that separateness? ♥

GLADYS HUNT

Fresh Strawberry Pie

9″ baked pie shell
1½ quarts fresh strawberries
1 cup sugar
3 tablespoons cornstarch
2 tablespoons lemon juice
sweetened whipped cream

Wash and hull strawberries. Reserve half (the best looking ones). Mash the rest. In a saucepan place mashed berries and sugar mixed with cornstarch. Cook over medium heat, stirring constantly, until mixture boils and is thickened and clear. Stir in lemon juice, cool. Add remaining strawberries, saving 4 or 5 for garnish. Pour into the baked pie shell. Chill. Before serving, top with a ruff of sweetened whipped cream and garnish with the reserved strawberries.

BERTHA G. & RICHARD S. TAYLOR

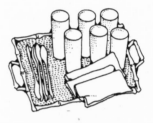

We eat on our screened porch as much as possible and particularly enjoy eating as we watch the sun set across the lake and share together about God's love, the beauty of His world, and the many blessings He has given us. Any family member that is not present is always remembered at mealtime. We take turns saying the blessing. ♥

DERRALL KINARD

Raspberry Rapture Pie

Crumb crust:

1¾ cups graham cracker crumbs
⅓ cup butter, softened
⅓ cup sugar

Raspberry filling:

1 (10 ounce) package frozen raspberries,
    thawed
1 cup sugar
3 tablespoons lemon juice
3 drops lemon extract
2 egg whites
1 cup (½ pint) whipping cream

Combine crumbs, sugar, and softened butter. Reserve ½ cup of the crumb mixture. Press the remainder into a deep (preferably collar-lined) 10 inch pie pan, forming a pie shell. Bake at 350F for 8 minutes. Cool thoroughly before filling.

Combine all filling ingredients except whipping cream and beat with an electric mixer at high speed for 20 minutes. Whip cream until stiff and gently fold into raspberry mixture. Pour into crumb crust. Decorate with reserved crumbs and freeze overnight. Let stand at room temperature 10 minutes before serving.

HELEN ENNS

Fresh Peach Pie

baked pie shell
1 cup sugar
3 tablespoons peach flavored gelatin
3 tablespoons cornstarch
1 cup water
2 cups fresh peaches, sliced
whipped cream or nondairy whipped topping

In a saucepan mix sugar, peach gelatin, cornstarch, and water. Cook over medium heat, stirring constantly, until mixture thickens. Cool.

Place fresh peach slices in baked pie shell and pour gelatin mixture over peaches. Chill until set. Serve topped with nondairy whipped topping or fresh whipped cream and garnish with a fresh peach slice.

HARRIET & DERRALL KINARD

Fresh Peach Pie

◄ *Being a peach-loving family and Derrall having a bookstore in Spartanburg, South Carolina, where we think they grow the best peaches in the world, I adapted a strawberry pie recipe to my family's liking.* ♥

HARRIET KINARD

Summer Pie

  Quick & Easy

prepared graham cracker crust
1 (20 ounce) can crushed pineapple, in its
    own juice, undrained
1 package lemon instant pudding
1 (9 ounce) container nondairy whipped
    topping

Combine pineapple and juice with lemon pudding. Add whipped topping. Fill prepared crust. Chill.

MARY & KEN REGAN

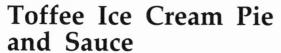

Toffee Ice Cream Pie and Sauce

MAKES one 9″ pie and 2½ cups of sauce; 6–8 servings

17–18 vanilla or brown edge wafers
½ gallon vanilla ice cream
1 cup chopped Heath English Toffee candy

Sauce:

1½ cups sugar
1 cup evaporated milk
¼ cup butter
¼ cup light corn syrup
dash of salt

Line bottom and sides of buttered 9″ pie pan with wafers. Spoon ice cream into wafer shell, sprinkling ½ cup of the toffee between layers of ice cream. Store pie in freezer until serving time. Prepare toffee sauce by combining in a saucepan sugar, milk, butter, corn syrup, and salt. Boil 1 minute, remove from heat, stir in remaining toffee. Cool, stirring occasionally. Serve sauce over pie wedges.

MARLA GELDER BLISS

Peanutty-Crunch Pie

"So easy, and very yummy."

SERVES 8

⅓ **cup peanut butter**
⅓ **cup corn syrup**
2 cups Rice Krispies cereal
1 quart vanilla ice cream
peaches or other fruit, for topping

In a bowl, mix peanut butter and corn syrup until combined. Add cereal, mix until well coated. Press mixture into bottom and sides of a buttered 9" pie pan. Chill until firm.

Spread slightly softened ice cream in pie shell. Freeze until firm. Serve topped with peaches or other fruit.

ANN & VERNON GROUNDS

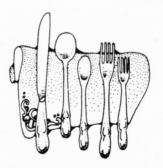

Ideas

● *Have a backward meal: dessert first. (Make sure it's a main course the children like.) The children will ask for a repeat of this, I can guarantee!*

● *Use your good china, crystal, and have a dining room candlelight dinner for just your family, because they are special too.*

● *Use candlelight and soft records anytime for a calming effect on your family during a meal. The menu need not be exotic. Spaghetti is elegant by candlelight!*

● *Plan an orange meal for Halloween, red for Valentine's Day, green (it can be done) for St. Patrick's Day.*

● *Put a Bible verse relating to thankfulness inside place cards at the Thanksgiving table. Have each one share theirs. This is a tradition at our house.*

● *Have each child plan a menu, shop with you, and prepare an entire meal. (Or if children are younger, one item of the meal.)* ♥

GRACE & DEAN MERRILL

Sugarless Banana Cream Pie

9" baked pie shell
2 cups milk
⅔ cup pure maple syrup (or ¼ cup syrup and
    ¼ cup honey)
¼ cup cornstarch
¼ teaspoon salt
2 eggs, beaten
2 tablespoons butter
2 bananas
½ teaspoon vanilla
whipped cream
½ teaspoon honey

In a saucepan scald milk. Add syrup and honey. Combine cornstarch and salt. Pour a little of the milk and syrup mixture into cornstarch and stir until smooth. Add to milk mixture and cook over low heat, stirring constantly. When thickened, slowly stir half of hot mixture into the beaten eggs. Stir into remaining hot mixture and boil one minute, stirring constantly.

Remove from heat, cool slightly, and add butter and vanilla. When completely cool, cut up bananas and put in pie crust. Pour the cooked mixture over bananas and chill.

Serve with whipped cream sweetened with ½ teaspoon honey.

MATILDA NORDTVEDT

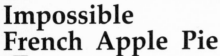

Impossible French Apple Pie

6 cups sliced apples
1¼ teaspoons cinnamon
¼ teaspoon nutmeg
1 cup sugar
¾ cup milk
½ cup biscuit mix
2 eggs
2 tablespoons margarine

Streusel:

1 cup biscuit mix
½ cup chopped nuts
⅓ cup brown sugar
3 tablespoons margarine

Mix sliced apples, cinnamon, and nutmeg. Place in a greased 10″ pie pan. In an electric blender mix sugar, milk, ½ cup biscuit mix, eggs, and 2 tablespoons margarine. Pour over apples. Prepare streusel by using fingers to mix 1 cup biscuit mix, nuts, brown sugar, and 3 tablespoons of margarine together until mixture is crumbly. Sprinkle over pie and bake at 325F for 55–60 minutes.

VERNA ESTES

Macaroon Apple Pie

A crustless pie with a coated top.

3–5 apples, peeled and sliced
½ cup sugar
¼ teaspoon cinnamon

Topping:

½ cup sugar
1 tablespoon butter
1 egg, beaten
½ cup flour
1 teaspoon baking powder
pinch of salt

Cover a buttered pie plate with sliced apples. Mix sugar with cinnamon and sprinkle over apples. To make topping: cream butter and sugar, stir in egg and flour sifted with baking powder and salt. Sprinkle over apples. Bake at 325F–350F until lightly browned, about 30–45 minutes.

Joyce Leensvaart

I love to cook. Think of cooking as a God given talent. Cooking is a gift I can share, and I share it as often as I can. ♥

Harriet Kinard

Elegant French Chocolate Pie

baked pie shell, cooled
2 squares unsweetened chocolate
⅔ cup margarine
1 cup sugar
1 teaspoon vanilla
3 eggs

Melt chocolate. Cream sugar and margarine, add chocolate and vanilla. Beat in 1 egg at a time, continue beating 5 more minutes. Pour into pie shell. Chill. Keep refrigerated. Serve topped with whipped cream.

Lois & Caryn Dykstra

French Silk Chocolate Pie

9" inch baked pie shell, cooled
½ cup butter, softened
1 cup chocolate chips, melted and cooled
2 eggs
2 cups nondairy whipped topping, thawed

With an electric mixer beat butter, and add the cooled chocolate. Add eggs one at a time, beating 5 minutes after each egg at high speed. Fold in whipped topping. Pour into pie shell and chill until firm, about 2 hours. Keep refrigerated.

Olive & Walter Liefeld

As our daughters were growing up we always had family devotions after our evening meal. Sometimes we all memorized a Bible verse together, later on, whole chapters. Also, reading through Romans, each taking a turn reading a chapter and paraphrasing, reading Pilgrim's Progress, *Ken Taylor's books, and C. S. Lewis'* Narnia *series. Now our daughters are asking for these books for their children.* ♥

Rea & Alan Johnson

Chocolate Cheese Pie

"A big hit for special occasions."

Chocolate Graham Crust:

1½ cups graham cracker crumbs
¼ cup brown sugar
⅓ cup melted butter
⅛ teaspoon nutmeg
1 square unsweetened chocolate, melted

Filling:

1 (6 ounce) package semisweet chocolate chips
1 (8 ounce) package cream cheese
¾ cup brown sugar
⅛ teaspoon salt (optional)
1 teaspoon vanilla
2 eggs, separated
1 cup heavy cream

Combine crust ingredients and press into a 9" pie plate. Chill.

Melt chocolate chips in a small saucepan, cool. Beat egg whites in a large bowl until stiff. Gradually add ¼ cup of the brown sugar and beat until glossy. In medium sized bowl whip cream and set aside. In another bowl beat together cream cheese, remaining brown sugar, salt, and vanilla. Add egg yolks and melted chocolate chips, blending well. Fold cream cheese mixture into egg whites. Fold in whipped cream. Pour into the chilled crust, reserving some filling for decoration. Chill. When filling is firm, drop mounds of reserved filling with a tapered spoon over top of pie. Chill 8 hours. Keep refrigerated.

JULIE L. & S. RICKLY CHRISTIAN

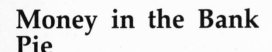

Money in the Bank Pie

"It takes just one pan to make this deliciously rich pie, but it tastes as though you messed up your whole kitchen."

unbaked 9″ pie shell
4 squares semisweet baking chocolate
¼ cup margarine
1 (12 ounce) can evaporated milk
1⅓ cups flaked coconut
3 eggs, slightly beaten
½ cup sugar
whipped cream or nondairy whipped topping

Melt chocolate and margarine over low heat in a medium saucepan. Add milk, coconut, eggs, and sugar, stir until well blended. Pour into pie shell. Bake at 400F for 30 minutes. Cool. Serve with whipped cream or nondairy whipped topping. Store in refrigerator.

LOIS & CARYN DYKSTRA

Create Traditions that Fit Your Family

My husband and I have discovered that traditions that seem to work happily in other families do not seem to suit us! For example, we thought that holding hands during grace seemed a nice custom, and when our children were old enough we tried to institute it. It never went smoothly, however, because one child, when his hands were washed, simply didn't feel like risking his cleanliness by holding other people's hands! I am embarrassed to say that for months we started each meal in a mood of mild (to severe) irritation because of the struggle involved (hold your brother's hand) until we finally realized that this was a nice custom, not something that had to be done! We dropped it, and our meals began with a peaceful prayer and happy moods. This seems so obvious, but yet it eluded us for so long that I feel it is worth mentioning: as you look around at other families' customs, try them! If they enrich your family life, wonderful! If they don't, then drop them without feelings of guilt! ♥

PHYLLIS & JAMES HURLEY

One-Bowl Brownie Pie

"This is a Landorf favorite dessert that was simple enough for the children to toss together, which made them feel they had really contributed to the pleasure of the entire family . . . a tasty gift of love!"

SERVES 6

2 eggs
1 cup sugar
½ cup butter or margarine, softened
½ cup flour
3 tablespoons cocoa
1 teaspoon vanilla
¼ teaspoon salt
½ cup chopped walnuts

You dump—and I do mean dump—all the ingredients, except nuts, into one bowl. Beat it with a mixer or by hand for 4 minutes. Add nuts and pour into a greased 8″ or 9″ pie pan. Bake 30 minutes at 350F. The pie will settle down in the middle as it cools. That's alright, it doesn't hurt the taste. Cut in wedges and serve topped with whipped cream or á là mode with a scoop of ice cream.

Variation for Pie Delicious: Omit cocoa and walnuts. Instead, add ¾ cup chocolate chips and 1 cup pecans.

JOYCE LANDORF
HARRIET & DERRALL KINARD

Pecan Pie

unbaked pie shell
¾ cup sugar
1 cup light corn syrup
1 cup pecans
3 eggs, beaten
2 tablespoons butter, melted
1 tablespoon lemon juice

Mix all ingredients and pour into unbaked pie shell. Bake 10 minutes at 450F, then lower temperature to 300F and bake 25 minutes more, or until a knife inserted in the center comes out clean.

MRS. T. T. (BENNIE) CRABTREE

Southern Chess Pie

9" unbaked pie shell
2 eggs, beaten
1 cup sugar
½ cup brown sugar
1 tablespoon corn meal
1 tablespoon flour
½ cup butter, melted
½ teaspoon vinegar
1 tablespoon vanilla or lemon flavoring

Mix filling ingredients together thoroughly. Pour into unbaked pie shell. Bake at 325F for 45 minutes, or until knife inserted in center comes out clean.

HARRIET & DERRALL KINARD

Picnics

A tradition we still follow is having guests or a picnic every Wednesday afternoon. My mother started a grocery store when I was a year old. We kept it for 57 years, until my brother was old enough to retire. We closed the store Wednesday afternoons. If we stayed at home, customers who knew we lived upstairs would come to the back door for groceries. In that day, very few people went picnicking once a week. But we had a truck and had room to pile in all the family and friends and off we went for a good time. We still love picnics and we still love having guests. If it isn't picnic weather, we eat at home and play games afterwards. ♥

DENA KORFKER

Pumpkin Chiffon Pie

"This is my one and only 'asked for' recipe. The pie turns out to be fluffy and delicious. I've been making it for at least 35 years."

9" pie shell, baked and cooled
1 tablespoon or envelope unflavored gelatin
¼ cup cold water
4 eggs
1 cup sugar
1 (16 ounce) can pumpkin
½ cup milk
½ teaspoon salt
½ teaspoon ginger
½ teaspoon nutmeg
1 teaspoon cinnamon
whipped cream or nondairy whipped topping

Soften gelatin in cold water. Separate eggs. In the top of a double boiler slightly beat egg yolks and mix in ½ cup sugar, pumpkin, milk, salt, ginger, nutmeg, and cinnamon. Cook over boiling water until thick. (Or, if speed is desired, cook in a saucepan, bringing mixture to boil and stirring constantly until thickened.)

When pumpkin mixture is thick, remove from heat and add gelatin, mixing together thoroughly. Let cool. Beat egg whites until stiff. Continue beating while gradually adding remaining sugar. When pumpkin mixture is cool, fold in egg whites. Pour into pie crust and refrigerate for two or three hours, or until ready to serve.

To serve, add a layer of whipped cream or whipped topping. Keep refrigerated.

GRACE RAMQUIST

Stir and Roll Pastry

For pie shells and double crust pies.

"This is an easy, no-fuss pastry recipe that has been passed down to me from my mother. It is always flaky and light and delicious."

2 Crusts or shells:

2 cups flour
1 teaspoon salt
¼ cup milk
½ cup oil

3 Crusts or shells:

3 cups flour
1½ teaspoons salt
⅓ cup milk
¾ cup oil

4 Crusts or shells:

4 cups flour
2 teaspoons salt
½ cup milk
1 cup oil

Combine all ingredients in mixing bowl. Pastry should be moist enough to easily mold into a ball. If more moisture is needed, add oil. Roll out crust between two sheets of waxed paper or plastic food wrap. Peel off top layer of waxed paper or plastic wrap and turn crust over into pie pan. Carefully remove bottom sheet of waxed paper or plastic wrap and mold crust to pan. Add pie filling and roll out top crust as before.

To bake for baked single crust pie shells: trim pastry, allowing a ½" extension beyond edge of pan. Fold pastry under, even with the edge of pan. Make a decorative edge with fingers, a fork or a spoon. Cover edge of pastry with 1½" wide

➤→

strips of aluminum foil to prevent overbrowning. Prick pastry all over with a fork at about 1" intervals. Bake at 475F 8–10 minutes. Cool.

ANNE WILCOX

Old-Fashioned Pumpkin Pie

"My grandmother's recipe."

unbaked 9" pie shell
1¾ cups pumpkin
¾ cup brown sugar, firmly packed
¾ teaspoon salt
1 teaspoon cinnamon
½ teaspoon ginger
½ teaspoon nutmeg or allspice
2 eggs, beaten
1 cup evaporated milk

Mix filling ingredients thoroughly with a rotary egg beater or wire whisk. Pour into unbaked shell. Bake at 450F for 15 minutes. Reduce heat to 325F and bake about 40 minutes more, or until a knife inserted in the center comes out clean.

H. JUDITH & ROLAND HARRISON

When I was growing up, the kitchen was always my favorite room in the house, because that's where Mamma usually was. It was always warm and actively interesting with churning, bread baking, or something. My desire is for my kitchen, too, to emanate cheerfulness, and to be filled with an atmosphere of peace for those who have been out in the rush and push of daily living. It delights me when someone comes in sniffing, wondering what smells so good. ♥

BRENDA KNIGHT GRAHAM

Raisin Tarts

MAKES 12 tarts

uncooked pastry for a double crust pie
¼ cup butter, softened
1 cup sugar
2 eggs
1 teaspoon vanilla
1 cup raisins
½ cup chopped nuts

Cream sugar and butter, add eggs, and beat for one minute. Stir in vanilla, raisins, and nuts. Line muffin pans (12 muffin size) with pie pastry. Fill and bake at 400F for 25–30 minutes.

ELEANOR & TOM MCCONISKEY

CANDY AND SWEET SNACKS

Peanut Butter Bon Bons 394
Favorite Fudge 395
Dad's Festive Fudge 396
Butter Toffee 396
Peanut Brittle 397
Party Popcorn 397
Microwave Caramel Corn 398
Oven Caramel Corn 399
Peanut Butter Popcorn 400
Gorp 400

Peanut Butter Bon Bons

MAKES 100 ½" balls.

1 (1 pound) box confectioner's sugar
3 cups Rice Krispies
2 cups peanut butter, plain or crunchy (if using crunchy, add a little extra)
½ cup butter or margarine
1 (12 ounce) package chocolate chips
1 (12 ounce) package butterscotch chips

In a mixing bowl combine confectioner's sugar with Rice Krispies. Melt peanut butter and margarine in saucepan over low flame. Pour peanut butter mixture over cereal mixture. Blend with hands. Form into balls about ½" in diameter. Chill until firm.

While peanut butter mixture is chilling prepare coating. Melt chocolate and butterscotch chips in a double boiler. (Can also make separate toppings of chocolate and butterscotch.) Coat balls by using 2 spoons, with the chocolate in one spoon and using the other spoon to turn the ball over. Keep chocolate thin by leaving burner on very low while covering the balls. Place on waxed paper or a lightly greased surface. Keep in a cool place.

JANEEN SHUPE

Favorite Fudge

MAKES sixty 1″ or thirty 2″ pieces

**4 squares unsweetened chocolate, finely
  shaved**
4 cups granulated sugar
1½ cups evaporated milk
½ cup butter (do not substitute)
1 teaspoon salt
2 teaspoons vanilla

Combine chocolate, sugar, evaporated milk,
butter, and salt in a large, heavy saucepan. Bring
to a rolling boil on high heat, and cook, stirring
occasionally, until a small amount of the mixture
makes a soft ball in cold water, 236F on a candy
thermometer. Cool until lukewarm, add vanilla,
and beat with an electric mixer on medium speed
until the fudge will just hold its shape and slightly
loses its gloss. Immediately pour onto a buttered
pan or cookie sheet. Cool slightly and cut in
pieces.

JO BERRY

*A little boy lived up the hill
from our store. Every night he
had to take a spoonful of cod
liver oil, which he hated. So his
mother let him have a sucker
(we call them lollipops today).
She didn't buy them by the
dozen. No, he came every
evening after we were all
upstairs (where we lived) to buy
one penny sucker! And he
wouldn't let me get it for him.
No, he had to go into the store
with me and decide which flavor
he wanted.* ♥

DENA KORFKER

Dad's Festive Fudge

2 cups sugar
⅔ cup evaporated milk
12 large marshmallows
½ cup butter or margarine
pinch of salt
1 (6 ounce) package chocolate chips
1 cup chopped nuts
1 teaspoon vanilla

In a heavy 2 quart saucepan mix sugar, evaporated milk, marshmallows, butter, and salt. Cook, stirring constantly, over medium heat to boiling. (Mixture will be bubbling all over the top.) Boil and stir 5 minutes more. Remove from heat. Add chocolate chips. Stir to melt. Stir in nuts and vanilla. Spread in a buttered 8"x8" square pan. Cool slightly and cut into pieces.

JOYCE LEENSVAART

Butter Toffee

1 cup butter or margarine, melted
1⅓ cups sugar
1 tablespoon light corn syrup
3 tablespoons cold water
½ cup walnuts or pecans

Cook above mixture in a heavy saucepan, stirring often with a wooden spoon, to 300F on a candy thermometer (hard crack stage). Add walnuts or pecans and pour in a thin layer on a buttered cookie sheet. Let cool completely and break into pieces.

CHERYL ROSE

Peanut Brittle

3 cups sugar
1¾ cups light corn syrup
1 cup water
1 pound raw Spanish peanuts
2 tablespoons butter
1 teaspoon salt
2 teaspoons vanilla
1 tablespoon soda

In a saucepan bring sugar, corn syrup, and water to a boil. Cook to 240F on a candy thermometer. Add peanuts. Boil, stirring constantly, to hard crack stage, 275F–300F. Remove from heat. Stir in butter, salt, vanilla, and baking soda. (Baking soda will cause mixture to foam up.) Pour on 2 buttered 10″x15″x1″ baking pans. Break in pieces when cool.

DANNY PENWELL

Party Popcorn

6 quarts popped corn
1 cup broken cashew pieces
16 ounces gumdrops
½ cup margarine
½ cup oil
16 ounces marshmallows

Place popcorn, cashews, and gumdrops in a large container. In a saucepan, melt margarine, then add oil and marshmallows. Stir until marshmallows are melted. Pour marshmallow mixture over popcorn mixture. Mix well. Pack firmly into a greased tube cake pan. Let harden. Turn out on a cake plate. Slice and serve.

CAROLYN OWENS

Popcorn-Flavored Popcorn

Most people have never tasted popcorn. What they think of as popcorn flavor is really butter and salt flavor. Not bad, but not popcorn. If you're going to eat butter and salt, just unwrap a stick of butter banana-style, dip it into a bowl of salt as if you were dunking a doughnut, and proceed ice-cream-cone style. Disgusting!

Popcorn is nutritious. Butter and salt give you more of what you don't need and cry out for a cold drink, which is likely to give you more of two other things you don't need more of, sugar and caffeine.

Pop the corn in an air popper. Munch guiltlessly, and sip from a tall glass of fresh, moderately cold water. You'll discover a delicate, sweet flavor you missed out on before. Try this five times—without having buttered, salted popcorn between times—before deciding whether or not you like it. I predict that you'll learn to love it. And it's good for you! ♥

RICHARD P. WALTERS

Microwave Caramel Corn

11 cups popped corn
1½ cups peanuts
1 cup brown sugar
½ cup butter
¼ cup light corn syrup
½ teaspoon salt
1 teaspoon soda

Use a microwave corn popper to pop corn. (Do not use a paper bag because it is a fire hazard.) Combine popped corn and peanuts in a lightly greased bowl or pan. Place brown sugar, butter, syrup, and salt in a 2 quart glass bowl. Microwave on high for 3 minutes. Stir the sauce and return to oven. Microwave for 4 more minutes at half power. Remove sauce from oven and immediately add soda. Stir quickly and pour over popped corn and peanuts. Allow to cool, stirring and separating a few times during cooling period. Store in an airtight container.

ANNE WILCOX

Good Looking Trail Mix

Ugly food tastes good. It has to. If ugly food tasted like it looks we wouldn't eat it.

Raisins are the ugliest things people eat. Raisins are really ugly. Proof: You never saw a mother raisin carrying a picture of her children. A raisin has never appeared in, let alone won, a beauty contest. Flowers are strewn in the aisle at weddings, never raisins, because flowers are beautiful and raisins are ugly. Raisins are so ugly they're afraid to look in mirrors. I happen to think, though it's just a personal opinion, that raisins are the exception to the "ugly is tasty" rule. You may disagree, but I think raisins taste like they look.

Oven Caramel Corn

5–8 quarts popped corn
2 cups brown sugar
½ cup light corn syrup
1 cup butter or margarine
½–1 teaspoon salt
½ teaspoon soda
1 teaspoon vanilla

Keep popped corn warm in a 250F oven while preparing caramel mixture. In a saucepan bring to a boil brown sugar, corn syrup, butter, and salt. Boil 5 minutes. Remove from heat and stir in soda and vanilla. Pour over popped corn. Mix to coat corn. Spread in lightly greased baking pans and bake at 250F for about 60 minutes, stirring about every 15 minutes. Remove from oven. Stir and separate into smaller pieces a few times as it cools to keep mixture from forming a single, solid piece. Store in an airtight container.

LORETTA R. WILSON
BARBARA & STEPHEN G. COBB

Variation for Cracker Jackeroos: Add 3 or more cups peanuts to popped corn.

DIANE HEAD

Trail mix, though, is wonderful. Trail mix is made to be carried to and eaten at beautiful places. Raisins are so ugly they do not deserve to go to beautiful places.

Recipe for good looking trail mix: one handful of almonds, equal amount of coconut flakes, same quantity dried banana slices.

This can be improved by substituting chocolate chips for the bananas. Or, substitute chocolate chips for the coconut. If you possibly can, substitute chocolate chips for both bananas and coconut. Chocolate is beautiful!

Raisins are very good for you. Eat lots of them, but don't look. ♥

RICHARD P. WALTERS

Peanut Butter Popcorn

2 quarts popped corn
½ cup sugar
½ cup light corn syrup
½ cup peanut butter
½ teaspoon vanilla

Place popped corn in serving bowl. In a saucepan bring sugar and corn syrup to a boil. Remove from heat and stir in peanut butter and vanilla. Pour over popped corn. Stir to coat.

PAT MCCARTNEY

Gorp

MAKES about 6 cups

1 (16 ounce) box granola with dried apples
    and cinnamon
1 (6 ounce) package mini-chocolate chips
1 cup peanuts
1 cup sunflower seeds
1 cup raisins
½ cup finely diced dried apricots, pears, or
    apples

Mix together in a large container. Store covered.

JOYCE LEENSVAART

MISCELLANEOUS

Digestibles
    Hot Fudge Sauce 402
    Chocolate Velvet Sauce 402
    Vegetable Sauce 403
    Barbecue Sauce 403
    Cranberry Chutney 404
    Sweet Dills 405
    Rhubarb-Pineapple Jam 405
    Crunchy Granola 406
    Adelle Davis's Granola 407
    Matilda's Granola 408

Indigestibles
    Play Dough 409
    Fingerpaint 409

Hot Fudge Sauce

"This has remained the favorite through the years with my family."

2 squares unsweetened chocolate
½ cup butter or margarine
1 (1 pound) box confectioner's sugar
1 (12 ounce) can evaporated milk
1 teaspoon vanilla

In a double boiler melt together chocolate and butter. Add confectioner's sugar. Stir in evaporated milk and vanilla. Cook over hot water about 1½ hours, stirring occasionally. Place in a jar, refrigerate, and use as needed. Keeps well.

WILMA ZONDERVAN TEGGELAAR

Chocolate Velvet Sauce

"I always keep the ingredients for this on hand, along with vanilla ice cream; guests can have hot fudge sundaes in about 5 minutes. I often make small amounts for one or two people."

1 cup chocolate chips
⅔ cup light corn syrup
⅔ cup evaporated milk

Heat chocolate and corn syrup in saucepan until chocolate melts. Remove from heat and stir in evaporated milk.

CARLA MOCKABEE

Vegetable Sauce

⅔ cup mayonnaise
½ teaspoon celery salt
¼ cup grated Parmesan cheese
¼ cup soft margarine
2 teaspoons lemon juice
¼ cup sliced almonds

Mix together ingredients and spread over partially cooked broccoli, brussels sprouts, artichoke hearts, or a combination of these. Can also be mixed in with cooked, chopped spinach or with green beans to make a casserole. Heat vegetables and sauce mixture in a 400F oven for 10 minutes (do not overcook sauce, as it can separate). Almonds can be reserved and sprinkled on top, or incorporated in the sauce as above.

SHIRLEY BLEDSOE

Barbecue Sauce

"A great Southern sauce for chicken."

½ cup oil
¾ cup chopped onion
¾ cup catsup
¼ cup water
⅓ cup lemon juice
3 tablespoons sugar
3 tablespoons Worcestershire sauce
2 tablespoons prepared mustard
2 teaspoons salt
½ teaspoon pepper

Saute onion in oil 10 minutes. Add rest of ingredients and bring to a boil. Boil gently for 20 minutes.

DORIS RIKKERS

We hold hands around the table, which gives us a feeling of togetherness and a common bond before the Lord. That is invaluable and more important than any food that could be placed on the table. ♥

YVONNE LEHMAN

Cranberry Chutney

"Especially appreciated by grownups at holiday dinners."

4 cups cranberries, washed and drained
1 cup raisins
1⅔ cups sugar
1 tablespoon cinnamon
1½ teaspoons ginger
¼ teaspoon cloves
1 cup water
½ cup chopped onion
1 large apple, peeled, cored and chopped
½ cup thinly sliced celery

In a large saucepan mix cranberries, raisins, sugar, cinnamon, ginger, cloves, and water and bring to a boil. Add onion, apple, and celery and bring to a boil again. Simmer 15 minutes, stirring often. Simmer the mixture until it is almost as thick as desired. It thickens a little more as it cools. Cool and refrigerate. If tightly covered keeps for weeks in refrigerator.

WILMA ZONDERVAN TEGGELAAR

Thanksgiving

One of the most memorable mealtime activities in my family has been Thanksgiving. Before the meal, Dad puts five or six kernels of corn on each of our plates and we each take turns saying one thing we're thankful for, one for each kernel, before we eat. ♥

SANDRA DRESCHER LEHMAN

Sweet Dills

Makes 1 quart

1½ **cups sugar**
¾ **cup vinegar**
1 **teaspoon celery seed**
1 **teaspoon mustard seed**
1 **teaspoon mixed pickling spice**
1 **quart dill pickles, drained and rinsed in**
   cold water

In a saucepan, boil sugar, vinegar, celery seed, mustard seed, and pickling spice for five minutes. Slice pickles in thick slices and pour syrup over pickles. Cover. Let cool. Refrigerate. Wait 3 or 4 days before serving.

WILMA ZONDERVAN TEGGELAAR

Rhubarb-Pineapple Jam

5 **cups rhubarb, cut in small pieces**
5 **cups sugar**
1 **(20 ounce) can crushed pineapple, undrained**
1 **large package red fruit-flavored gelatin**

In a large saucepan boil rhubarb, sugar, and pineapple for 20 minutes. Remove from heat. Add flavored gelatin powder. Stir until dissolved.

JULIE & KALMAN TOTH

Crunchy Granola

MAKES enough to fill about four to five 1-pound coffee cans.

3 cups rolled oats
1 teaspoon cinnamon
3/4 cup unsweetened wheat germ
¾ cup brown sugar
1 cup coconut
1 cup bran cereal
1 cup chopped nuts
⅓ cup oil
⅓ cup honey
⅓ cup boiling water
2 teaspoons vanilla

Mix together all dry ingredients. Stir together oil, honey, and boiling water. Add to dry mixture and stir well. Spread in two 10"x15"x1" baking pans and bake at 350F for 20–25 minutes. Remove from oven and sprinkle vanilla over mixture. Stir while warm. Cool. Store in airtight containers.

Variations: Before baking you can add banana chips, dates, and dried fruit. After baking and cooling add raisins, chocolate or carob chips.

MARCI & WAYNE RICE

Crunchy Granola

◄ *This is a great dry snack or breakfast cereal. But it is more than a cereal to our family—it has become a Christmas tradition. Our son Nathan began making this for all his grandmas, grandpas, aunts, and uncles about five years ago. He calls it "Nate-ola," and now his sister Amber is also included in the shopping, mixing, and baking. We wrap the "Nate-ola" in 1 pound coffee cans. All the relatives are anxious for it each Christmas.* ♥

MARCI & WAYNE RICE

Adelle Davis's Granola

Several years ago nutritionist Adelle Davis gave this basic recipe on a T.V. interview show. Feel free to vary and adapt it to your own taste.

5 cups rolled oats
1 cup soy flour
1 cup non-instant nonfat dry milk (instant is OK, too)
1 cup wheat germ
1 cup chopped almonds, walnuts or peanuts
1 cup sesame seeds
1 cup sunflower seeds
1 cup coconut
1 cup oil
1 cup honey (or a bit more)
1 cup water

In a large container mix all dry ingredients. Stir together oil, honey, and water. (Hot water blends the liquids together better.) Add to dry mixture and mix together well. Bake in two lightly greased 9"x13" baking pans at 300F for about 60 minutes or until lightly browned, stirring 2 or 3 times during baking. Or bake at 350F and stir more frequently, watching mixture carefully to prevent burning, especially toward the end of the baking time.

VIRGINIA & LE ROY EIMS
PATRICIA GUNDRY

Matilda's Granola

Eat as a snack, as a breakfast cereal, or mixed with your favorite dry cereal.

4 cups quick oats
4 cups old fashioned oats
1 cup bran
1 cup wheat germ or whole wheat flour
1 cup peanuts, or other nuts
1 cup sunflower seeds
¾ cup oil
¾ cup molasses and honey together (any
proportions)
¾ cup water
2 teaspoons vanilla
1 cup raisins

Mix dry ingredients together. Mix liquid ingredients together. Add to the dry ingredients, mixing well. Bake in two greased 9"x13" pans at 300F until lightly browned, stirring frequently, about 30–35 minutes. When cool, add raisins.

MATILDA NORDTVEDT

Play Dough

"This is the best recipe for play dough I've found, which has entertained my toddler for many an hour."

1½ cups water
½ cup salt
1 tablespoon oil
food coloring
2 cups flour
2 tablespoons powdered alum

In a saucepan heat water, salt, oil, and food coloring* to boiling. In a bowl mix together flour and alum. Stir hot liquid *into* flour mixture. Set aside until cool enough to handle, knead until smooth. Store tightly covered in margarine tubs.

*To make four colors instead of one, add color after dough is mixed. Divide dough into four pieces and knead into each piece about 4 drops of food coloring.

MELODIE DAVIS

Fingerpaint

1 cup water
½ cup flour
liquid laundry starch
food coloring

In a saucepan bring water to a boil. Add flour. Stir over low heat until thick and shiny. Remove from heat. Mix in an equal amount of liquid laundry starch. Add food coloring as desired.

JOYCE LEENSVAART

INDEX OF RECIPES

Adelle Davis's Granola, 407
Almond Chicken, 154
Almond Tassies, 313
Angel Bavarian Cake, 327
Annie's Yogurt Waffles, 95
Apple Cake, 350
Apple Pound Cake, 349
Applesauce Cake, 351
Apricot Nectar Gelatin Salad, 51
Autumn Fish "Slew," 224

Bacon and Cheese Oven Omelet, 119
Bagels, 88
Baklava, 311
Banket, 312
Barbecue, 207
Barbecued Beef, 208
Barbecued Meatballs, 194
Barbecue Sauce, 403
Basting Sauce, 171
Batter for Deep-Fried Onion Rings or
    Zucchini, 242
Beef-Mushroom Stew, 210
Beef Soong, 205
Beef Stroganoff, 214
Berry Favorite Brownies, 259
Best Banana Bread Ever, 111
Best Biscuits, 98
Best Brownies Ever, 257
Beth's Cheese Ball, 15
Betty's Salad and Dressing, 37
Blueberry Buckle, 103
Blueberry Oatmeal Bread, 104
Blueberry or Cherry Cream Cheese
    Dessert, 323
Blueberry Sauce, 321
Bonnie's Easy Baked Chicken, 173
Boston Brown Bread, 107
Braised Short Ribs, 191
Broiled Baked Bean Sandwich, 151

Broiled Gulf Scallops, 226
Brussels Sprouts with Almonds, 248
The "B's" Cheese Crepes, 320
Buttercup Cookies, 274
Butter Farm Coffee Cake, 365
Buttermilk Pancakes, 95
Butter Pecan Cookies, 275
Butter Pecan Waffles, 94
Butterscotch Brownies, 260
Butterscotch Cookies, 275
Butter Toffee, 396

Cabbage Borscht, 62
California Zucchini Bread, 100
Can Can Chicken, 172
Carrot Bread, 105
Carrot Bundt Cake, 343
Carrot Cake I, 342
Carrot Cake II, 342
Carrot Mushroom Soup, 57
Casserole Mexico, 202
Cheese and Broccoli Soup, 63
Cheese Fondue, 132
Cheese Pops, 17
Cheese Pouf, 117
Cheese Straws, 18
Chef Pinzon's Cheese Soufflé, 122
Cherry Cool Comfort, 323
Chicken Adobo, 163
Chicken and Mushrooms in Madeira
    Sauce, 169
Chicken Enchiladas in Green Sauce,
    160
Chicken Enchiladas Rancheros, 161
Chicken Marengo, 170
Chicken Paprikash, 158
Chicken-Rice Soup, 69
Chicken Soup Hunt, 70
Chili Dogs, 134
Chili-Mac, 145

Chilled Rock Cornish Game Hens, 170
Chinese Fried Walnuts, 21
Chocolate Cheese Pie, 385
Chocolate Cream Cupcakes, 353
Chocolate Eclair Dessert, 330
Chocolate Heart Cookies, 286
Chocolate Sheet Cake, 354
Chocolate Shortbread, 267
Chocolate Slice, 329
Chocolate Velvet Sauce, 402
Chocolate Zucchini Cake, 357
Christmas Breakfast, 121
Christmas Porridge, 306
Clam Chowder, 65
Cole Slaw De Luxe with Dill Dressing, 39
Consommé Rice, 233
Cookie Day Cookies, 284
Cooperation Salad, 46
Corned Beef Party Buns, 151
Corn Pudding I, 254
Corn Pudding II, 254
Country Egg Soufflé, 121
Crabby or Shrimpy Dip, 16
Crab Meat Joni, 227
Cracker Jackeroos (variation), 399
Cranberry Chutney, 404
Cranberry Coffee Cake, 347
Cranberry Jell, 52
Cream Cheese Frosting, 341
Cream Cheese Glaze, 343
Creamy Beef Enchiladas, 203
Crepes Marquis, 130
Crunchy Granola, 406
Crunchy Ice Cream, 335
Crunchy Salad, 40
Cucumber Salad, 50

Dad's Festive Fudge, 396
Danny Penwell's Pumpkin Pie Cake, 337
Date Bread, 106

Debbie's Layered Broccoli Casserole, 249
Dill Dressing, 39
Dinner in a Skillet, 198
Dinner Rolls, 78
Divinity Pie (variation), 375
Donita's Zucchini Casserole, 244
Double Chocolate Cookies, 293
Dream Bars, 264
Dream Cake, 316
Dutch Baby, 116
Dutch Fried Cabbage, 241
Dutch Krinkle, 314
Dutch Nutmeg Cake, 367

Easy Chicken Divan I, 174
Easy Chicken Divan II, 175
Easy Cinnamon Rolls, 113
Easy Coffee Cake, 363
Easy Homemade Pizza, 137
Easy Koulourakia, 280
Easy Pineapple-Cherry Dessert, 317
Ed's Mongolian Tea, 28
Elaine Watson's Sunday Morning Bread, 73
Elegant French Chocolate Pie, 384
Elegant Frosty Punch, 24
English Pancakes, 96
Ethiopian Beef and Vegetable Alecha, 211
Everybody's No Bake Cookies, 296

Family Favorite Low Calorie Ice Cream, 332
Farina Dumplings, 67
Favorite Fudge, 395
Fettuccine Alfredo, 131
Fingerpaint, 409
Flemish Almond Cookies, 283
Fosmire's Favorite Chicken Kiev, 168
French Cherry Pie, 374
French Onion Soup, 64
French Silk Chocolate Pie, 384
Fresh Peach Pie, 378

Fresh Strawberry Pie, 376
Fried Greek Meatballs, 196
Fritata, 123
Frosted Cinnamon Rolls, 82
Frozen Bread Dough Pizza, 141
Frozen Cheese Cream, 333
Fructsoppa, 307
Fruit Crumble, 304
Fruity Lemon Cheesecake (variation), 325
Fudge Drop Cookies, 294
Fudge Pudding with Ice Cream Sauce, 310
Funny Cake, 315

Generic Animal Crackers, 290
German Broccoli, 41
Gingerbread People, 288
Ginger-Soy Sauce, 20
Gladis's Hong Kong Brownies, 258
Golden Pot Roast, 208
Golden Raisin Buns, 92
Goombay Walnut Chicken, 156
Gorp, 400
Grandma Dee's Imperial Cookies, 276
Grandma Lou's Hot Potato Salad, 43
Grandma's Fresh Fruit Cake, 346
Grandma's Macaroni and Cheese, 128
Great Aunt Margaret's Cereal Cookies, 290
Gretchen's Oatmeal Molasses Cookies, 273
Guacamole, 12

Halley's Kentucky Fruitcake, 370
Hall's Baked Omelet, 120
Ham-Broccoli Casserole, 187
Hamburger Doo-Lollies, 133
Heath Bar Sugar Cookies, 274
Helen's Fancy Pancake, 319
Herbed Chops and Rice, 184
Hibernia Bread, 108

Hit of the Party Cookie Bars, 270
Holiday Cranberry Salad, 49
Honey Oatmeal Bread, 85
Honey Wheat Bread, 86
Hoot Owl Cookies, 281
Hot Chicken Salad Casserole, 176
Hot Cocoa Mix, 29
Hot Fruit Salad, 49
Hot Fudge Sauce, 402
Hot Sausage Balls, 18
Hungarian Gulyás, 213

Ice Box Buns, 83
Ice Cream Grasshoppers, 333
Ice Cream Sauce, 310
Impossible French Apple Pie, 382
Indonesian Dinner, 218
Indonesian Soy Sauce (Ketjap Manis), 157
Indonesian Stir-Fry, 157
Irish Crescents (variation), 277
Irish Lamb Stew, 221
Irish Soda Bread, 109
Italian Broccoli Casserole, 251

Janeen's Cheese Spread, 14
Jane's Corn Bread, 99
Jan's Chocolate-Caramel Brownies, 261
Japanese "French Fries," 20
J.D. Douglas's Apricot Dessert, 300
Jiffy Cranberry Salad, 52
Joanne's Vegetable Dip, 15
Johnny Cash's "Old Iron Pot" Family Style Chili, 148
Judith's Cream of Chicken Soup, 68
Judith's Cream of Mushroom Soup, 56
Julie's Octopus Cookies, 295

Kendall's Chili, 146
Korean Skewered Beef, 220
Kraut 'n' Pork Chops, 186

Latayne's Chili, 147
Layered Vegetable Salad, 36
Lazy Daisy Frosting, 366
Lebkuchen, 287
Lemon Frosting, 92
Lemon Soy Sauce, 20
Light Fruit Cake, 369

Mab's Meaty Soup, 61
Macaroon Apple Pie, 383
Mama Jeannie's Pizza, 138
Mandarin Orange Salad, 48
Marinated Flank Steak I, 216
Marinated Flank Steak II, 217
Mary Carroll's Whole Wheat Pizza,
    136
Mashed Potato Cake, 361
Matilda's Granola, 408
Matzo Ball Soup, 66
Melba's Dessert Topping, 337
Melba's Torte, 317
Meri's Many Bean Salad, 34
Mexican Chef's Salad, 35
Mickey's Macaroni Casserole, 129
Microwave Caramel Corn, 398
Microwave Crispy Chicken, 171
Milk Chocolate Cake, 360
Milky Way Cake, 356
Moist and Crispy Chicken, 172
Mom's Saucy Meatballs, 193
Money in the Bank Pie, 386
Mother's Old-Fashioned Bread Pud-
    ding, 309
Mother's Shortcake, 347
Mrs. Howard's Rolls, 81
Mrs. Truman's Ozark Pudding, 302
My Grandmother's Tea Cakes, 285
Mysaka, 204

90-Minute No-Knead Bread, 74
Nipponese Eggplant, 245
No-Bake Onos, 295
Non Plus Ultra, 289
Noodle Kugel, 305

Nystrom's Round Steak, 216

Oatmeal Caramelites, 262
Oatmeal Date Cookies, 282
Old-Fashioned Creamy Rice Pudding,
    308
Old-Fashioned Potato Pancakes, 240
Old-Fashioned Pumpkin Pie, 391
Olé Dogs, 135
Olie Bollen I, 89
Olie Bollen II, 90
Olivia's Broccoli-Mushroom Salad, 41
Olivia's Cornbread, 98
Olivia's Pizza, 142
One-Bowl Brownie Pie, 387
1, 2, 3 Counting Banana Bread, 110
Open-Faced Sourdough Seafood
    Sandwiches, 149
Orange Cake, 352
Orange Pineapple Salad, 51
Oriental Chicken, 155
Oriental Punch, 25
Oreo Pie, 336
Outdoor California Glazed Ribs, 179
Oven Barbecued Chicken, 163
Oven Caramel Corn, 399
Oven Cinnamon French Toast, 124
Oven French Fries, 234
Oxtail Pepper Stew, 212

Pan Chicken, 159
Pan Rolls, 77
Pantry Pie (variation), 374
Parmesan Cheese Loaf, 76
Parmesan Chicken Breasts, 158
Parmesan Potatoes, 237
Party Popcorn, 397
Party Rye Pizza, 143
Pastel de Chocolo, 162
Patchwork Quilties, 272
Pavlova, 328
Peach, Blueberry, or Cherry Cobbler,
    299
Peach Glazed Spareribs, 180

Peanut Brittle, 397

Peanut Butter Bars, 268

Peanut Butter Bon Bons, 394

Peanut Butter Chocolate Chip Cookies, 279

Peanut Butter Lovers' Wheat Germ Muffins, 90

Peanut Butter Popcorn, 400

Peanut Butter Rice Krispie Bars, 269

Peanutty-Crunch Pie, 380

Pear Bars, 263

Pecan Pie, 388

Philip Yancey's Summer Squash Casserole, 243

Piad Liang Shia (elegant shrimp), 228

Pie Delicious (variation), 374

Pigtails, 215

Pineapple Drop Cookies, 294

Pita Sandwiches, 150

Pizza Bread, 144

Pizza Meatloaf, 207

Play Dough, 409

Popover Chicken, 166

Poppy Seed Dressing, 54

Poppy Seed Torte, 318

Porcupine Beef Balls, 195

Pork Chops and Orange Rice, 183

Pork Chops Southern Style, 185

Potato Puff, 236

Potato Salad, 42

Potato Soup (variation), 65

Powerful Whole Wheat Pancakes, 97

Praline Pound Cake, 367

Pumpkin Cake, 341

Pumpkin Chiffon Pie, 389

Punch du Jour de Blender, 26

Quick & Easy English Trifle, 326

Quick Cinnamon Rolls, 80

Quick Picnic Salad, 48

Quick Pineapple Cake, 348

Raisin Tarts, 392

Raspberry Rapture Pie, 377

Red Dressing For Tossed Salad, 53

Request Punch, 25

Restuffed Potatoes, 235

Return Engagement Beef Casserole, 209

Rhubarb Coffee Cake, 344

Rhubarb-Pineapple Jam, 405

Rhubarb Upsidedown Cake, 345

Rice Krispie Cookies, 278

Rice Pilaf, 233

Rotini Salad, 44

Russian Tea, 28

Salesman's Garlic Bread, 76

Salisbury Steak Supper, 198

Salsa, 12

Sandra's Breakfast Casserole, 119

Sarma, 181

Scalloped Spinach, 251

Scalloped Tomatoes and Vegetables Italia, 246

Scandinavian Summer Salad, 38

Seven Layer Bars, 271

Seven-Layer Sabrosa Spread, 13

Sharon Engel's Blueberry Muffins, 93

Shelley's Layered Broccoli Casserole, 250

Shelley Smith's Pizza, 140

Sherbet Cream Cake, 334

Sherried Beef, 215

Shirley's Whole Wheat Muffins, 91

Shrimp Dip, 16

Shrimp Jambalaya, 225

Six Week Bran Muffins, 91

Skillet Lasagna, 199

Slim Lemon Cheesecake, 325

Snowball Cookies, 277

Soft Chocolate Chip Cookies, 291

Sonja Henie Cookies, 278

Sour Cream Cocoa Cookies, 292

Sour Cream Coffee Cake, 362

Sour Cream Dressing, 38

Sour Cream Potatoes I, 238

Sour Cream Potatoes II, 239
Sour Cream Potatoes III, 239
Sour Noodles, 45
Southern Chess Pie, 388
Spaghetti and Vegetables, 200
Special Baked Chicken, 173
Special Spinach, 252
Spice Tea, 29
Spicy Oatmeal Cake, 366
Spinach Dip, 17
Squash and Apple Bake, 240
Stir and Roll Pastry, 390
Stir-Fry Cabbage and Zucchini, 241
Strawberry Crepes, 322
Strawberry Yogurt Pie, 375
Stuffed Breast of Chicken, 167
Stuffed Cabbage, 197
Stuffed Tomatoes á là Graham, 247
Sugarless Banana Cream Pie, 381
Summer Pie, 378
Sunday Morning Casserole, 118
Sunny Carrot Salad, 47
Sunny Lemon Bars, 265
Super Quick Coffee Cake, 364
Surprise Chocolate Cake, 359
Susan Feldhake's Cornmeal Pizza
    Crust, 139
Swedish Almond Bread, 102
Swedish Limpa Rye Bread, 87
Swedish Pancakes, 96
Sweet and Sour Chicken, 164
Sweet and Sour Chicken Wings, 165
Sweet and Sour Pork, 178
Sweet & Sour Short Ribs of Beef,
    192
Sweet Dills, 405

Tabouli, 32
Tangy Lemon Bars, 266
Tasty Ham Buns, 152
Teriyaki Meatloaf, 208
Thick Mexican Salsa, 13
Three Bean Bake, 252

Three or Four Bean Salad, 33
Tim's Famous Chili, 147
Toffee Ice Cream Pie and Sauce, 379
Toffee Squares, 331
Topsy Turvey, 201
Tourtiere, 182
Tropic Chops, 186
Tuna Cooler, 44
Tuna for Two, 229
Tuna Lasagna, 230
Tuna Soup, 64
Turtle Cake, 355
Turtle Sundae Dessert, 336
Twyla's Christmas Fruit Cake, 368
Twyla's Quickie Stew, 59

Uldine's Cheesecake, 324
Uldine's Light Avocado-Carrot Salad,
    40
Uldine's Mushroom Soup, 57
Ursula's Cinnamon Topped Banana
    Bread, 112

Van Raalte Dressing, 53
Vegetable Beef Soup, 60
Vegetable Sauce, 403
Vegetarian Pizza, 19
Vietnamese Rice, 127

Walnut Honey Buns, 79
Wassail, 27
Weinacht Stollen, 84
White Bread, 75
Wild Bean Spread, 14
Wild Rice-Broccoli, 234
Willie-Mae, 303
Wilma's Easy Baked Beans, 253
Winter Bean Soup, 58
World's Best Walnut-Zucchini Bread,
    101

Zucchini Chocolate Bundt Cake, 358
Zucchini San Louie, 242